THE ART OF
RENE LALIQUE

THE ART OF
RENE LALIQUE

PATRICIA BAYER & MARK WALLER

Grange
BOOKS

A QUANTUM BOOK

Published by Grange Books
An imprint of Grange Books plc
The Grange
Grange Yard
London SE1 3AG

ISBN 1-85627-930-8

This book was produced by
Quantum Books Ltd
6 Blundell Street
London N7 9BH
Printed in China

CONTENTS

The work of my grandfather, René Lalique, has always provoked great excitement and continues to do so, not least my own, which I share with many amateur and professional collectors all over the world. He was a creative giant who knew how to make full use of all the resources available to him at a time when revivalism was very much the fashion.

A René Lalique jewel is a perfect microcosm of imagination, poetry and subtlety. He could use materials and colors with consummate skill. I can honestly say that I am as deeply moved by one of my grandfather's jewels as I am by Egyptian sculpture dating back thousands of years, or an Old Master.

I believe that this is how collectors are born. Enthusiasm breeds excitement and excitement in turn produces the longing to contemplate and then to possess. I am happy to say that these feelings, far from fading as the years pass, only increase in their intensity.

Lalique knew how to move with the times and as a result his work has a certain continuity. After devoting himself entirely to the art of jewelry, he dedicated himself to the art of glass with much the same enthusiasm.

My father Marc succeeded him and his creations are equally renowned. It was he who, after the war, decided on the change from glass to crystal, a medium which opened up new artistic possibilities.

Having been brought up by these marvelous artists, it was only natural that I should become equally inspired. Design and Lalique have become my life, and my homage to my genius grandfather, René Lalique. He elevated the decorative arts to the level of the fine arts and is recognized today as an undisputed master.

I would like to thank all his admirers and those who have dedicated work to him.

M. Lalique

Portrait of René Lalique, 1931, by the designer's daughter, Suzanne Lalique, oil on canvas. Collection The Hon. Margery Holman.

This lovely portrait shows the artist sitting at his desk, pen to paper and inkpot at hand. He has a concentrated look on his bespectacled face, and is nattily dressed in a tie, waistcoat and jacket. The vase *Albert* appears on the right, an elegant goblet on the left.

LALIQUE THE MAN

1

The number of artists whose styles overlap – yet alone define or epitomize – more than one distinctive movement within their field is a small one. For the most part a painter or sculptor remains the exponent of one style and one medium throughout his working years, except for *rarae aves* like Leonardo, Michelangelo or Picasso. Within the decorative arts, where styles and movements tend to be more protracted and less easy to categorize – and the techniques often more difficult to master – the possibility of diversity is even slimmer. René Jules Lalique (1860–1945), however, was a designer *extraordinaire*, who in his professional career spanned both the florid Art Nouveau and rectilinear Art Déco styles, first as an innovative goldsmith and later as a prolific glassmaker. Lalique was also an exemplary businessman, in quality of craftsmanship, quantity and variety of output, aesthetic vision, and overall commercial and critical success rivaled only, perhaps, by his contemporary American counterpart, Louis Comfort Tiffany (1848–1933). Today the name of Lalique lives on. His works have come to be more and more appreciated as the prices they fetch have risen and his legacy is perpetuated by the glassmaking firm, Cristal Lalique, run by his descendants.

Lalique's roots lay in the small town of Ay, on the north bank of the river Marne in the northeastern French province of Champagne, whence his mother's family came. An only child, he was born there on 6 April 1860, his family moving to the outskirts of Paris two years later, but returning to the country for holidays. Unfortunately – and perhaps strangely for one who was to rise to such prominence – few details are known either of Lalique's family or of his youthful years.[1] It is certain that his father was a merchant selling novelty goods, that his primary schooling took place at the Lycée Turgot near Vincennes, that he won an award there for drawing in around 1871, and that, at the age of 16, he was apprenticed to the renowned Parisian goldsmith, Louis Aucoc (1850–1932), and enrolled at the famed Ecole des Arts Décoratifs in Paris. In that same year, 1876, Lalique's father died, an event which may well have prompted René's mother to advise him to take up an apprenticeship.

The two years at Aucoc's firm no doubt provided Lalique with a good basic knowledge of both the materials and working methods of a jeweler. The primarily neo-rococo *joaillerie* sold by Aucoc was not, however, innovative, either technically or stylistically; Aucoc was a high-priced goldsmith whose wealthy and modish clientele demanded what was at the time fashionable – heavy and showy cut gems which dominated their precious-metal settings, not at all the dramatic, organic jewelry for which Lalique was to become known and admired.

In 1878 Lalique moved to Sydenham, a suburban village south of London in an area that contained many French immigrants. According to Henri Vever (1854–1942), a respected goldsmith working with his brother Paul (1851–1915) in much the same vein as Lalique, the teen-aged René attended the "Collège de Sydenham",[2] most likely the School of Art established in the Crystal Palace, that monumental glass-and-iron symbol of a new age which had housed the first great Industrial Exhibition in 1851 and had been removed to Sydenham three years later. Art schools in Great Britain were at the time more progressive than those in France, which may have been the reason Lalique went to London, but he returned to Paris in 1880, after the Sydenham school had closed its doors. At Sydenham he had devoted much of his time to drawing and illustrating from life and nature, something he had enjoyed since he was a young boy. This early devotion to drawing – which resulted in his selling some gouache miniatures of flowers painted on ivory to dealers in Epernay[3] – holds much significance: Lalique proved to be a superb draughtsman, as the multitude of sketches and finished drawings for both his jewelry and glass confirms.

On his return to Paris at the age of 20, Lalique studied sculpture under Justin Lequien at the Ecole Bernard Palissy. At the same time he designed wallpaper and textiles for a relation of his named Vuilleret, thus adding to his already-extensive repertory of techniques, media and styles. Then, in 1881, he decided to devote himself to designing jewelry, the pursuit that was almost fully to occupy him for the next two decades and to gain him a prominence unequaled by his contemporaries. For the first few years, with the help of a friend named Varenne, he worked on a freelance basis for numerous *joailliers de luxe*, including Aucoc, Boucheron, Cartier, Jules Destape, Gariod, Jacquet and Renn. In late 1885 he bought an atelier in Place Gaillon from his patron, Jules Destape (who soon after moved to Algeria), and a year later, with the assistance of a small staff of workmen – some of them previously employed by Destape – his own workshop officially began operations.

Having opened his own firm, Lalique was free to design jewelry as he wanted, without any restrictions from employers or clients. With an élan unprecedented among goldsmiths, he exploited the spirit and motifs of the burgeoning Art Nouveau style (with more than a passing nod to Symbolism). Lalique's designs, which were regularly reproduced in the trade publication, *Le Bijou*, inspired praise and imitation from numerous colleagues, among them Alphonse Fouquet and his son, Georges (who took over his father's firm in 1895 and became a well-known Art Nouveau jeweler, probably second only to Lalique, though his technique was not so fine or delicate). And his clientele grew as Art Nouveau took root. Large, heavy gems ceased to be the rage, and unconventional, nature-inspired pieces, of new and often inexpensive materials, became the *nouvelle vague* among the fashionable rich, with René Lalique at the crest of the creative wave.

The workshop inherited from Destape soon proved to be inadequate for Lalique's needs and in 1887 he leased a second atelier on the Rue du Quatre-Septembre. Both workshops appear to have been in operation until 1890, when Lalique, whose staff by then numbered about 30, acquired an even larger space at 20 Rue Thérèse. In the same year Lalique married Augustine Ledru, the daughter of the sculptor, Auguste Ledru,[4] and the newlyweds moved into a flat on the third floor of the Rue Thérèse premises.

In the spacious new atelier, Lalique's experiments with jewelry continued and his fame and patronage grew. Among his clients during the next dozen years or so were Siegfried Bing (1838–1905),[5] the German-born entrepreneur whose Paris shop, *La Maison de l'Art Nouveau*, gave the revolutionary new style its name, the great tragic

1. Even in articles and books by his family members, there have not emerged a multitude of facts concerning Lalique's personal life, perhaps evidence of a deliberate reticence on his and their part.

2. It was so called by Henri Vever in his *La Bijouterie Française au XIXme Siècle*, Paris, 1908, Vol. III.

3. Marc and Marie-Claude Lalique, *Lalique par Lalique*, Lausanne, 1977, 16, 20.

4. Little is known of Mme Lalique, including her date of birth (she died in 1909 and is buried aside her husband at Père Lachaise cemetery in Paris). There are several portraits of her, including a photograph showing her with her husband and a bronze plaque executed by Lalique.

5. The art historian, Gabriel Weisberg, has researched "S. Bing" most thoroughly and proven conclusively that his first name was not Samuel, as is often used (he himself allowed it to be used), but Siegfried (*see* Weisberg, *Art Nouveau Bing*, New York, 1986).

actress, Sarah Bernhardt (1844–1923), renowned for the daring fashions and jewelry that she wore, the opera singer, Emma Calvé (1858/1866–1942), and Calouste Gulbenkian (1869–1955),[6] the Armenian financier and petroleum-magnate whose discerning acquisition of some 150 Lalique pieces formed what is today the finest and most representative collection of the man's work, in Lisbon.

The *fin-de-siècle* decade of the 1890s also witnessed Lalique's initial interest in glass. He had already incorporated glass in some of his jewelry, when in 1893 he began to experiment with the ever-fascinating material on its own – in the form of a perfume vial and stopper cast in the *cire-perdue,* or lost-wax, method.[7] In the first half of this decade Lalique made a number of objects in *cire-perdue* glass, including a goblet, relief panels and sculpture, and he also cast *cire-perdue* bronzes, such as plaques, mirrors, sword guards and sculptures. It is likely that Lalique was first exposed to the lost-wax process by his father-in-law and brother-in-law, both of whom were sculptors in bronze. (Although the exact date of the piece is not known, a *cire-perdue* bronze portrait figure of Lalique by his friend, Théodore-Louis-Auguste Rivière,[8] showing the subject at around 35 to 40 years of age, captures the benign yet formal spirit of the man in a medium of which Lalique was especially fond and knowledgeable.)

The artistic and social circles in which Lalique moved were diverse and fascinating. His friends and admirers included the Symbolist writer, Robert de Montesquiou; the editor of *Figaro*, Miguel Zamakoïs; the politician, Ehepaar Waldeck-Rousseau; the painter, Georges-Jules-Victor Clairin; the architects, René Binet and Henri Guillaume, and other noted writers, musicians and artists. Lalique was given commissions by a host of international patrons, both individual and corporate. Among his clients were industrialists, entertainers, *parfumeurs* and royalty. At times in his long career he collaborated with other creative talents, such as the American sculptor, Gaston Lachaise (who worked briefly for him in 1905)[9], and the Art Déco metalworker, Edgar Brandt. Still, Lalique was unique among his design contemporaries, for he ran his atelier with a firm hand and discerning eye. He may have employed dozens of workers (hundreds, later, in the production of glass), but for more than half a century he oversaw the design of every piece bearing his name (and the execution of at least the prototype of multiple pieces). Hence the high quality and impeccable design of his entire body of work.

By the turn of the century, Lalique's name was synonymous with Art Nouveau, with excellent craftsmanship as well as with experimentation and innovation. At the Exposition Universelle Internationale of 1900 in Paris, that great exhibition which heralded the dawn of the 20th century, his pieces were universally praised. Besides jewelry, bronzes and occasional glass pieces, Lalique was producing unusual decorative objects, at times combining several materials in new and exciting ways and using motifs such as bats, butterflies and human-insect hybrids which figured widely in Symbolist painting and literature. There were hair combs of ivory and horn with enamel and glass blossoms; a full-length mirror with two serpents coiled around it as a frame; a sublime chalice of ivory, enamel and gold; small metal keys; and a blown-glass and silver bowl in the form of a mass of wriggling snakes with mouths agape.

Portrait of Augustine Ledru, the future Mme René Lalique, 1887–88, by Georges Clairin, oil on canvas. Collection Glenn and Mary Lou Utt, USA.

This oil painting was executed – probably at Lalique's request – by Georges Clairin, a good friend of Lalique's and Sarah Bernhardt's. It is believed to have been done before René and Augustine Ledru were married in 1890. Mlle Ledru is depicted in casual, colorful dress with a jaunty mien – quite unusual for Clairin, whose female subjects (Bernhardt among them) were generally painted in formal, elegant, even theatrical attire.

6. Gulbenkian was supposedly introduced to Lalique by Sarah Bernhardt. *See* Dr. Maria Teresa Gomes Ferreira's introduction to the catalogue, *Art Nouveau Jewelry by René Lalique*, Washington, D.C., International Exhibitions Foundation, 1985, 13.

7. Nicholas M. Dawes, *Lalique Glass*, New York, 1986, 3–4.

8. The piece is inscribed "A Mon Ami Lalique".

9. Hilton Kramer, *The Sculpture of Gaston Lachaise*, New York, 1967.

living quarters. Architectural elements were designed and cast by Lalique's firm for the new space, the first in an impressive line of commissions for interior fittings.

In 1905 Lalique opened his first retail shop at 24 Place Vendôme, next to the establishment of the perfume manufacturer, François Coty, who, much as Lalique transformed jewelry in the Art Nouveau era and glass in the Art Déco period, revolutionized the scent industry. It was not long before the *parfumeur* was commissioning Lalique to design labels and perfume bottles for his blossoming House of Coty (founded in 1904), and the collaboration and friendship of the two men continued for many years. By the 1920s, Lalique was designing bottles and flasks for other perfumers as well, including D'Orsay, Houbigant, Roger et Gallet and Worth.

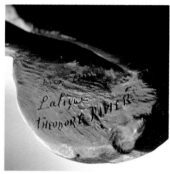

Portrait of René Lalique, *c.* 1900–04, by Théodore-Louis-Auguste Rivière, *cire-perdue* bronze, 14in (35cm). Collection Glenn and Mary Lou Utt, USA.

Detail of Rivière bronze, showing the sculptor's inscription: *à mon ami/Lalique/ THEODORE RIVIÈRE.*

Finding that his own facilities were sorely lacking for the production of glass, the fascinating and challenging material that was now occupying most of his design and production time, Lalique rented his first glassworks in 1909, at Combs-la-Ville near Fontainebleau. Initially the factory's output was dominated by commercial perfume bottles, but within a year Lalique was producing his own unlabeled bottles, flacons and powder containers for the retail trade, and was successful enough to be able to purchase the factory.[10]

During World War I the Combs-la-Ville glassworks was closed, but it reopened in 1918 and the following year saw a great increase in production. By then Lalique's eager clientele was becoming truly international. He began to show his works in glass throughout Europe and at American galleries and museums, and the demand for his works grew so rapidly that the firm had to expand once more. In 1921 a new factory in Wingen-sur-Moder, in the Alsace region of France, started production and Lalique began to market his glass aggressively throughout the world, with outlets offering his wares in the United States, Great Britain and South America as well as continental Europe. Mass-production of high-quality, moderately priced glassware began in earnest, although the genesis of every piece could be traced back to the pen and eye of the master himself, who continued to produce designs in his Paris studio.

In the 1920s Lalique began to manufacture works in glass other than perfume bottles and related ornamenture. Jewelry, mirrors, paperweights, ashtrays, inkwells and, of course, vases of all sizes – some hand-blown, others blown into a mold, some still of *cire-perdue* glass, others in vivid hues – were made, as well as clock cases, picture frames, lamps and chandeliers, goblets, plates and other tableware.

By 1902 Lalique's experiments with glass were already more than one-man endeavors. In the village of Clairfontaine, he worked with a staff of four at a family estate that was to be a small-scale atelier of sorts for some 10 years. That year also marked the completion in Paris of an impressive new facility at 40 Cours la Reine (today called Cours Albert 1er), a seven-storey, renovated neo-Gothic structure which contained workshops, a display space and shop, and Lalique's

10. It is quite probable that some of the finances needed to start the glass business were obtained from outside sources such as Coty and Gulbenkian, both of whom were men of immense wealth and influence.

Small sculptures and statuettes proved popular, as did related automobile mascots, their streamlined but always rich design complementing that of the splendid vehicles they adorned. The rich variety of Lalique's mass-produced glasswork was shown to advantage at the 1925 Exposition des Arts Décoratifs et Industriels Modernes in Paris (whence the style, Art Déco, received its name in the 1960s).

Throughout the 1930s, Lalique – now in his seventies and suffering from debilitating arthritis – remained at the helm, even though his firm had grown so large that it employed some 600 workers. Many of the objects produced had, in fact, been designed a decade or so earlier; new products consisted in the main of simple tableware and vases. As the fashion for showy, decorative pieces waned, Lalique's vases – now often intended for floral displays, as opposed to being solitary centerpieces – came to be press-molded, a cheaper and quicker means of production.

In the last years of his life, Lalique's output became less exciting and innovative, but his reputation was enhanced by a retrospective exhibition of his glass held in 1933 at the Musée des Arts Décoratifs in Paris. For a living artist to be honored in that way was a rare and fitting tribute to Lalique's great eminence. A great many of his works were displayed, some on glass tables of his own design (Lalique designed several pieces of furniture during his career in both glass and wood). An altar, one of a few ecclesiastical projects which he undertook, was also included in the exhibition.

Lalique had first demonstrated his flair for interior design in his own Cours la Reine showroom, and in subsequent years he was asked to contribute to the interior decoration of several firms, notably Coty's Fifth Avenue showroom in Manhattan (1913), the Oviatt Building in Los Angeles (1928) and John Wanamaker's department store in Philadelphia (1932). He was also commissioned to design decorative glass panels for the Compagnie Internationale des Wagons-Lits in the late 1920s and tableware, lighting fixtures and glass paneling for the luxury liner, *Normandie,* launched in 1935. Lalique's renown in America was at its peak in the 1930s, helped there by the superb display of his glass at B. Altman's in New York (1935), engineered in large part by the master's only son, Marc (1900–77),[11] who had managed the Wingen factory since 1922 and was involved in the technological and marketing, as well as design, aspects of the business.

The Combs-la-Ville workshop was permanently closed in 1937 and the Wingen Glassworks, which was temporarily shut down in 1940, did not reopen until several years after Lalique's death in May 1945. Marc succeeded his father as head and chief designer of the firm and supervised the reconstruction of the factory after its heavy destruction during the war. He introduced new techniques (notably a new crystal) and did away with older ones, though many pre-war designs remained in production. Marc was neither so prolific nor so inspired a designer as his father, but some of his pieces of the 1960s (not unlike the inventive Scandinavian designs of the period) bear his own distinctive stamp. In 1956 Marc's daughter, Marie-Claude (b. 1935), joined the firm and, after her father's death in 1977, she became its principal designer, a role she successfully continues to fill to this day.

1 Design in pencil for enameled glass charger, decorated with birds in gilt enwreathed by stylized tendrils and florettes in black gouache on board. 18⅞ × 18⅛in (48 × 46cm). Galerie Moderne.

1

11. He also had a daughter, Suzanne (date of birth variously listed as 1892, 1893 and 1899), who was a noted theater designer as well as a ceramics designer for the Haviland Company, into whose family she married.

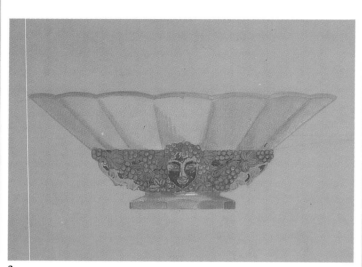

2

2 Design for glass bowl with bacchanalian masks amid fruiting vines below flaring faceted sides, in pencil shaded green, watercolor on paper. 19⅝ × 13 in (50 × 33cm). Galerie Moderne.

3 Design for perfume bottle with tiara stopper, watercolor and white gouache on paper. Collection Glenn and Mary Lou Utt, USA.

3

4

4 Design for Madonna and Child glass statuette, in pencil, wax crayon and white gouache on wax paper. 16¾ × 12¼ in (42.5 × 42cm). Galerie Moderne.

5 Design for glass jardinière, elongated with twin Pegasushead lug handles nearly identical to the mascot "Longchamps", the wings decorating the bowl; pencil and shaded green gouache on paper. The Pickard-Cambridge Family Collection.

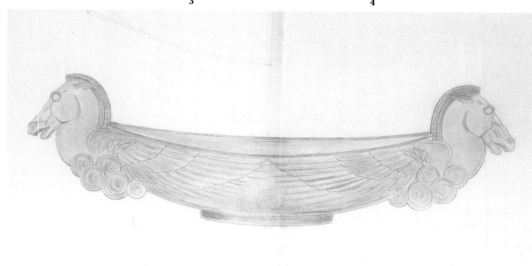

5

6 19 studies for pendants and brooches of dragonflies, butterflies and decorative devices, in ink on paper, three sheets overall. Kagan Collection, USA.

7 Design for perfume bottle with stopper modeled as an elephant, blue watercolor, white gouache, pencil on paper. Collection Glenn and Mary Lou Utt, USA.

8, 9 Two designs for perfume bottles, in blue and indigo watercolors, ochre, white gouache, pencil on paper. Collection Glenn and Mary Lou Utt, USA.

10 *Knot of Serpents* corsage ornament, *c.* 1898, silver-gilt and *champlevé* enamel, 8½ × 5½in (21 × 14cm); signed *LALIQUE*. Calouste Gulbenkian Museum, Lisbon. This oversized brooch is the *chef d'oeuvre* among Lalique's serpent-jewels. Originally each of the nine interlacing snakes spat out a row of pearls from its gaping jaws.

THE JEWELRY

2

11

The jewels of René Lalique are among the richest and most telling of Art Nouveau creations. The myriad – and largely one-of-a-kind – brooches, pendants, necklaces, diadems, lorgnettes, haircombs, watch cases and other *bijouterie* bearing the master's signature comprise a singular *oeuvre* shaped by a vivid imagination and honed by virtuoso technical skills. Lalique's innovative combination of previously under-utilized, even scorned, "lesser" materials, like glass, horn and tortoiseshell, with rare gems and metals (such hybrid jewels are called *bijouterie,* as distinguished from all-precious *joaillerie*), as well as his use of natural, fantastic, neoclassical and literary images in a sublime but never mannered or caricatured way, makes his work an outstanding achievement in the long history of the goldsmith's art.

The goldsmith's work that was produced in France, and throughout most of the West, before the Art Nouveau period essentially followed a long-established line of classical, baroque and rococo jewelry. It was opulent, ostentatious, and often rather unimaginative, although sculptor-designed pieces, such as gold chimera- and dragon-shaped brooches, were produced and might be said to presage Lalique's fantastic creatures.[1] One principle that many turn-of-the-century goldsmiths adopted as their own – the jewel as a miniature work of art – preceded the Art Nouveau period, but it was probably best exploited by Lalique. A stunning example is the *Dragonfly* pectoral (*c.*1898; Gulbenkian Collection), whose head terminates in a carved-chrysoprase woman's torso, evoking a terror and fascination on the same level as Fernand Khnopff's drawing of the winged *Sleeping Medusa* or Odilon Redon's several versions of a long-tressed, skull-topped *femme fatale* as Death.

It has been said, perhaps rightly, that Lalique made his jewels, not to be worn, but to be admired, and that they have, therefore, the inherent "disregard for function" which characterizes much French work of the period.[2] But although Lalique's jewels were derided as flamboyant, impractical and unwearable by some, most critics and connoisseurs of the period found them and their creator, as the writer, Gabriel Mourey, did, "ever fertile in imagination, of infinite fancy, constantly advancing, with undiminished freedom and originality".[3]

Lalique's jewelry must be seen in the context of the development of the Art Nouveau style. Art Nouveau received its name from the entrepreneur and connoisseur *par excellence,* Siegfried Bing, who owned a shop called *La Maison de l'Art Nouveau* at 22 Rue de Provence, in Paris. Earlier in his career Bing had collected, promoted and sold Japanese art, just as Arthur Lasenby Liberty had in England. But at his first *Salon de l'Art Nouveau,* in December 1895, he exhibited both fine and decorative art by such seminal Western figures as Tiffany, Gallé, Beardsley, Mackintosh, Rodin, Khnopff, Toulouse-Lautrec, Vuillard and, of course, Lalique.

Art Nouveau, called *Jugendstil* ("young style") in Germany, *Paling stijl* ("eel style") in Belgium and sometimes *style nouille* ("noodle style") in France, was essentially a reaction against the traditional design that had held sway for years, design that was, as Bing wrote, "decoration ... copied from what was in vogue in previous centuries".[4] Its *leitmotif* was the line – the curving, undulating, often

12

11 *Serpents* box, *c.* 1900, gilt-copper and enamel, 1¾ × 6¼ × 2¾in (4.5 × 15.5 × 7cm). Calouste Gulbenkian Museum, Lisbon.

12 *Head of Medusa, c.* 1900, bronze, 6⅞ × 4⅝ × 3¼in (17.4 × 11.8 × 8.2cm); signed: R. LALIQUE. The Virginia Museum of Fine Arts, Richmond, Gift of Sydney and Frances Lewis.

1. Charlotte Gere and Hugh Tait, "Romanticism to Art-Nouveau", in *The Jeweller's Art, An Introduction to The Hull Grundy Gift to The British Museum,* London, 1978, 18.

2. *Ibid.*

3. Gabriel Mourey, Aymer Vallance, et al., *Art Nouveau Jewellery & Fans,* New York, 1973 reprint, 2.

4. Peter Selz and Mildred Constantine (eds.), *Art Nouveau and Design at the Turn of the Century,* New York, 1975 (revised edition), 11.

asymmetrical line which seemed to cut through the constraining, confining patterns of the past and symbolize the path into never-before-explored artistic territory. Nature provided a significant theme or background for this new style. The Art Nouveau designer looked at nature in a new and challenging way, depicting both flora and fauna, whether exotic or mundane, whether a marquetry hare on a Louis Majorelle buffet or a triad of glittering swallows on a Lucien Gaillard head ornament, in an elevated, out-of-the-ordinary manner. Art Nouveau strove, in addition, to present a noble synthesis of all the arts, much as its immediate predecessor in Great Britain, the Arts and Crafts Movement of William Morris and John Ruskin, had aspired to reconcile art and society by producing well-made, inexpensive hand-crafted objects in the age of industry and mass-production. Art Nouveau designers could be quite outrageous in their quest for this synthesis – the Belgian, Van de Velde, and the Parisian, Guimard, designed their wives' apparel to make them an integral part of their environment.

Lalique exploited his own personal designs in a diversity of ways: some of his floral motifs appeared on paper, in jewelry, in architectural ornament and in glass. For their dazzling depiction of some of nature's loveliest and most frightening creatures, Lalique's jewels are often far superior to the creations of his contemporaries in wood, glass, metal and ceramic. In part, his unique vision can be traced to his kinship with the Symbolist writers and artists of the time. The aim of art, according to Symbolists like Mallarmé and Verlaine, was to suggest felt reality, that is, to depict its "veiled essence", the idea behind the form. Many of Lalique's fantasy creatures do just that, alluding to a dream world beyond physical appearances, much like the hybrid creations of Odilon Redon. One of the Symbolists' most important subjects was Woman in her many guises, especially at one with nature and the embodiment of both seduction (as the *femme fatale*) and salvation (as the innocent virgin). Her long, serpentine hair was a popular manifestation of Art Nouveau's whiplash-curve motif, and Lalique's jewelry is rife with long-tressed, languorous women, most notably and supremely in the bronze of *Medusa* (*c.*1900) whose head is a mass of writhing serpents. But to say that Lalique was a Symbolist artist is incorrect. He used elements of the Symbolist vocabulary in some of his goldsmithswork, but in other pieces he remained painstakingly faithful to natural detail. He was also happy to use Christian iconography, Oriental themes and classical imagery. Like the Art Nouveau style itself, Lalique was eclectic and at times unorthodox in his choice of subjects, although his craftsmanship was of a consistently high standard.

Goldsmiths of the Second Empire and the early Third Republic generally subjugated whatever innovative talents they might have possessed to the manipulation of the precious gem they had at their disposal, namely, the ostentatious diamond. In the wake of South Africa's "diamond rush", there was from the late 1860s a strong demand for cut diamonds throughout Europe and the West, and goldsmiths tended to work almost exclusively with these brilliantly cut stones. Lalique did not forsake diamonds altogether, but it was his genius to rediscover semiprecious colored stones such as opal, chalcedony, agate, jade, chrysoprase and moonstone and to use

them in exciting combinations with other materials. Those included ivory (also obtained in vast quantity from Africa), horn and baroque pearls; translucent, opalescent, *champlevé* and *plique-à-jour* enamel; precious stones such as sapphire, aquamarine, amethyst, topaz and, of course, gold and silver.

In 1880, when Lalique returned from his two-year sojourn in London, he found that the Parisian climate was becoming more sympathetic to the creation of finely crafted *objets d'art*. In the face of the dawning machine age, interest had been reawakened in individual workmanship, an echoing of the Arts and Crafts Movement that Lalique had witnessed in England. This Gallic revival, one of the seeds of Art Nouveau, manifested itself in the formation of various groups and salons devoted to, or at least mindful of, the decorative arts – *les arts mineurs*. When the Musée des Arts Décoratifs opened in 1882, the time was ripe for Lalique's full flowering as a goldsmith. Although he studied sculpture and continued to work as a graphic designer, he primarily used his talents in the early 1880s as a free-lance jewelry designer. At one time, indeed, he considered producing a book of patterns for the goldsmith's trade,[5] and although the project was abandoned, he did submit a year's worth – about two jewelry designs a month – to the respected trade publication, *Le Bijou*.

By 1885 Lalique had purchased Jules Destape's workshop, and in the following five years his enterprise expanded to comprise the capacious Rue Thérèse premises. Although he had begun to exhibit his jewels as early as the Exposition of 1889 (anonymously, under the names of the large firms for which he worked as a freelancer), it was not until the Paris Salon of 1894 that Lalique displayed his own works under his own name. He immediately won lavish praise from critics and gained numerous commissions from fashionable *grandes dames* of the Third Republic (the more conservative bourgeoisie tended to be chary of the Art Nouveau style, which it felt might not prove a sound financial investment). Lalique was well on his way to becoming the most prominent and innovative master in his field, but he was always to remain, in the words of Roger Marx, a "free-spirited goldsmith-poet as well as refined and discerning scientist".[6]

Sarah Bernhardt was doubtless Lalique's most famous female client and she provided him with the opportunity to apply his talent to relatively large-scale, often audacious, pieces that could be seen by the audience. She commissioned luxurious diadems, necklaces, belts and other stage "props", which he tailored specifically to the roles she was enacting – the Théodora crown of 1884, as well as *parures* for the parts of Iseyl and Gismonda.

Despite the boldness of his theatrical extravagances, Lalique's ruling notion was that a jewel worn by a woman should contribute to the harmony and total effect of her entire ensemble, a kind of "*gesamt-kunstwerk* within reason". The stage pieces for Sarah Bernhardt and the museum-pieces, so to speak, for Calouste Gulbenkian (which were never intended to be worn), were one-of-a-kind distractions which seemed to breathe a life of their own, and were exceptions to his general rule. They were outnumbered by the hundreds of other subtler, but no less lovely, pieces of *bijouterie* he produced: the brooches of shimmering aquamarine thistles or vivid enamel butter-

5. Dora Jane Janson, "From Slave to Siren", *Art News*, May 1971, 70.

6. Roger Marx, "La Parure de la Femme, Les Bijoux de Lalique", *Les Modes*, VI (June 1901), 9.

13

14 Winter Woodland
pendant, *c.* 1899–
1900, gold, enamel,
glass, pearl, 4½ ×
2¾in (11.3 × 6.7cm);
signed *LALIQUE*.
Calouste Gulbenkian
Museum, Lisbon.
Several of Lalique's
jewels depict
miniature landscapes
in the most expert,
highly detailed
fashion. This one
shows a frost-covered
lake and tall trees in
ice-blue glass, framed
by an enameled-gold
tree with snow-laden
limbs.

15 Owls bracelet, *c.*
1900–01, gold,
chalcedony, enamel,
glass, 2½ × 8in (6 ×
20cm); signed
LALIQUE. Calouste
Gulbenkian Museum,
Lisbon.
This piece had a
literary genesis; it was
inspired by
Baudelaire's poem,
"Les Hiboux."

13 Dragonfly Corsage
Ornament, *c.* 1897–
98, gold, enamel,
chrysoprase,
moonstones,
diamonds, 10¾ ×
10½in (27 × 26.5cm);
signed *LALIQUE*.
Calouste Gulbenkian
Museum, Lisbon.
The head of this
hybrid dragonfly
terminates in a
carved-chrysoprase
torso of a helmeted
woman, while its feet
are the talons of a wild
beast. The effect of
this massive jewel,
which Calouste
Gulbenkian acquired
from Lalique in 1903,
is both erotic and
terrifying.

14

15

18

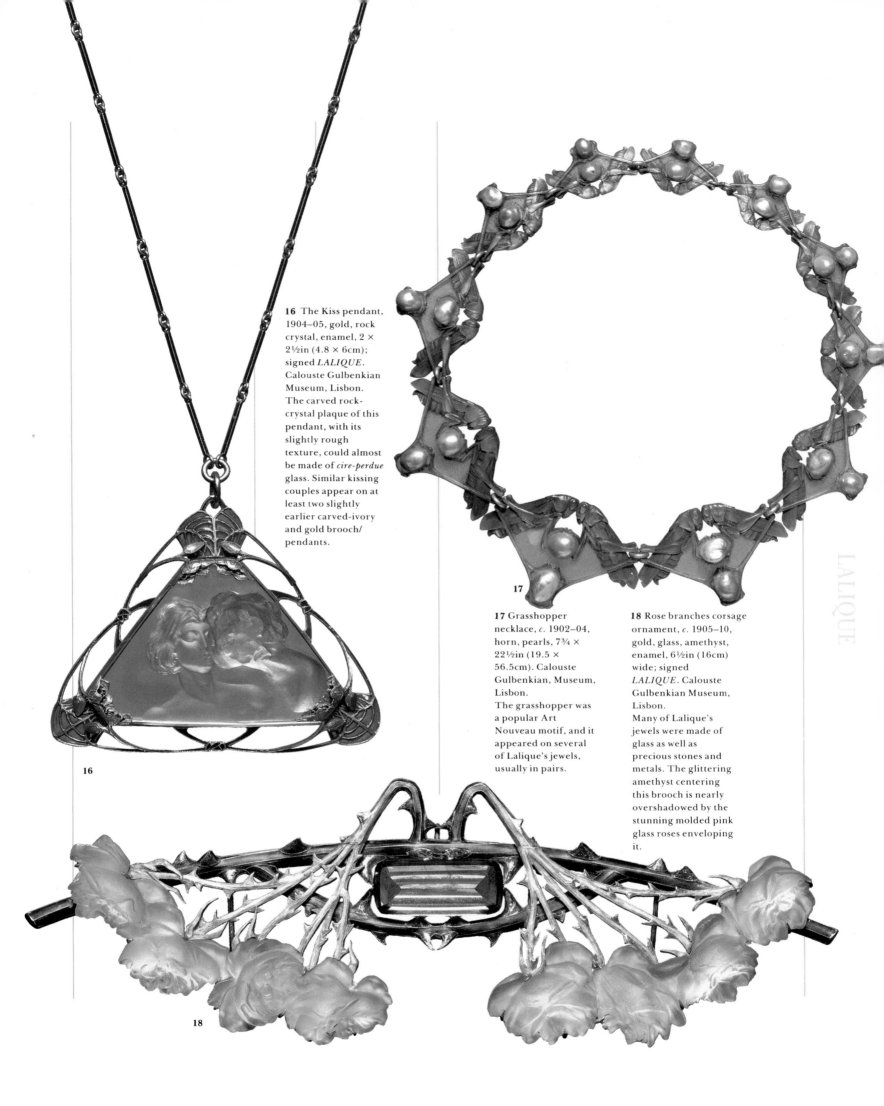

16 The Kiss pendant, 1904–05, gold, rock crystal, enamel, 2 × 2½in (4.8 × 6cm); signed *LALIQUE*. Calouste Gulbenkian Museum, Lisbon. The carved rock-crystal plaque of this pendant, with its slightly rough texture, could almost be made of *cire-perdue* glass. Similar kissing couples appear on at least two slightly earlier carved-ivory and gold brooch/ pendants.

17 Grasshopper necklace, *c.* 1902–04, horn, pearls, 7¾ × 22½in (19.5 × 56.5cm). Calouste Gulbenkian, Museum, Lisbon. The grasshopper was a popular Art Nouveau motif, and it appeared on several of Lalique's jewels, usually in pairs.

18 Rose branches corsage ornament, *c.* 1905–10, gold, glass, amethyst, enamel, 6½in (16cm) wide; signed *LALIQUE*. Calouste Gulbenkian Museum, Lisbon. Many of Lalique's jewels were made of glass as well as precious stones and metals. The glittering amethyst centering this brooch is nearly overshadowed by the stunning molded pink glass roses enveloping it.

LALIQUE

flies, the pendants of carved-ivory women, the dog collars of playful frogs, the bracelets of wise owls, the horn haircombs bedecked with naturalistic blossoms. Each of these provided the "spot of color in which the *tout ensemble* of a lady's apparel [found] its fitting culmination: the final touch that [accented] and [revealed] the general harmony of the whole".[7] Quality craftsmanship and intrinsic, intriguing beauty characterized all of Lalique's jewels, and whatever precious stones or metals he might employ (and they were always used more sparingly than the so-called "lesser materials"), they were never allowed to get in the way of the aesthetic effect of   piece.

Throughout his three decades as a goldsmith, Lalique continually experimented with new methods and new materials. He used horn in place of tortoiseshell and elevated that material to a near-luxury state; he employed embroidery techniques on metal; he applied enamels to any variety of metallic surface. And as his reputation grew, his rebellion against the proliferation of diamonds in *joaillerie* came to be officially approved by the board of jewelers. In July 1900, by order of the Chambre Syndicale de la Bijouterie de Paris, the use of precious stones or materials alongside semiprecious or "vulgar" stones and materials was formally permitted for the first time.

To detail the output of René Lalique the goldsmith is to review the entire repertory of Art Nouveau themes and inspiration. Brightly plumaged peacocks, glistening-shelled beetles, tensely coiled enamel serpents, realistically rendered flowers and trees, devastatingly devouring (or innocently playing and dancing) women and tightly embracing couples all make their appearance in his jewelry. But there are also more complicated, multi-dimensional, even painterly pieces, such as a miniature wooded landscape in gold, enamel, opal and brilliants which could be attached to a collar (but is probably lovelier on its own); or an ivory-carved pendant of a horseman emerging from the creamy dust, a nude fallen figure about to be trampled below and the entire scene surrounded by a gold frame of three horses' heads with stylized manes; or a superb plaque camouflaging a pair of indigo-blue enameled eagles behind gold and green pine-tree branches, and having in the center of it all a huge, stunning opal. Indeed, like many of the painters of the second half of the 19th century – Whistler and some of the Pre-Raphaelites, for instance – Lalique created both the work of art and the frame enclosing it, a revolutionary concept in the goldsmith's art.

The subjects Lalique chose for his *bijouterie* mostly came from nature. His home was aswarm with plants and from a very young age he had been a shrewd observer of flowers, trees and animals in all their guises and stages of growth. Pol Neveu wrote of Lalique's devotion to nature in *Art et Décoration* in 1900:

> For Lalique nothing is worthless and despicable in the spectacle of things. He seems to have strolled through fields, scrutinized with an attentive eye the streams of the Saintonge region, so as to question its aquatic life. He studied the germination, blooming, diseases and deaths of plants, the habits and movements of birds and insects . . . He has a knowledge of rural life which he acquired in the gardens, woods and in his atelier. As a sensible Champenois he has cherished animals and plants with a touching but informed faith.[8]

Lalique's floral vocabulary is perhaps his richest and, in the main, the most faithful to nature. Works range from a simple hatpin consisting of three silver-birch leaves in horn, their gold seed cones enameled in a complementary autumnal hue, to a bracelet of five bluish-violet *champlevé*-enamel irises on gold, all on a carved-opal background, and a lovely diadem in the shape of an apple-tree branch which, but for its composition of horn, gold and diamonds, might just have fallen to the ground and been retrieved.

The myriad combs, diadems and other hair ornaments that Lalique produced, mostly of horn embellished with gold, enamel, ivory, glass and stones, are the most realistically nature-laden of his *bijouterie*. In these designs Lalique was strongly influenced by the irregular design system of flowers which characterized *japonisme*, that borrowed Oriental style which, thanks in part to Siegfried Bing, had a vogue in turn-of-the-century France. Outstanding also (though more regular) is the Gulbenkian's diadem in the form of three orchids. The middle flower of *Orchids* (c.1903–04) is carved ivory inset with a topaz dewdrop, the outer blossoms are of carved horn, and the overall symmetry and perfection of the piece bring to mind one of Georgia O'Keeffe's monumental flower paintings – mysterious, symbolic, even slightly erotic. In another Gulbenkian comb, *Sycamore Fruit* (c.1899–1900), Lalique has carved the mundane wing-shaped fruits of the tree out of chalcedony, joined them with onyx seeds and dark-blue enamel and gold rods, and playfully nestled small gold beetles in the leaves, as in a Dutch still-life painting of the 17th century. Still another Gulbenkian comb, *Wisteria* (c.1902–04), exhibits a device often used by Lalique: certain carved areas are left "blank", that is, in their originally hued state, whereas other primary areas are built up or emphasized by means of fixing vividly colored enamels or other materials to the surface. Here the carved-horn leaves are left in their natural blond shade, the color being added by the twice-flowering wisteria, whose blossoms are of molded blue glass, stems of dark-blue enamel and gold, and calyxes set with tiny diamonds. The Cleveland Museum's *Lilies of the Valley* comb (c.1900) uses the same method. The edges of the carved-horn leaves are merely tipped in green enamel, but the stem and blossoms of the flower are in gold and white enamel. Two lovely combs of horn, silver and enamel show the blossoms not at their freshest, but in the initial stages of decay, their withering petals folding over ever so gently.

Flowers and other plant forms are also displayed on various brooches, bracelets and pendants, though more often than not these incorporate other insect and animal motifs as well. The Gulbenkian's dog-collar plaque (c.1899–1900), which features a carved-chrysoprase woman's head in profile, is framed by three blue-and-black enamel and gold poppy blooms, as well as by a flowering blue-enamel hair ribbon and the woman's own gold tresses. The flowers are often not the focus of these chiefly figural or animal *objets*. In the *Female Figure with Wisteria* pendant (c.1898), for instance, the carved-ivory nude, though partly hidden by the blue-enamel flowers and leaves, is nonetheless the main subject. Despite its name, the Gulbenkian's *Orchid Blossom* pendant (c.1900–01) is identified chiefly by its bottom petal, which is not of *plique-à-jour*, pale-blue enamel and gold

7. Nilsen J. Lauvrik, *René Lalique – Master Craftsman*, New York, 1912, 4.

8. Pol Neveu, "René Lalique", *Art et Décoration*, VIII, (November 1900), 129–36 (translated by V. Cozzi-Olivetti in "Lalique", *Metalsmith*, Fall, 1980).

19

like the four petals above, but of molded frosted glass in the ethereal form of a woman's head and breasts.

Some of Lalique's bejeweled flower pieces tend to become rather stylized, sometimes even too perfectly symmetrical, in comparison with the more freely designed, true-to-nature hair accessories. A chest ornament of *Thistles* (c.1905–06), for instance, centers on a huge aquamarine which is attached to enamel, gold and diamond thistle sprigs terminating in enameled-glass flower buds. What gives this pectoral significance is its blatant display of precious stone side by side with common material. The same is true of *Rose Branches* (c.1905–10), which is set with an amethyst in the middle, but is more notable for its octet of striking rose-frosted glass flowers.

One especially outstanding *japoniste* jewel created by Lalique is a necklace from the 1890s, made up of nine spherical *ojime* in ochre lacquer carved with a stylized-wave motif and embellished with tiny mother-of-pearl insets (*ojime*, part of the traditional Japanese costume, are bell-shaped toggles which separate the little seal container called the *inrō* from the carved *netsuke* from which it hung – the whole of which was worn suspended around the girdle). The *ojime* beads alternate with 20 pairs of dark-green-enamel twisted links, between some of which are circular peridot bezels. This necklace is not only noteworthy for its obvious Japanese borrowing (the *ojime*), but also for its translating a common Japanese motif – the crested wave of the beads – into the curvilinear Art Nouveau vocabulary.

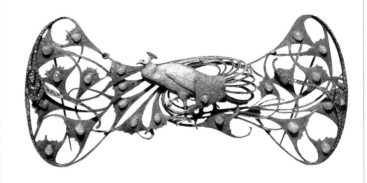

20

19 Cock's Head diadem, *c.* 1898, gold, enamel, amethyst, 3½ × 6¼in (9 × 15.5cm). Calouste Gulbenkian Museum, Lisbon. The subject of this elaborate – and unwieldy – diadem was adapted by Lalique from Oriental art. The cock's golden beak grasps an amethyst and its delicate openwork gold and enamel comb is as delicate as a spider's web.

20 Peacock corsage ornament, *c.* 1898–99, gold, enamel, opals, diamonds, 3¾ × 7½in (9.2 × 19cm); signed *LALIQUE*. Calouste Gulbenkian Museum, Lisbon. The exotic and haughty peacock was a popular motif with many Art Nouveau designers. Lalique's lavish chest ornament is undoubtedly one of the loveliest interpretations of the bird.

Interestingly, Lalique was to adapt another article of Japanese dress – the *tsuba*, or sword guard – to his all-glass pendants of the Art Déco period.

The animals that Lalique depicted in his jewels spanned nearly all the species of the zoological kingdom, from grasshoppers to polar bears, and at times beyond, to mythical dragons, sphinxes and bizarre hybrid beasts. Insects, amphibians, reptiles, birds and mammals were subject to his scrutiny and his craftsman's technique, with a decided emphasis on creatures beloved by Art Nouveau designers: the curvilinear swan, seahorse and snake, the brilliantly hued butterfly, peacock, beetle and dragonfly, the fearful bat and serpent. Sometimes Lalique interpreted literary characters. The *Owls* bracelet (*c.*1900–01) in the Gulbenkian was inspired by the poem, "Les Hiboux", from Baudelaire's often-illustrated *Les Fleurs du Mal*:

> *Sous les ifs noirs qui les abritent,*
> *Les hiboux se tiennent rangés,*
> *Sans remuer, ils se tiendront*
> *Jusqu'à l'heure mélancolique*
> *Où, poussant le soleil oblique,*
> *Les ténèbres s'établiront.*[9]

Along a five-part gold frieze perch four molded frosted-glass owls, symbols of darkness and night, among pine cones and branches.

A charming collar (*c.*1900) in the Virginia Museum of Fine Arts may very well depict the story of the "Frog Prince". Sixteen strands of tiny pearls surround a rectangular central plaque featuring a regal and smiling young woman's profile, and her head is crowned with a huge green-enamel frog. A bevy of his slithering companions fill the openwork field around the woman and her "Crown Prince", and the overall effect is humorous and even a little touching.

Most of Lalique's creatures are without any specific literary allusion and should be appreciated for their sheer beauty, the delicacy of their execution, and the imaginative way in which they are arranged or combined with other natural or abstract elements. Two facing *Grasshoppers on a Plum Tree Branch* (*c.*1902–03), a horn, enamel and gold diadem in the Gulbenkian Collection, become an elevated, almost poignant, pair in Lalique's hands, and the same couple is multiplied 11 times over in the Gulbenkian's *Grasshoppers* necklace of the same vintage, which takes on a dizzying, abstract quality enhanced by the baroque pearls that each pair of grasshoppers holds between them with their feet. A chest ornament of *Two Blister Beetles* (*c.*1903–04) facing each other, resting on branches of rose-enamel and glass berries and holding a large red tourmaline in the middle, also manifests a certain abstract quality, although the insects themselves are quite realistically rendered.

Butterflies and moths can be found on several Lalique jewels. One of the most striking is perhaps the blond horn and enamel stomacher showing seven butterflies, all carved from one piece of

21

horn, but only two of them embellished with enamel and one of these to a lesser extent than the other. The aforementioned "blank and built-up" technique is here employed most effectively to depict the maturation process of the butterfly itself – the carved, unadorned creatures representing the early stages of development, the fully finished and colored butterfly the one just emerged from its cocoon. Two sides of a single coin are shown on a watchcase that Lalique designed in about 1899–1900. The reverse of the gold case is covered with a swarm of dark-blue *champlevé*-enamel bats (dotted with appropriately nocturnal moonstones), the dial side with a coterie of frothy blue-and-white-enamel butterflies on a gold surface. The winding stem is topped by an intricately coiled serpent, its mouth agape. Bats and moonstones were also conjoined on a haircomb of *c.*1900, and an ankle bracelet of *c.*1902–06 depicts a bevy of the creatures amid opal-studded, five-pointed stars.

The snake is one of the strongest, most horrific subjects in Lalique's Art Nouveau (and to a lesser extent Art Déco) repertory, be it the above-mentioned fillip on the bat-and-butterfly pocket watch or the decidedly stronger pair of facing cast- and chased-silver serpents acting as the frame and clasp of a lady's evening purse (*c.*1901–03), whose entwining coils are continued in gray silk and silver metallic thread on the gray-suede body of the bag. The confronting-serpents motif was used by Lalique on a large scale as well. A standing bronze mirror (*c.*1899–1900) in the Gulbenkian has two

9. Charles Baudelaire, "Les Hiboux", in *Les Fleurs du Mal*, Paris, 1857.

such creatures forming its frame. In another example, two serpents whose bodies asymmetrically coil as one, and whose open fangs clutch a baroque pearl, form a stunning horn, pearl, silver and paste brooch. But the masterpiece among Lalique's serpent-jewels is the Gulbenkian's *Knot of Serpents* pectoral (*c.*1898), comprising nine interlacing snakes whose silver-gilt *champlevé*-enamel bodies of blue, green and black fan out from a top knot, their jaws hideously agape. Originally each serpent was represented as spitting a row of baroque pearls out of its mouth.

Birds of various types, but especially peacocks, roosters and swans, figure in Lalique's jewelry designs, as they do in his works in glass (though parakeets, swallows and other less mysterious flyers ordinarily adorn his vases). One of Lalique's best-known – and doubtless unwieldiest – diadems is in the shape of a proud *Cock's Head* (*c.*1898). Never before in the West had this barnyard fowl been treated so luxuriantly as on this Gulbenkian piece. The cock's golden beak grasps an amethyst and its openwork gold and enamel comb is as delicately wrought as a spider's web. More than the cock, the exotic and haughty peacock was a popular motif with many Art Nouveau designers, as it had earlier been with artists of the Aesthetic Movement. Designers such as Morris and Tiffany chose to depict only the brilliantly hued peacock feather – sometimes nearing the point of abstraction. Lalique was eager to display the bird in all its glory, as he did in a stunning chest ornament (*c.*1898–99; Gulbenkian Collection), in which the bird's enamel and gold tail feathers, richly studded with opals, swirl about the body in a bow-like pattern. The mysterious and delicate opal, often called "the aurora borealis captured in stone", is an apt mineral counterpart to the multicolored peacock. Lalique ingeniously paired the two on a pendant-brooch whose center is a

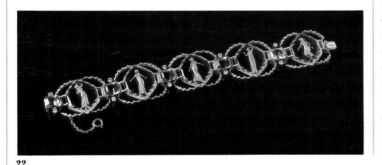

22

triangular opal around which two facing peacocks nestle their blue-and-black enamel bodies.

The swan, symbol of pride, is also the very embodiment of grace, the flowing line incarnate as it glides majestically over the water. It was therefore an irresistible subject for Art Nouveau designers. Lalique made dramatic use of it in a necklace of *c.*1897–99 which was shown at the 1900 Exposition Universelle in Paris (today it is jointly owned by the Metropolitan Museum of Art and Lillian Nassau). A pair of standing black swans flanks an elongated golden female nude in each of the nine segments of this showpiece. The woman's dark-blue *champlevé*-enamel hair swirls around her head – echoing the curves of the purple-and-black enamel swans – and pale green *plique-à-jour*-enamel wings emanate from her body and shelter the birds. Dividing each group is a round Australian opal framed by gold tendrils, and violet amethysts hover over each opal and between each pair of swans.

It is, of course, the woman who stands out in that necklace and indeed it is she who, almost to the exclusion of the male sex, populates the Art Nouveau domain, whether as a long-haired seductive nude, or a flower-crowned innocent, or a fetchingly veiled Loïe Fuller (the bewitching American dancer who came to personify the style). Lalique is thought to have been the first goldsmith since the 16th century to represent the female nude in jewelry. He did so frequently. He carved them in ivory and gave them rapturous demeanors; he coupled them in erotic dances; he veiled them with caressing vines and blossoms; he represented them as shameless pagan nymphs; and he paired them with birds and beasts (sometimes even with human males!).

Lalique's women were not always nude. A plethora of fully or partly clothed women sparkled on his combs, pendants, brooches and other *bijoux:* regal ladies with strong profiles carved in colored stone; classically draped maidens trailing floral garlands, one playing an aulos; Breton peasants in traditional costume; genuflecting angels deep in prayer; a wheat-crowned Ceres; silver torsos of Night and Day personified; a golden Ophelia reclining under a willow tree. Indeed, many of Lalique's plants and animals – serpents, swans, dragonflies, lotus blossoms, roses – are often Symbolist allegories of Woman in her various and mysterious guises, so that even when he is not depicting her directly, her spirit is often present. An element of

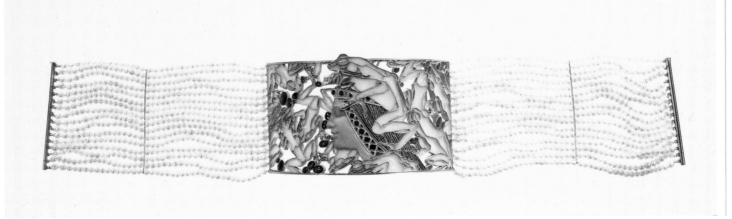

23

playfulness or humor is brought to the odd piece as well, as in a gold pendant of two women blowing opal bubbles from long pipes, or the plaque of the lady (described earlier) with her amphibious "Crown Prince".

In addition to the jewels themselves, Lalique executed a variety of unusual bejeweled objects, from mirrors and purse frames to precious lorgnettes with serpent handles and, even more ambitious, the stunning silver, horn and steel dagger of 1901. Female nudes, armed warriors and grotesque bats decorate the guard of the sword, which was first shown at Messrs T. Agnew & Sons in London in 1905, an exhibition which captivated the English critics. Lalique also designed a bookbinding in silver, elephant horn and leather, tiny metal keys and sculptured centerpieces, which usually depicted mythological characters, in silver, glass and other materials.

24

24 Details of desk and chair showing an ammonite-fossil motif and sorb-tree pinnates, designed by René Lalique and made by Léon Jallot (?), c. 1902–05. French walnut and leather, desk 29 × 40 × 33in (73.6 × 101.6 × 83.8cm), chair 36in (91.4cm). Collection Glenn and Mary Lou Utt, USA.

The two pieces were part of the furnishings of Lalique's Cours la Reine premises.

By 1895 Lalique was firmly established in the pantheon of great designers of the day, was perhaps even its leading light. Exhibitions of his jewelry increased, as did his clientele, critics were profuse in their praise, and various honors, including the *Chevalier de la Légion d'Honneur*, were bestowed on him – all before the turn of the century. Soon after creating pieces for Sarah Bernhardt in the mid-1890s, Lalique met Calouste Gulbenkian, and the artist-patron bond, as well as close friendship, which the two men formed led to the creation of objects that had, perhaps, been beyond Lalique's wildest imaginings. Lalique and Gulbenkian shared a profound love of nature. Each of them was a perfectionist. The client, Gulbenkian, did not in any way exert influence on the artist by virtue of what he chose to purchase, though he acquired 150 Lalique pieces during the two decades from 1899 to 1920 (some glass was bought up until 1937). Some pieces were purchased directly from Lalique, others from exhibitions, and they include the bulk of the goldsmith's most important work. To be able to view today, in Lisbon, so many works in one place is a rare privilege, one for which later designers, eager to study Lalique's jewels *en masse*, have been grateful. The Italian goldsmith, Vittorio Cozzi-Olivetti, and the premier American metalsmith, Albert Paley, for instance, are two artists whose work has been influenced by a close examination of Lalique's art, just as Lalique might have been inspired by the Renaissance sculptor and goldsmith, Benvenuto Cellini.

The Gulbenkian also possesses a superb collection of Lalique's preliminary designs for his jewelry, and indeed the master's many extant drawings form a valuable segment of his *oeuvre*. Lalique's talent as a draughtsman emerged quite early in his life and it served him well throughout his career as goldsmith and glassmaker. When a drawing is placed next to its finished product, one is amazed to note in each the precision of line and detail, as well, often, as the delicacy of color which permeates them. The similarity of many of the polished drawings to the final jewels attests to Lalique's vigorous discipline. (Lalique did, it is true, employ a group of talented craftsmen to help him realize his designs.) Many of the drawings are accompanied by detailed descriptions of the materials to be used, and side elevations are sometimes provided, especially for works in bas-relief. There are also more simple sketches for hundreds of pieces, these generally uncolored and many to a page. But the finished drawings – usually done in pen, pencil and ink, and gouache on a goldenrod-hued paper – are stunning works of art in themselves, a measure of Lalique's many-sided genius.

Less well known is the wooden furniture which Lalique designed for his own use. Two desk and chair sets are extant, one being the actual worktable on which he produced many of his sketches. This drawing desk with matching chair, c.1902–05, was part of the furnishings at 40 Cours la Reine, where Lalique was working by early 1903. Earlier he had helped to decorate and furnish the Rue Thérèse premises, as his family described in *Lalique par Lalique:*

> Helped by two relatives, René Lalique personally decorated his residence, covering walls and ceilings with frescoes, paintings, relievo motives. He designed his own furniture, combining functional and decorative purposes.[10]

10. *Lalique par Lalique*, 21.

The French walnut and moss-green leather desk and chair from the Cours la Reine house are adorned with ammonite-fossil motifs, as well as twigs, pinnates and blossoms of the sorb, or service, tree. The design complemented the overall pine and fir-tree decorations that pervaded the new premises (motifs not uncommon to Lalique's goldsmithswork). No doubt Lalique knew of the sorb tree from his family's holiday villa in the south of France, where the genus *Sorbus domesticus* abundantly grows, and perhaps from various publications as well (most likely Eugène Grasset's *La Plante et Ses Applications Ornamentales,* published in 1896–1901 and including colored drawings of the tree). The genesis of the ammonite-fossil motif used by Lalique for this furniture is more difficult to trace; similar shell designs appear much less frequently in his Art Nouveau repertory than they do later in his Art Déco glassware.

The desk and chair were solely intended for Lalique's private use and were not reproduced in any contemporary publications, as were the large African mahogany desk and gondola-style armchair, also from Cours la Reine, with their traditional shapes and Art Nouveau decoration (floral on the desk's carved legs and the chair's arms and top, chameleons on the desk drawer's mounts). These pieces both bear the stamp of Léon Jallot, the well-known designer who had worked for Siegfried Bing and also may have been the maker of the drawing desk and chair, neither of which is signed. They may also have been produced, in part or wholly, by M. Briançon, Lalique's friend and the foreman at his workshop from 1890 to 1910, Lalique's master chiseler, M. Deraisme, his father-in-law or brother-in-law, the Messrs Ledru, or even, perhaps, the architect of 40 Cours la Reine, the firm, Feine.

Another superb example of Lalique's furniture design is a tripartite screen of *c*.1900. The provenance of this painted and gilt leather screen unfortunately is not known, although it too may have belonged to the designer himself, judging from the pine motif at the top (and prevalent throughout 40 Cours la Reine). The 6ft-high screen is of a warm golden leather, and it is decorated with a flock of jackdaws, a trio of finely detailed birds perched on branches in the foreground, others flying in the background, these on the whole slightly defined – in much the same "blank and built-up" manner in which floral and faunal subjects were variously delineated on hair combs and other goldsmithswork. The upper border of the screen is covered with a symmetrical arrangement of pine cones and branches, while the lower features branches, roots and floating daisy-like blossoms, the latter fading out into the background. A lovely landscape of trees is visible in the distance, vestigial silhouettes in deep contrast to the minutely detailed borders and foreground. This recently discovered screen not only bears witness to Lalique's multifaceted design genius, but is also an outstanding piece of Art Nouveau furniture. Still another piece of furniture designed by Lalique is an interesting display case and stand comprising a four-legged wooden stand carved with sunflowers and leaf-covered corbels, surmounted by a bronze and glass vitrine fitted with glass panels molded with apple blossoms. At least three such vitrines exist, two in museum collections (London's Victoria and Albert Museum and the Chrysler Museum in Norfolk, Virginia). Nearly 5 feet tall, the vitrine and stand date from *c*.1910;

25

again, their original owner is not known.

Looking at the extensive and varied output of Lalique's first career as a goldsmith, it is not difficult to see that there was a quiet, diversified genius at work. Thinker, innovator, risk-taker, perfectionist, tastemaker – Lalique the Art Nouveau jeweler was all these and more. But during the years when he was making a name for himself in *bijouterie*, he was feeling the pull of another challenge, of a new material which he had already begun to incorporate in some of his jewels, namely, glass. The possibilities for varied shapes, textures, surfaces, colors and shadings in this material were endless. Soon Lalique was not content laboriously to produce the odd *cire-perdue* vase, nor merely to mold opalescent or frosted-glass figures and attach them to bracelets and pendants. He wished to devote himself fully to the production of glass. Doubtless Lalique the goldsmith's frustration with the many lesser imitators he had spawned also led him to consider working in another medium, although the chief reason for turning to glass was most likely an economic one – quite simply, the possibility of appealing to a wider market.

Amazingly, after just a few years' time, the most acclaimed goldsmith at the 1900 Exposition Universelle in Paris was to become the *maître verrier* of 20th-century France.

26 *Tête de paon* car
mascot, *c.* 1928, 7in
(17.7cm). The
Pickard-Cambridge
Family Collection,
National Motor
Museum, Beaulieu,
Hampshire.

EXPERIMENTS WITH GLASS

3

The decade of the 1890s was one in which Lalique experienced both the flush of success and the frustrations which accompany experimentation. The former, of course, was gained as a goldsmith, the profession whose peak he reached at the 1900 Exposition Universelle in Paris. In a mere six months, a staggering 50 million people visited the fair, which is today considered the apogee of the Art Nouveau style. Lalique's jewels garnered countless words of praise at the Exposition, and so did several other objects which were products of his second, and at this time still shadow, career as a glassmaker. Among the goldsmithswork, ivories and bronzes were works both wholly and partly made of glass.

The creation of a 4in-long perfume vial with stopper (c.1893) is the main subject of a somewhat romantic and heightened account of Lalique's search for a new material:

> Throughout the past years, he had been seeking for a medium in which he could not only bring his art to its height, but at the same time remove it from the luxury class, make it available to a wider public. Experimenting constantly, working feverishly, Lalique tried every medium which came to hand. Metals, shell, horn, various woods . . . he had used them all with conspicuous success. Still he was not satisfied.
>
> Finally on one occasion he was executing a new design . . . a buckle of gold set with gem-like rock crystal. Out of this came the idea which charted his future . . . pure crystal glass. Here was the medium he sought . . . the material he knew so well, for had he not for years worked with enamels . . . glass transformed with oxides? Scientifically he knew the composition: sand, potash, lead . . . he understood it, he recognized its possibilities, he foresaw its artistic future in the hands of the master designer. In his own kitchen he made his first experiment with pure glass . . . a tiny tear bottle, a droplike gem. It was moulded in a simple cooking pan over the fire in his stove in Rue Thérèse. He piled on the wood, hotter grew the flame . . . in that fire not just a treasured work of art was formed, a great artistic idea was coming to life. In the intense heat, Lalique worked, alone, oblivious to his surroundings. Suddenly he became aware of crackling timber. His studio was afire, his experiment in danger. While his landlord rushed to put out the fire, Lalique saved his original experiment in glass.[1]

Whether Lalique was at the time seeking a medium he could market to the general public and whether the fiery episode actually occurred are not known; but it is clear that the master was dissatisfied with the fruits of de luxe goldsmithswork alone. This was first manifested by his subtly embellishing his jewels with small figures or plaques of cast pâte-de-verre, as well as clear, opalescent or colored glass. The Flower Thistle pendant (c.1898–1900; Gulbenkian Collection) is one of the earliest of these hybrid pieces. Its iridescent, molded-glass thistle-wings surround a large, sapphire-framed moonstone in the shape of a teardrop and are themselves bedecked with diamond-set antennae. The typical Art Nouveau pendant, Female Head with Poppy Blossoms (c.1898–1900; Gulbenkian Collection), centers on the woman's molded-green-glass face. Her long, tousled hair of silver is crowned with four dark-blue enamel and chased-silver blossoms, and a baroque pearl, as bulbous as a popped kernel of corn, is suspended from the flowing locks which curl under her chin.

A small number of all-glass relief plaques, some of them with attractive metal frames, were also created by Lalique during the experimental 1890s, probably at the tail end of the decade. One frosted-glass plaque with an intaglio molded design (c.1900), measuring 18in × 16½in, depicts six singing angels, four of whose handsome profiles echo the female visages on some of his jewels. This piece is noteworthy, too, for its bronze frame with vertical side-strips of stylized Art Nouveau blossoms and for the manner in which the horizontal frieze of the seraphic group is surrounded above and below by a great deal of empty space, giving the piece a painterly, almost ethereal, effect. Plaques such as this, related technically to the architectural reliefs which Lalique designed for his Cours la Reine premises, foreshadow the later Art Déco figural reliefs, such as those for the Compagnie Internationale des Wagons-Lits. The later works, however, are undeniably products of the rectilinear Art Déco style, with stylized neoclassical overtones, whereas the early panels are more sentimental, romantic, indeed 19th-century, in character.

At the 1900 Exposition, Lalique also displayed larger objects which resulted from his experiments with glass. One spectacular vase (its location today is not known) was made from opalescent glass blown into an armature of metal. The frame consisted of a coterie of long, twisting snakes, their curling tails shaping the base, their multi-fanged heads acting as the rim. The glass between the sinuous vertical lines of the serpents' bodies undulated both concavely and convexly. This piece, even so, related more to the goldsmithswork of Lalique, the glass serving merely as a filler between the other far stronger – visually and structurally – elements of the vase.

The glass sculptures which bridge the gap between Lalique the jeweler and Lalique the glassmaker are surprisingly traditional in content and, for the most part, technique. They are by no means Art Nouveau in appearance, but then the qualities of the material (at least in the way that Lalique looked at it) did not lend themselves to the organic, curvilinear, colorful aspects of the style. In contrast to the sparkling Art Nouveau studio glass which was being produced by Daum, Tiffany and Emile Gallé (who was undisputed maître verrier of Art Nouveau glass), Lalique sought to inject his own taste and technology into decorative pieces. In his search to understand and master this challenging medium, and to control its limitless possibilities, Lalique dispensed with the organic, polychromatic hommage-à-nature approach of Gallé and others and adopted a more rigorous, organized, even serial approach. The earliest all-glass pieces were small statues and figurines which were cast from wax maquettes. They often depicted vaguely classical nymph- or warrior-like figures. Examples are the two statuettes in the Gulbenkian's collection called Pan and Maiden on Dolphin, both of which date from the first decade of the century. Such subjects were not new to Lalique, of course, but neither were they typically Art Nouveau. They looked back to Renaissance classical motifs and forward to the neoclassical aspects of Art Déco.

---

1. B. Altman and Company, René Lalique, Sculptor in Glass, New York, 1935.

28

27

27 *Tzigane* flacon, for
Corday, *c.* 1930, 8½in
(21cm). Collection
Mary Lou Utt, USA.

28 *Gros poisson algues,*
c. 1923, 11½in
(29cm). Courtesy
Christopher Vane
Percy.

29 *Borromée* vase,
c. 1925, 9in (23cm).
Collection Mary Lou
Utt, USA.

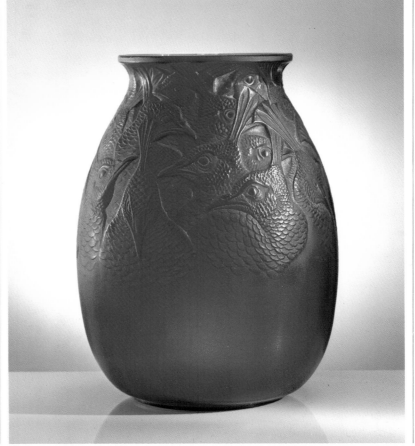

29

30 *Tourbillons* vase,
c. 1925, 8in (20cm).
Private collection,
London.

31 *Actinia* vase, *c*. 1933,
10¼in (26cm).
Galerie Moderne.

32 *Tortues* vase,
c. 1924, 11in (27cm).
Collection Laurie and
Joel Shapiro, Detroit.

Lalique's mass-
produced vases could
be pure Art Déco
compositions, like
Tourbillons and
Actinia, or their
naturalistic designs
could approach
abstraction, such as
the bevy of tortoises'
backs comprising the
amber *Tortues*.

In his early glasswork Lalique employed a wide variety of production methods, from *cire-perdue* and *pâte-de-verre* to hand-blown and mold-cast. He used both metal and ceramic molds, the latter primarily for *cire-perdue* pieces. Works which combined two or more materials, such as the metal, glass and enamel hybrids, were often subjected to numerous, time-consuming tests, in which temperature and the application of direct heat were continually altered until the desired effect was achieved.

In 1902 Lalique took his glass experiments a giant step further, by working along with a staff of four on the casting of glass reliefs at the family estate in the village of Clairfontaine, some 25 miles southwest of Paris, near Rambouillet. Raw materials were used to produce glass at the estate, as opposed to the vitreous blocks which were bought for the smaller Paris atelier (still very much a goldsmith's studio). It was at Clairfontaine that Lalique designed his first decorative architectural panels, greatly elaborating on the method of using paving slabs of glass, or *dallages*, as elements of building interiors (such massive square "stones" had been on view at the 1900 Exposition, having been produced for the trade by French and American flat- and window-glass manufacturers). The first panels made at the estate were of frosted glass and were used as the glazing for the metal entrance doors at Lalique's Cours la Reine premises. One can still view the gently pendant pine branches cast in bas-relief on 72 separate glass blocks, and the harmonious continuation of the pine-tree motif upward, in stone on the building's façade, in wrought iron on its balcony. A writer in *Art et Décoration* at the time concluded: "The effect is charming, of an exquisite simplicity, and at the same time the most subtle refinement."[2]

With the death of the great Emile Gallé in 1904, a fecund era of French Art Nouveau glass design had drawn to an end, and Lalique, whom Gallé himself had in 1897 called "the supreme exponent of the *Beaux Arts*",[3] was preparing to don the unofficial mantle of *le maître verrier* in France. Although the Fauve-painter-turned-glass-artist, Maurice Marinot (1882–1960), assumed Gallé's position as the premier *studio* glassmaker in the Art Déco period (all in all he created some 2,500 exquisite pieces by hand from 1911 to 1937), Lalique's methods of mass-producing Art Déco glass for the modern consumer changed the attitudes toward glassmaking altogether; and many people rated him higher than, or at least equal to, Gallé for revolutionizing and perfecting the manufacture of art glass. To manufacture art glass would have been considered a contradiction in terms a decade or so earlier, but Lalique's methods compromised neither the inherent qualities nor the natural beauty of glass.

Guillaume Janneau, in his 1931 book, *Modern Glass*, succinctly analyzed Lalique's glassmaking aesthetic and accorded Lalique his rightful place in the history of glassmaking:

Few artists have been so sensitive to the austere charm and the delicate chastity of the absolute transparency of glass, or have responded to it with the sincerity and subtlety of René Lalique. He is the champion of uncoloured glass, and as such, no less than through his actual formulae, his work marks a fresh stage in the history of glass-making. When René Lalique was bringing to light the results of his first experiments, Emile Gallé's formula consti-

2. Tristan Destève, "La Maison de René Lalique", *Art et Décoration*, XII (July–December 1902), 163 [authors' translation].

3. "Les Salons de 1897: Emile Gallé", *Gazette des Beaux-Arts*, XVIII (1897), 248.

tuted the epitome of the art of glass-making in the eyes of connoisseurs. His complicated and skilled productions, in which the
substance itself was disguised, were regarded, not without reason,
as masterpieces in the technical sense. In this direction every
possibility had been exhausted. No one could carry the art further
than Gallé, whose magic touch transformed glass into precious
stones. Lalique, however, revealed the beauty of glass as glass. His
relief technique, with its adroitly selected design, gave full effect
to rich material and rare craftsmanship. In a style which was
altogether French, and with an instinct for broad effect unknown
to the Venetians of the sixteenth century, he created a formula no
less exquisite than that of Murano.[4]

The "altogether French" style which Janneau was alluding to, Art
Déco, did not come to be referred to as such until some four decades
after the 1925 Paris Exposition, whose abbreviated title provided its
name. But by the end of the first decade of the new century its seeds
had already been sown, and sown in part by Lalique.

Just as the influences on French Art Nouveau were multifaceted
– Oriental design, Symbolist thought, Arts and Crafts philosophy
and, of course, nature in her many guises – so the Art Déco style
derived from a variety of sources. Classical and Egyptian motifs,
African art, the Ballets Russes and Cubism were among the influences embraced and adapted by Art Déco designers. The eclectic
style that emerged, unlike Art Nouveau, did not wholly ignore the
technology of the machine age. However, there were many premier
talents – such as the furniture makers, Emile-Jacques Ruhlmann and
Clément Rousseau; the metalworkers, Jean Dunand and Armand-
Albert Rateau; the silversmith, Jean Puiforcat; the studio glass artists,
Marinot and François-Emile Décorchement (the latter worked in
pâte-de-verre), and the ceramicists, Emile Decoeur and Emile Lenoble –
who used the finest materials and most elaborate techniques to produce outstanding, often one-of-a-kind pieces which today are considered the masterpieces of the style. And even though Lalique's
mass-production of glass did not echo the more restrained working
methods of artists like Ruhlmann and Dunand, the glass vases, statuettes, chandeliers and other works he produced were seen as complementary and not antithetical to theirs – as witnessed by the many
ensembliers who used Lalique glass to enhance their sumptuous interiors. Indeed, "luxury goods fashioned with consummate craftsmanship"[5] could be considered the motto of Art Déco designers, and
Lalique's glass, despite the vast quantities in which it was produced,
certainly met that criterion.

Paris was the undisputed capital of the new style, which was a
significant component of the "cacophony of aesthetic statements
[which] burst forth between 1910 and 1930",[6] as Penelope Hunter-
Stiebel has described that fertile period. No less than Cubist, Con-
structivist, Vorticist, Bauhaus and De Stijl artists, the Parisian designers who "band[ed] together in the Société des Artistes Décorateurs [Lalique and furniture-maker Léon Jannot were among its
members] were equally intent on creating an aesthetic for the
modern world. They absorbed influences from the more radical
modernists, but at the same time revived craft techniques of the past
and sought new forms by distilling the traditional vocabulary."[7]

The traditional vocabulary used by Lalique the glassmaker was
not so very far removed from that which he had used as a goldsmith.
Neoclassical figures, which were depicted on bejeweled pendants
and in bronze and cire-perdue-glass statuettes, continued to appear in
great numbers on his mass-produced vases and perfume bottles,
table lamps and car mascots, and mirror and picture frames. Floral
motifs were also abundant, though they often became less naturalistic and more stylized. A veritable menagerie of animals – birds, insects, reptiles, fish and mammals – was depicted as well, often greatly
abstracted and geometricized, but not without attention to detail.
The splendid solitary peacock of the Gulbenkian chest ornament,
for instance, can be compared to the Three Peacocks centerpiece of
some 30 years later. This elaborate glass surtout, 36in long and of
demilune shape, is accompanied by a bronze illuminated stand and
depicts the trio of birds in a stylized, yet somehow naturalistic,
manner. The stylization occurs in the abstracted tail feathers which
occupy most of the space, yet a realistic touch is added by the ran-
dom grouping of the peacocks, one in left profile in the foreground,
the upper left bird in right profile, and the one next to it viewed
from the back. The bird on the Gulbenkian pectoral, on the other
hand, is more naturalistic in hue and overall detail, while its feathers
fan out in a rather stylized manner to heighten the appearance and
shape of the jewel. Another depiction of peacocks is the Borromée
vase in electric-blue, opalescent-white and also clear glass, with its
disorderly flock of birds whose tail feathers are totally absent and of
whom only a jumble of heads and necks can be seen. One of these
heads, isolated in clear and frosted glass on a 7in-high statuette
(which could be used as an automobile mascot, a paperweight or a
bookend), presents a regal profile.

On the whole, Lalique's glass designs were derived from nature,
even if nature was stylized almost beyond recognition. They remain
some of the most stunningly Art Déco works in any medium: Tortues,
for example, in which a bevy of tortoises' backs nears pure abstraction in an amber hue, or cigarette jars in the Lierre pattern, in which
the intertwining plant tendrils appear more as five-point stars than
mere ivy leaves. Fish, which were not seen frequently on Lalique's
jewels, took wonderfully to his glass – like fish to water. These include the beautifully sculpted Gros poisson vagues (Large, Fish, Waves),
with its slippery surface, a menu holder with a bas-relief fish half-
above, half-under water, an opalescent-glass bowl adorned with
shimmering fish in a whirling radial pattern, and the Penthièvre vase
(c.1927), whose school of fish is a dazzle of zig-zags with vaguely
aquatic eyes and tails.

There is no doubt that Lalique was one of the premier exponents
of the Art Déco style. He singlehandedly developed a great deal of
its vocabulary, he made invaluable contributions to interior as well as
architectural design of the time, and he inspired, whether for artistic
or mercenary reasons, or both, a number of other firms to follow in
his wake. Included among these glassmakers were André Hunebelle,
Etling, Verlys and Sabino in France, Jobling in Great Britain, even
Steuben in the United States. Such inspiration and imitation attest to
Lalique's superiority in the design of glass, and to his esteemed place
in the pantheon of all Art Déco designers.

4. Guillaume Janneau, Modern Glass, London, 1931, 9.

5. Penelope Hunter-Stiebel, "Twentieth Century Decorative Arts", The Metropolitan Museum of Art Bulletin, Winter 1979/1980, 17.

6. Penelope Hunter-Stiebel, "Surpassing Style, Four Art Deco Masters: Ruhlmann, Dunand, Marinot, and Puiforcat", Antiques, October 1985, 733.

7. Ibid.

33 *Cire-perdue* vase with plums, *c.* 1913–20, 8in (20.4cm); wheel-cut: *LALIQUE*. Collection Glenn and Mary Lou Utt, USA.

THE TECHNIQUES

4

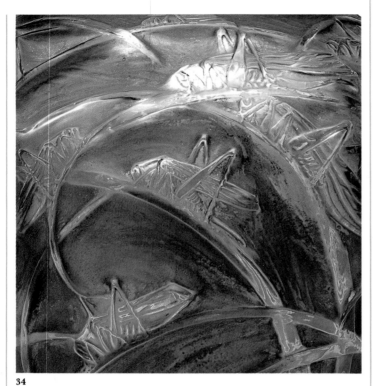

34

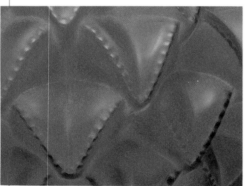

35

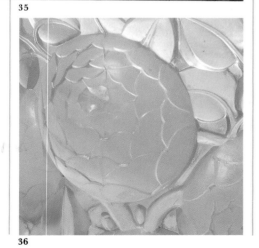

36

34 Detail of *Sauterelles* vase, early 1920s, 10¾in (27cm). Galerie Moderne.

35 Detail of *Languedoc* vase, *c.* 1926-27, 9in (22.5cm). Collection I. Chisholm, London.

36 Detail of *Oran* vase, *c.* 1925, 10½in (26cm). Galerie Moderne.

The details of these three vases show the sharpness and clarity Lalique was able to obtain through his molding methods. After being taken from the mold, *Sauterelles* was stained with a dark-blue and *Oran* with a light-blue *patine*, but the vivid green hue of *Languedoc*, as well as *Oran's* opalescence, were attained directly in the molding process.

o comprehend fully the importance of Lalique as a glassmaker and to understand why Guillaume Janneau called him the "champion of uncoloured [and coloured] glass", the creator of this "immaterial ether, the frozen breath of the Polar night",[1] it is useful to look in some detail at his most frequently used techniques and at some illustrative examples of his work.

The techniques employed by Lalique illustrate a near-complete history of glassmaking. These include the earliest pieces made entirely of *cire-perdue* glass, whose basic technology was developed in ancient times; the hand-blown delicacies mounted in metal armatures; the huge cast-glass blocks used as architectural elements; the layers of glass blown into a mold to achieve a lovely, semi-opaque effect, and the highly sophisticated mass-produced *demi-cristal* glass made exclusively by the Lalique Company before 1945. Likewise, the decorative elements added to glassware were varied, attractive and at times quite difficult to achieve. For instance, sepia-hued *patines* (a type of enamel) were used to heighten *cire-perdue* figures (a method Lalique may have learned about from Oriental ivory-staining); engraved handles and other decorations – including green-glass frogs in one instance – were applied to vases; raised areas of a design were polished, leaving a reserve of frosted or patinated glass in the recesses; black, blue or brown enameling was employed to highlight relief, and, rarely, metal foil was encased within glass to produce a dramatic effect (this too is an Eastern technique, and is still used by some Indian goldsmiths).

Glass is an artificial compound created by the fusion of a silica (such as flint, quartz or sand) with an alkaline flux (potash or soda) in a furnace. Additional ingredients will create various desirable effects, such as hardness, sheen or, in the case of metallic oxides, color. When the metal is in a molten state, it is quite pliant (although sticky) and can be drawn out from a lump into long threads, or blown into bubbles which can be shaped with pincers or tongs, or made to conform to a mold. To ensure strength and prevent brittleness, all glass must finally be slowly cooled, or annealed, in a warm oven or chamber. The two methods of blowing and molding glass have come a long way from their humble, ancient beginnings, by virtue of the increased efficiency, advanced tools, and diverse additives used in the process, yet the basic principles remain the same, thus linking the studio glass produced today in France by such talented artist-craftsmen as Gilles Chabrier and Claude Monod to the earliest glass cast in Egypt in 1500 BC.

PATE-DE-VERRE GLASS

The term *pâte-de-verre* literally means "glass paste". To produce it vitreous glass is first crushed to a fine powder, then an adhesive medium is added to make the glass a moldable plastic, and finally the paste -- which has the consistency of damp salt -- is put into a mold.[2] Unlike *pâte-de-cristal*, a clear glass which is composed of larger granules and is sometimes embellished by a marbling of color, *pâte-de-verre* is opaque and, unless polished, has a matt surface.

1. Janneau, *Modern Glass*, 9.

2. The authors are indebted to Elaine J. Lewin, whose "Research Project to Rediscover and Reintroduce the Lost Art of Pâte de Verre", written for the Royal College of Art, London, in 1979, provided much information on *pâte-de-verre* glass.

Pâte-de-verre was first used in ancient Egypt, but was not "redis-covered" until the 19th century (it had been rendered obsolete by blown glass in the first century BC), when the sculptor, Henri Cros (1840–1907), used it to produce large-scale polychrome reliefs. A number of Art Nouveau and Art Déco designers followed in Cros' footsteps, though they usually produced much smaller pieces, such as vases, ashtrays or bowls. They included Albert Dammouse (1848–1926), François-Emile Décorchement (1880–1971; his two grand-sons continue to work with *pâte-de-verre* glass today), the Daum fac-tory, Gabriel Argy-Rousseau (1885–1953), Alméric Walter (1859–1942) and, in the United States, Frederick Carder of Steuben Glass.

Lalique himself performed a few experiments with *pâte-de-verre*, using cullet, or waste glass, which he melted into fire-clay molds. Nicholas Dawes, in his excellent book, *Lalique Glass*, concludes that by 1893 "Lalique was incorporating glass into his jewelry in the form of cast *pâte-de-verre* shapes in opaque colors",[3] but it is difficult to be sure which jewels include such glass, and which a non-paste glass molded in the usual manner. It is safe to say, however, that Lalique worked with *pâte-de-verre* glass early in his goldsmithing career, but that he did not progress from making the odd jewelry embellish-ment with it to using it for self-contained vases and the like – most likely because of its limited commercial production possibilities.

CIRE-PERDUE GLASS

Lalique used this "lost-wax" process, which was adapted from *cire-perdue* bronze casting, for more than 20 years. He produced pieces in bronze as well as glass at the start of his career, such as the lovely *Portrait of Mme R. Lalique*, in which the artist's wife's regal profile, facing right, is crowned with an upswept tumble of curls. The per-fume vial mentioned in Chapter 3 was of *cire-perdue* glass, as were other small pieces from the 1890s (few are extant today, unfortu-nately), including a figural seal of *c*.1895–1900, which closely resem-bles popular bronze seals of the day.

Whether Lalique learned the "lost-wax" process from his father-in-law or brother-in-law, the Messrs Ledru, who were sculptors in bronze, is not definitely known; he may have been exposed to the method, before his marriage in 1890, while studying modeling tech-niques under Justin Lequien Père at the Ecole Bernard Palissy.

The *cire-perdue* process was first used exclusively to cast bronze, probably as early as the 2nd millennium BC. A wax model was made around a core of burnt clay and then encased within an "envelope" of clay mixed with plaster. The entire object was then baked, the molten wax run off through an opening at the bottom, and the molten bronze poured through the resultant cavity via another hole

37

3. Dawes, *Lalique Glass*, 4.

37 From left to right, three examples of *c.* 1930 vases with relief borders at their bases: *Lilas*, 9½in (24cm); *Renoncules*, 6¼in (15.5cm), and *Graines* 8in (20cm). Galerie Moderne.

38 *Cire-perdue* vase
with bees, 1919, 3¼in
(8cm); engraved:
Lalique 42–19. Private
collection, London.

39 *Cire-perdue* vase
with four leafy
branches, 1923, 3¼in
(8.2cm); wheel-cut:
R. LALIQUE 434–23.
Private collection, London.

40 *Cire-perdue*
"Hawthorn" jar and
cover, 1920, 5½in
(14cm); wheel-cut: *R.
LALIQUE 102–20/ 103*.
Private collection, London.

38   39   40

at the top. The outer layer of clay was then cut away, and the core inside was broken up and released through an opening made for that purpose. A hollow bronze figure was the final result, exactly producing the original, now destroyed, wax model. The process suffers from the disadvantage that only one cast may be produced at a time.

The *cire-perdue* method used by Lalique to make one-of-a-kind frosted-glass objects – perhaps his most sought-after works today – was essentially the same as that used for bronze sculptures. First, a design was carved by hand in modeling wax. The finished maquette was then set on a special tray and a retaining wall, usually of wood or metal, was constructed around it. Then the wax mold was "invested", that is, encased within a semiplastic refractory clay mixture – normally consisting of plaster of paris, quartz and water – which was kept in check by the wall. The clay was allowed to harden, so that even the finest details on the wax mold would be impressed on its inner walls. Once dried, the clay shell had two holes bored into it, one at the top, another at the bottom. The invested mold was then placed on its tray in front of the heat of a kiln, melting the wax and releasing it through the bottom opening of the shell. Later, molten glass was poured into the now-empty clay shell and allowed to anneal. Once that was done, the clay was carefully broken up to reveal the solid-glass sculpture underneath. *Cire-perdue* vases were made slightly differently from figurines or plaques, however, in that the glass was *blown* into the mold, rather than poured or cast into it, thus resulting in a hollow vessel. Finishing touches – polishing, applying additional pieces of glass, highlighting with a colored *patine* – were sometimes added. Lalique did not, of course, reveal every detail of his "lost-wax" craftsmanship – a *confidence d'artiste* which it was his to keep secret and with which he enticed clients and frustrated imitators.

The authors believe that the maquettes for the majority of the *cire-perdue* works were carved by Lalique, who would work pre-made wax blanks, sometimes modeling from scratch, sometimes adding only finishing touches. The high quality of the carving exhibited on many of the *cire-perdue* pieces attests to this belief, and is almost as good a proof as fingerprints (some of which appear on the sculptures, although they have never been tested as to their identity!).

A stunning *cire-perdue* glass shade for a lighting fixture, now in the Gulbenkian, was without a doubt realized from a maquette sculpted by Lalique himself. An explosion of blossoms covers the shade, creating a highly naturalistic and detailed piece which approaches the *japonisme* of some of the master's *bijouterie*. Likewise, a hanging light bowl (*c.*1910–20) is decorated with realistic prunus blossoms which strongly resemble the flowering twigs of the Gulbenkian's *Apple Tree Branch* diadem. Examples in blown *cire-perdue* glass also exhibit touches of *japonisme*, if only in their traditional ovoid or cylindrical shapes with lids. For example, a *Dragonfly* vase with cover (*c.*1910–13), in the Metropolitan Museum of Art, pays homage to both nature and the Orient in its form and motif, as does the lovely *Japanese Hawthorn* jar and cover from 1925 (private collection, London). Neoclassical motifs are also common, as they were in Lalique's goldsmithswork. The Gulbenkian's *Medusa* vase (*c.*1909–10) is decorated with four profiles of the horrific Gorgon, and amid her hair of snake-tendrils are twisting, fighting and cowering male nudes. The quartet of pink-tinted masks was cast separately and applied later to the body of the piece, as was the case with a small number of *cire-perdue* works.

Today Lalique's *cire-perdue* glass pieces – which are few in number and for that reason alone highly collectable – are sometimes worth well into five figures. The humble, but historically significant, perfume vial and stopper with the charming fish design (*c.*1893),[4] for instance, sold for $37,000 (or £16,150) at auction in New York in early 1980, a sculpted cougar (*c.* 1910) fetched $39,000 (£17,030) at the same Phillips sale, and a vase molded at the bottom with three fish heads attained a price of $56,000 (380,000 French francs) at a 1986 Paris auction.

The exact number of *cire-perdue* Lalique glass pieces is not known. Estimates range up to 500, but only 100 or so, which are in either private collections or public museums, are fully documented. They

---

4. The gently iridescent bottle was on loan to the Louvre from 1925 to 1945 and later belonged to Lalique family friend, Elie Khouri.

range from vases, bowls and platters to ashtrays, sculptures and boxes, and they were quite visible at various salons and expositions in the early 1920s. Many of the *cire-perdue* works are classified by two sets of molded numbers (which had been incised on the wax maquettes) and might therefore seem to be parts of a limited series. But by the very nature of their one-of-a-kind status, this cannot be so. The first two or three numerals represent either a control number or the number of the drawing or sketch from which the work was derived,[5] and the last two numerals the year in which it was made. This type of numbering was used from around 1919 to 1926 and is usually found on the base of a piece, next to or alongside Lalique's generally wheel-cut signature (usually his surname in block capitals). Those *cire-perdue* pieces produced earlier in the century are often marked by a barely legible "Lalique" in script; the faintness is often due to the matt, pitted surface of the glass (which often reveals dramatic fingerprint impressions, though whether they are Lalique's cannot be proven, as previously mentioned).

ARCHITECTURAL GLASS

Lalique began producing large blocks of glass for use in interior and exterior architectural design at Clairfontaine. For this purpose he increased the dimensions of his molds – something he could not have done in his more limited Paris atelier. The molds were made of steel and the glass was poured into them in a molten state, thus allowing for "pieces of far greater size and importance [to be] produced than is possible under other methods. The cost of one such mold may easily run into three or four thousand pounds."[6] So wrote Mrs. Gordon-Stables in 1927, hoping "to dispel to some extent the delusion that Lalique glass is somewhat highly priced".

To decorate the blocks, which invariably had a satin or frosted finish which produced multiple internal reflections, the method of sand-blasting was usually employed, whereas smaller works with frosted surfaces were treated with special acids to produce the desired texture. It is not possible to tell in every case exactly how a finish was realized (again, Lalique was guarded in terms of his methods), but one sales brochure reads: "Special fluoridic baths, endless time at the polisher's wheel and considerable handwork are involved in achieving the proper contrast between satin and clear."[7]

The glass in Lalique's interior decorations was often used in conjunction with steel, the blocks being set in the framework of the metal, which was often broken up into grid-like partitions. The thickness of the panels – which were far easier to mold, to anneal, and to transport than huge, unwieldy single slabs – both prevented breakage and enhanced their luminosity, as Gabriel Mourey wrote in 1926:

> Lalique has opened up new realms for [the architectural glass] industry . . . by using glass of great thickness, either leaving its transparency and brilliance, or frosting it or enriching it with engraved designs; by pressing glass into steel molds which reproduce relief decorations in all their delicacy and perfection.[8]

41

41 *Cire-perdue* vase with fish-head base, 1923, 7¾in (19.5cm); wheel-cut: *R. LALIQUE*, incised: *437–23*. Kagan Collection, USA.

MOLDED GLASS

The entirety of Lalique's mass-produced works was either blown or pressed into a mold. The shape of a piece was of utmost importance to him, as well as its surface decoration, and the types of molding procedures available and then elaborated on by Lalique allowed for great variety in his output.

Essentially, a mold-blown piece is produced by blowing a bubble of molten glass into a metal mold. The process is especially well-suited to producing Oriental-style shapes with narrow necks and swelling bodies, many of which Lalique produced in the 1920s. Many smaller vases were mouth-blown, whereas all the larger designs were

5. It is not certain whether the first series of digits refers to an actual design number, as suggested by Mirek Malevski (in an unpublished manuscript) or to consecutive design numbers, as suggested by Nicholas Dawes (*Lalique Glass*, 32).

6. Mrs. Gordon-Stables, "Lalique", *Artwork*, May 1927, 33.

7. Quoted in Dorothy Clendenin, "The Hood Ornaments of Lalique", *Road & Track*, June 1974, 52.

8. Gabriel Mourey, "Lalique's Glassware", *Commercial Art*, July 1926.

42

42 *Druides* vase, *c.* 1925,
7½in (19cm). Galerie
Moderne.

43 *Formose* vase,
c. 1926, 6¾in (17cm).
Galerie Moderne.

Both these spherical
vases are "cased", that
is, they comprise two
(in some cases, three)
layers of different-
colored glass which
make for a rich,
nearly opaque effect.

43

produced in partly automated molds, thus allowing for vessels with slightly thicker walls. Such automation of blown glass also allowed for the "casing" method, in which two, and sometimes three, separate gathers of molten glass were applied to the blowing tube, or pontil rod, and the layered gather then put into the mold. A lovely semi-opaque or opalescent effect could be achieved in this manner, especially in those pieces which encased a shimmering white gather between two colors, as in the jade-green *Alicante* and *Druides* vases (*c.*1925), or the stunning agate and opalescent cased *Formose*, the exterior of which was molded with a shoal of shibunkin fish.

After the Wingen-sur-Moder Glassworks was established in 1921, Lalique successfully introduced the press-molding method of glassmaking – that is, pressing or forcing the molten glass into the mold with the use of a vertical plunger. Not only was this process more efficient, but it allowed for extremely sharp detail in relief decoration and it imparted heavier walls to hollow pieces and greater overall thickness to solid sculptures. Depending on its weight, one or two men were required to produce a press-molded vessel, all of whose shapes tended to taper at the bottom (in order to ease entry and exit of the plunger). The technique was described in the French publication, *Mobilier et Décoration*:

This is the process which he uses: The molten glass is poured directly into a steel mold from a melting pot, at which point it is

forcibly compressed. On making contact with the wall of the mold, the glass cools and retracts a little. Then the mold is quickly opened up in order to prevent any breakage – but not too quickly, or else the still-soft mixture will lose its shape. The process, as it has been seen, demands a skillful turn of hand.[9]

Besides their tapering shapes, press-molded vases have even inner surfaces, which do not conform to the design on the exterior (as they do in mold-blown pieces).

Massive, solid vessels of bold, decidedly Art Déco, designs were produced by the press-molded method in the 1920s, among them the dramatic *Tourbillons* (*c.*1925), available in colored or clear glass (with or without black enameling) and today one of Lalique's best-known and more desirable pieces, the black-enameled version having been shown at the 1925 Paris Exposition. *Eucalyptus* (*c.*1922) is one of Lalique's earliest press-molded vases and it retains a high degree of naturalism in its long, gentle fronds. Yet three years later *Moissac*, with its vertical-stripe motif of conjoining leaves, is characterized by a stylization of nature which approaches abstraction. Whatever their shape or design, however, all of Lalique's molded pieces were of high quality, which was maintained by the frequent replacement of molds. That was no doubt a costly custom, but excellence and the name Lalique were synonymous.

9. "René Lalique", *Mobilier et Décoration*, September 1925, 31– 32.

TINTED GLASS

An article on Lalique written in 1912 observed that his "whole purpose seems to bring out the pure crystalline quality which glass alone is capable of presenting in final exquisite perfection".[10] That "crystalline quality" was inherent in most of his works, blown or molded, and was achieved by using a potash glass body with a lead oxide content of around 12 per cent, half the lead content required for glass to be called crystal under French law. Duly named *demi-cristal*, Lalique's glass was suitable for both mold-blowing and press-molding, since it was relatively inexpensive, highly ductile when semi-molten, yet smooth enough to be removed easily from the mold when annealed. It was not so pure and sparkling as pure lead crystal, but it took definition better, and its other qualities – colors, textures, motifs and shapes – more than made up for its questionable lack of "sparkle".

The vast majority of Lalique's works are clear, opalescent or of pale hues. But an explosion of color emerged from his palette for a brief spell around 1912 to 1914 and then again for some time in the 1920s and 1930s, with shades ranging from the richest amber to the boldest blue, from the rubiest red to the most emerald of greens. These were jewels of quite a different sort from the master's *bijouterie*, but they were every bit as dazzling, perhaps even more so, considering that they were made of the commonest raw materials, magically transformed by Lalique's painstaking and advanced production methods. Today, collectors value the vividly colored pieces almost as highly as those of the rarest *cire-perdue*, despite the fact that there are many more of them available.

To achieve colors in glass, certain, usually metallic, oxides are added to the basic mixture before firing: cobalt for blue, uranium for yellow, chromium for red, etc. Lalique's first use of color, however, was part of the external decoration on glass: the wash, or *patine*, with which he was staining or coloring pieces by the first years of the 20th century (and which he continued to use for the next couple of decades, sometimes combining more than one shade of *patine* on a vase). A type of enamel, *patine* was a natural extension of the enamels he had used to embellish his goldsmithswork.

Color next entered Lalique's technical vocabulary in about 1910, on the occasional powder box and perfume bottle (black was a rare but desirable shade for boxes as well as for the choicest perfume containers). He also produced a limited number of vases in a wide range of colors. *Courges*, with its amoeba-like gourd motif, dates from *c*.1913 and was available in a number of hues, including red, green, yellow, plum and turquoise. After World War I, an extensive range of colored pieces was produced, and today connoisseurs consider the large, brightly hued vases the finest of their kind, "whose design, execution, and overall quality were unmatched in the 1920s and have not been equaled since".[11]

Large numbers of production pieces, in addition to the monumental vases, were also available in colors. Ashtrays, paperweights and pendants were composed of molded tinted glass, and there were clear-glass brooches, buttons, pins and other jewels whose color derived from a piece of foil mounted between the glass and the

44 *Eucalyptus* vase, *c*. 1922, 6½in (16.5cm). Galerie Moderne.

44

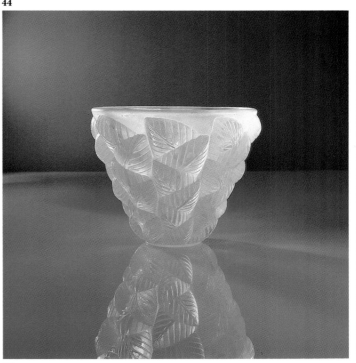

45

45 *Moissac* vase, *c*. 1925, 5½in (13cm). Galerie Moderne. Photo by John Kegan.

Both of these vases are early press-molded examples of Lalique glass. Whereas *Eucalyptus* is characterized by naturalistic feathery fronds, the opalescent *Moissac* – produced only several years later – has a decidedly abstract leaf pattern.

10. Raymond Riordon, "A New and Great Craftsman in France", *The Craftsman*, October 1912, 81.

11. Dawes, *Lalique Glass*, 48.

LALIQUE

46

47

46 Lemonade set, jug and six glasses, late 1920s. Galerie Moderne.

47 *Blidah* pitcher, late 1920s, 8in (20cm). Galerie Moderne.

Lalique produced "services à orangeade", as they were called in his 1932 catalogue, in both clear and colored glass. The *Blidah* set also would have comprised a matching round tray and at least a pair of tumblers.

metal backing. They had a widespread appeal, and their shimmering iridescence was much imitated at the time by costume jewelers in France, Great Britain and elsewhere.

A large assortment of functional wares was also produced in color, from decanters, bowls and platters to an orangeade or lemonade service in the *Blidah* or *Bahia* patterns – available in an orangeish shade of glass.

The use of colored glass decreased sharply in the late 1930s, in part for reasons of cost, and only the rare vase was produced in other than clear glass.

OPALESCENT GLASS

The pearly, opalescent quality found in many of Lalique's vases, platters and statuettes is very close to that of *blanc de lait* glass, which is reminiscent of Chinese porcelain; and its mysterious, blue-white sheen is evocative of moonstone, a gem of the feldspar family which Lalique often used to stunning effect. Opalescent glass was made in Venice in the early 16th century, by the end of the 17th century it was made throughout Europe, and by the 19th century it had become a tradition in France. It comes as an astonishment to learn that Lalique used it for more than 90 per cent of his production ware in the 1920s and 1930s. His *Suzanne* figurine of the mid-1920s, representing the Biblical Susannah among the elders, is one of his best-known works in any type of glass. Designed to be lit from behind or underneath, the figure is erotic yet ethereal, very much a product of early Art Déco stylization – and the classic Lalique woman.

It may be useful to examine the composition of opalescent glass, if only to comprehend the complexities and painstaking chemical processes which accompany the production of any type of glassware, clear, colored or opalescent. Essentially, phosphates, fluorine and aluminum oxide are added as "opacifying" agents to the glass mixture, often with a trace of cobalt to obtain the internal bluish sheen. On some pieces, including Lalique's, the opalescence is more intense on those parts in relief, for instance, figures against a background. This is because the density of the opalescence depends on the rate of cooling of the exterior in relation to the center. The opal within cools more slowly, thus making for more transparent opalescence in the thin walls and a richer effect on the thicker surface areas.

Unfortunately, we do not know the exact ingredients of Lalique's opalescent glass (nor of his other types of glass, whose compositions were all kept secret), but the following formula is considered typical for opalescent glass:[12]

Ingredient	Percentage
SAND (SiO_2)	67
POTASH (K_2O)	8.5
SODA ASH (Na_2O)	10
LEAD OXIDE (PbO)	3
QUICKLIME (CaO)	5
ALUMINUM OXIDE (Al_2O_3)	1.3
PHOSPHORUS PENTOXIDE (P_2O_5)	4
SULPHUR TRIOXIDE (SO_3)	0.16
CHLORINE (Cl_2)	0.1
FLUORINE (F_2)	0.4
MANGANESE DIOXIDE (MnO_2)	0.04
WHITE ARSENIC (As_2O_3)	0.2 to 0.6
COBALT (CoO)	Trace

An interesting anecdote, told by John Baker and Kate Crowe in their guide to Jobling art glass,[13] illustrates Lalique's guarded attitude towards his formulae and methods and his desire for his firm to maintain unmatched, and unmatchable, standards of glass-production. In 1931 the Jobling firm of Sunderland, England, was interested in manufacturing and selling opalescent glass similar to Lalique's. The firm developed its own "Opalique" glass and by early 1932 was producing lighting panels in it. Jobling wrote to Lalique to suggest that his firm manufacture Lalique's products in Great Britain on a royalty basis. Lalique roundly refused the offer. Jobling, however, worked at perfecting his Lalique-type glass and by 1935 "Opalique" was registered as a trademark. A variety of glass ornaments and utilitarian wares were produced by Jobling in the "Opalique" style, at prices far lower than Lalique's, but in no way representing a threat to his opalescent output. A price comparison shows that Jobling's "Opalique" animal figures had trade prices of 10–25p, while Lalique's deer statuette (or *presse-papier*) retailed for approximately £2.62 – a considerable difference in cost, but then, their clienteles probably never overlapped.[14]

48 *Montmorency* vase, c. 1926–27, 8in (20cm). Galerie Moderne.

The milky blue-white sheen effected on this opalescent vase could be found on most of Lalique's vases and statuettes in the 1920s and 1930s. Because of chemical changes in the cooling process, the opalescence is always more intense on those parts of an object in relief – such as the luscious raised berries on *Montmorency*.

48

12. Chart drawn in *Opalescence, Le Verre Moulé des Années 1920–1930*, Brussels, 1986, 7. The formula coincides almost exactly with one shown in John Baker and Kate Crowe, *A Collector's Guide to Jobling, 1930s Decorative Glass*, Tyne and Wear County Council Museums, 1985, 11.

13. Baker and Crowe, *A Collector's Guide to Jobling*, 11–12.

14. *Ibid.*, 55.

49

Lalique's first atelier was the one he bought on Place Gaillon from his patron, Jules Destape. In 1886 he began working in that space, designing and producing his goldsmithswork with the assistance of a small work force. The workshop soon proved inadequate for his needs, and in 1887 he leased another space on the Rue du Quatre-Septembre. He occupied both spaces until 1890, when the premises at 20 Rue Thérèse were acquired. By then Lalique was employing some 30 workers, who assisted with the goldsmithswork and also the bronze-casting with which Lalique was increasingly involving himself. The 1890s witnessed the first experiments in glass, some of which took place in Rue Thérèse, and by 1902 his work in that medium had expanded enough to warrant yet another space, the atelier at Clairfontaine. There Lalique worked with a staff of four (mostly casting large glass reliefs), who were probably, according to Nicholas Dawes, "a foreman, or *chef de place,* two *ceuilleurs,* who supervised the melting and pouring of glass, and a *gamin,* or boy helper".[15]

The premises at 40 Cours la Reine followed, and they were completed in around 1902. Workshops, a display space, and living quarters comprised the multi-story structure, for whose renovation Lalique, in collaboration with the architect, Feine, was directly responsible. This remained his Paris residence for the rest of his life, but a separate retail shop was opened in 24 Place Vendôme in 1905, opposed to which Francois Coty set up his own retail premises two years later, at number 23.

Lalique's first major commissions from Coty, for perfume bottles, were made in the workshops of Legras and Company of St.-Denis, whose facilities were better-equipped to handle the demands of such mass-production. The Legras firm had over a thousand employees working for it, a number which must have overwhelmed Lalique. In 1909 his own rented Combs-la-Ville Glassworks, near Fontainebleau, employed some 50 to 100 workmen, mainly in the production of perfume bottles. The methods used for making bottles were adapted from those used in the French wine trade and pharmaceutical industries. Lalique's most sophisticated elaboration of this basic technology was the use of precision-cast metal molds. The molds were not inexpensive, but neither were Lalique's products; he raised the standards of his machinery to meet his own quality product's standards.

A year later, in 1910, Lalique purchased the Combs-la-Ville Glassworks and his commissions from *parfumeurs,* as well as production of vessels of his own (*cire-perdue* and mold-blown), increased. In addition, Lalique continued to cast decorative panels at Clairfontaine – for Coty, among other clients. Combs-la-Ville closed down in 1915 and when it reopened four years later it entered a period of rapid growth. *Cire-perdue* glass was still made at Combs-la-Ville in the 1920s, but Lalique had by then set his sights on even greater mass-production and work began on the construction of another glassworks in 1919. This was located in Alsace, the province recovered from Germany and now a prime location for new industry (the French government offered money-saving inducements to firms setting up there). The new factory was situated in the town of Wingen-

49 *Styx* flacon, for Coty, 1910–13, 4¾in (12cm). Collection Mary Lou Utt, USA.

This is one of the earliest perfume bottles Lalique designed for François Coty. The mass-production method he employed for making his fragrance flacons was adapted from those used in the French wine business.

LALIQUE

15. Dawes, *Lalique Glass,* 9.
16. Maximilien Gauthier, "Le Maître Verrier René Lalique à l'Exposition", *La Renaissance de l'Art Français et des Industries de luxe,* September 1925.

sur-Moder (where Cristal Lalique still produces glass to the present day).

More efficient methods of mass-producing glass were developed at Wingen. In 1925, in an interview with a French magazine, Lalique said that his objective was to lower the price of his glass while increasing and diversifying the designs – to make his art available to all at modest prices.[16] In the 1920s the production of Lalique glass expanded by tenfold and the work staff trebled. Lalique's son, Marc, was made plant manager at Wingen in 1922 and many of the innovations in manufacturing introduced there were the fruit of his engineering and technological acumen. Press-molding was first used at Wingen in 1921 (it was used only there) and some 200 of Lalique's vase designs were realized at the factory in that productive decade.

By 1930 Lalique's production was at its peak, although the bulk of the works produced had been designed in earlier years. The production of *cire-perdue* and colored glass all but ceased after the Depression, as did that of mold-blown vases, ornate centerpieces and massive chandeliers (the latter two due to changing tastes). Easy-to-produce, press-molded vases were the order of the day at Wingen in the 1930s, with a dozen or so new designs introduced to the public every year.

The factory at Combs-la-Ville closed its doors for good in 1937, and in 1940 World War II forced the Wingen Glassworks temporarily to cease operations. By the time it reopened in the late 1940s, after the extensive repair of war damages, Lalique had died and his son, Marc, was at the helm. The Wingen factory thrives today, employing some 450 people, under the artistic supervision of Marie-Claude Lalique (she has a studio at Wingen, as well as an atelier in Paris, where she produces two or three designs a year).

50

50 *Dahlia;* for Nina Ricci, after 1945. Collection Mary Lou Utt, USA.

Dahlia is a René Lalique design and was featured in the 1932 catalogue.

51 *Duncan* flacon 4, *c.* 1932, 7½in (19cm). Collection Mary Lou Utt, USA.

The *Duncan* garniture set included flacons, as well as boxes and trays. It was produced after 1945 as well, but Marc Lalique changed the shape of the stopper, from that of a hemisphere to a large rectangle.

51

43

52 *Source de la fontaine*, *c.* 1925, 28in (70cm). Galerie Moderne.

This statuette takes its name from the fountain Lalique designed for the 1925 Paris Exposition. At least 15 versions of the female figure – all with aquatic attributes – made up the fountain.

THE EXHIBITIONS

5

LALIQUE

Exhibitions of Lalique's designs – at international expositions and fairs, at the Parisian salons, and in his own and other retail establishments – were a key factor in establishing his worldwide success and fame. Favorable reviews and articles on the master's creations, in newspapers and art publications, kept the name of Lalique in the discerning public's eyes for some 50 years, from the first dazzling descriptions of his jewels at the 1900 Paris Exposition Universelle to respectful obituaries in *The New York Times* and other papers on 10 May 1945.

Lalique first exhibited his work – a modest assortment of exquisite watercolors for jewels – in 1884, at an Art and Industry exhibition of contemporary goldsmithswork which accompanied a showing of the French Crown Jewels at the Louvre. The designs were admired by many who saw them, including the renowned *joaillier*, Alphonse Fouquet. Lalique next displayed some jewelry at the 1889 Paris Exposition (for which the Eiffel Tower was erected), but these were presented under the names of the firms for which he was at the time doing freelance work. In 1893 he produced a series of jewelry designs for the journal, *Le Bijou*, further advancing his reputation among members of the trade.

It was not until the 1894 Salon of the Société des Artistes Français that Lalique exhibited works of art under his own name, including an ivory relief panel depicting a scene from the opera, *Die Walküre*. A large selection of jewels was presented at the salon the next year, and from then on the art of René Lalique was regularly unveiled to an eager audience. He participated in the salons first as a goldsmith (until about 1909) and later as a glassmaker (well into the 1920s) and he was awarded various medals of distinction. His work was promoted by Siegfried Bing at his Rue de Provence gallery, and his exhibits continued to be reviewed in the European art and design journals which had begun to proliferate in the early 1890s (partly in response to the growing respectability of and interest in arts and crafts).

Without a doubt the apogee of Lalique's career as a goldsmith was the Exposition Internationale Universelle of 1900 in Paris, which welcomed the dawn of the new century and commemorated the 30th anniversary of the Third Republic with displays of recent technological achievements and contemporary art and design. Lalique contributed jewelry as well as ivories and bronzes to the fair, where he was honored with both a Grand Prix and the Rosette de la Légion d'Honneur. According to critics of the time, the sumptuous jewels he displayed, as well as their dramatic setting, were among the most arresting attractions at the entire fair. The patinated-bronze grillwork of the vitrine in which the jewels were displayed was itself a masterpiece of Art Nouveau, dominated as it was by five sultry, sinuous female nudes posing in front of feathery backdrops which terminated far below their feet in long webs of openwork wings. One account further describes this exhibit:

> This grille served as a background screen in front of which the jewels were displayed on a ground of white moiré silk. Lambrequins of gray were applied with velour bats. The rug and the draperies were of gray and on the wall at the back was a large painting by Georges Picard which represented small sylphs fro-

licking by moonlight among the trees at the border of a lake. A mirror reflected two huge bronze serpents. In this spectacular setting Lalique exhibited twenty horn combs ornamented with enamel, opals, amethysts, and chrysoprase; and a variety of collars and diadems.[1]

The *Cock's Head* comb, *Dragonfly* pectoral and *Knot of Serpents* corsage ornament – all in the Gulbenkian Collection – were among the one-of-a-kind bejeweled fantasies on view at the exposition.

The noted critic, Gabriel Mourey, described Lalique's contribution to the 1900 Exposition rather sedately (though there is no doubting his appreciation of the master, since he continued to praise Lalique's genius throughout several decades of articles and reviews):

> Facing the glass-cases where Lalique had exhibited a true wealth of jewels with the supremely refined taste which he had always devoted and still devotes to the presentation of his works, an enthusiastic crowd had assembled, from morning till night, for six months. And the lookers-on had every right, indeed, to display such enthusiasm. All the art critics of the day and the others too have celebrated the gifts of freshness, splendor, fancy, variety, and versatility which had turned into small but undoubted masterpieces all those pendants, diadems, brooches, gorgets, combs and hairpins through which Lalique had entirely renovated the art of the goldsmith.[2]

After the 1900 Exposition in Paris came a series of triumphant displays of Lalique jewels: at the Turin Exposizione (1902), the St. Louis World's Fair (1904), the Liège fair (1905), and in London (1903 and 1905). He continued to exhibit jewels at the Paris salons (in 1901 his display window "was framed by two large crystal snakes, to the astonishment of the visitors"[3]), and soon his renown had spread to America, where a review of his contribution to the 1903 Salon appeared in *The Craftsman*:

> These articles of feminine adornment strike a note never before sounded or even attempted in what has been seen, until now, [as] one of the minor arts. They do away with the last trace of suspicion, that it is a barbarous instinct which prompts the wearing of jewels and ornaments. It is not exaggeration to say that each of these little creations is a hymn in praise of Nature, composed by one who is capable of feeling the great and of rendering the small.[4]

Two significant events occurred in Lalique's career in 1905: he opened his first retail shop at 24 Place Vendôme and a major exhibition of his works was held at the prestigious T. Agnew & Sons gallery in Bond Street, London. The London exhibition was reviewed in the *International Studio* and, despite several negative comments, such as that of the "unpleasant decadence" suggested by some of Lalique's "beautiful natural forms and flowers in unnatural-looking material" and a "feverish haste of creation" leading to a "lack of style",[5] the reviewer complimented the master on "his great imaginative skill", on his genius, and on his "daring originality . . . as a designer":

> Whether there is a market in England for the more beautiful of the adornments in which M. Lalique has shown his skill we cannot say, but in any case the exhibition was a success. For, to pass from jewelled pendants to an ornamented and elaborate dagger, from

1. Charlotte Gere and Hugh Tait, "Romanticism to Art-Nouveau", in *The Jeweller's Art, An Introduction to The Hull Grundy Gift to The British Museum*, London, 1978, 18.

2. *Ibid.*

3. Gabriel Mourey, Aymer Vallance, et al., *Art Nouveau Jewellery & Fans*, New York, 1973 reprint, 2.

4. Peter Selz and Mildred Constantine (eds.), *Art Nouveau and Design at the Turn of the Century*, New York, 1975 (revised edition), 11.

5. Dora Jane Janson, "From Slave to Siren", *Art News*, May 1971, 70.

6. Roger Marx, "La Parure de la Femme, Les Bijoux de Lalique", *Les Modes*, VI (June 1901), 9.

53 Brooch/cloak clasp, *c.* 1904–05, gold, glass, *plique-à-jour* enamel, 2 × 6¾in (4.8 × 16.85cm); signed: *LALIQUE*.

Galerie Moderne.

This stunning jewel was featured in the Paris Salon d'Automne of 1905,

one of the many exhibitions where Lalique triumphed, first as a goldsmith and later as a *maître verrier*.

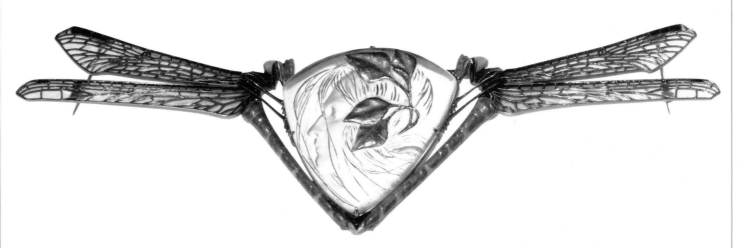

53

dishes with beautiful silver figures to pieces with exquisite ornamentation in gold, all carried to a level of execution not surpassed in modern things, was to be at an exhibition showing the success of a fine artist in every department of his chosen work.[6]

Lalique himself designed the *cire-perdue* bronze medallion announcing in simple script the opening of his Place Vendôme gallery. Bearing at the top the profile of a downcast, leaf-bedecked female head, the medallion is at once classicizing and Art Nouveau. The invitation issued to his 1912 exhibition of glass, his first significant display of works in the medium, presented a marked contrast from the earlier roundel. Not only was this circular medallion made of pressed glass (a shade of sea green), but on one side was a molded text whose print was very much in the early Art Déco manner and on the reverse an all-over decoration of mistletoe which presaged the stylized floral designs on some of his later vases.

In 1912 Lalique also used glass in his interpretation of "the modern style" at the Salon of the Société des Artistes Décorateurs. This salon was held twice a year at the Pavillon de Marsan of the Musée des Arts Décoratifs, and it proved to be an important showcase for Lalique's designs for several years.

The Place Vendôme showroom turned into a successful operation for the marketing and selling of Lalique objects, which by 1915 consisted almost entirely of glass. Before World War I there were surprisingly few retail establishments selling Lalique wares, only Place Vendôme and a smattering of *de luxe* jewelry stores in European cities. By the 1920s, however, all that had changed. More fairs and expositions in France and abroad had brought Lalique more praise and business, and he set up agents and retail businesses in France, Great Britain, the United States, Argentina and other places.

The Crystal Shop and Breves Galleries were agents of Lalique in London, and in America Ovington's (an East Coast chain of stores), Saks Fifth Avenue, Wanamaker's (in Philadelphia), Jacques Jugeat and B. Altman & Company (both in New York) and Los Angeles's Alexander and Oviatt's offered Lalique ware to a responsive public.

An impressive selection of museum exhibitions enhanced Lalique's reputation as a *bona-fide* artist-designer, not just a successful self-promoting business man, just after World War I. In 1919 he showed his works extensively at galleries and museums in Europe (including Copenhagen's Museum of Industrial Art) and the United States. Two summer 1919 shows at the Brooklyn Museum and Knoedler Galleries in New York must have produced a wave of "Lalique fever" among those lucky enough to view them, judging from the tone of the reviews they received. The *International Studio* reviewed the Brooklyn show:

> The current exhibition ... includes 28 pieces of glass by the French jeweler René Lalique. This glass was unknown in the United States until the San Francisco Exposition of 1915, and has rarely been seen in this city since that date ... Lalique has produced glass of wholly original character, and the most beautiful so far known to modern times. Its beauty depends upon form and design more than upon colour, which is frequently that of clear glass, but occasionally of a light copper-coloured stain said to be a form of enamel ... The composition of the glass has been achieved after many years of experiments and is, so far, a secret of Lalique, who personally designs all the drawings and patterns.[7]

Maria Oakey Dewing (wife of the American Impressionist painter, Thomas Wilmer Dewing) waxed poetic about the Knoedler show:

LALIQUE

54 Medallion
announcing the
opening of Lalique's
Paris gallery, *c.* 1905,
cire-perdue bronze,
2½in (6.5cm) dia.

Collection Laurie and
Joel Shapiro, Detroit.
The roundel reads:
*Invitation à l'exposition
de R. Lalique 24 Place
Vendôme.*

54

In the glass of René Lalique we see the adventure of the imaginative artist who has lifted the veil between the real and what the real holds for the seer, the vision beyond the tangible.

That glass can be the medium for such sentiment is the surprise – that nature can be so captured and bent to this poetic use – that technique may be so rigid and so fluid – that in so hard a material as glass the quality of moonlight, the tender downiness of little birds, the exquisite fragility of flowers may be expressed.

These familiar things are used as words in a song suggesting more than themselves, showing that they as well as the pure contour of the vase are speaking of something greater of which they are but a symbol, that evasive but eternal beauty to which the inspired hand may point in using marble, or paint, or musical instruments, or glass. We had not heretofore placed glass so high.[8]

If the 1900 Paris Exposition was the crowning achievement of Lalique's career as a goldsmith (and the peak of the Art Nouveau style as well), then the 1925 Exposition Internationale des Arts Décoratifs et Industriels Modernes capped his career as a glassmaker and was the pinnacle of the Art Déco style. How elegantly Lalique fit into – and bridged – the two styles, and how fortunate he was to have the two greatest expositions of the 20th century as his showcases!

Although 21 foreign countries took part in the 1925 Exposition, the summer fair, which was financed by the French government, was primarily intended as a spectacle of French design and decorative arts. Its emphasis was on quality workmanship, luxurious materials and elegance, and among its star displays were interiors by Süe et Mare and Robert Mallet-Stevens, furniture by Pierre Chareau, Armand-Albert Rateau and Emile-Jacques Ruhlmann, silver by Jean Puiforcat, lacquerware and metalwork by Jean Dunand, and, of course, glass by René Lalique. Lalique's touch was felt throughout

the exposition, from the entrance, whose *porte d'honneur* was embellished with panels of his frosted glass, to his centerpiece outdoor fountain on the Esplanade des Invalides, and from his contributions to the Parfumerie Française and Sèvres pavilions to his own sumptuous pavilion.

Gabriel Mourey, ever the champion of Lalique, wrote that it was at the 1925 exhibition that the master:

made the most brilliant demonstration of the innumerable applications of glass to architecture and interior decoration. The fitting up of the department of Perfumes, the decoration of the dining-room exhibited by the factory of Sèvres, the monumental fountain which preceded the entrance to the Court of Trades were signed by him. As for his own pavilion, it was indeed, in its obstinate and refined simplicity, the expression of his supple and strong talent, which delights both in measure and pluck. The white marble of the flag-stones, the bright woods of the ceilings, the glass-doors vignetted with silvery flowers, the E-wrought-iron of the glass-cases, the large glass-shield of the luminary at the ceiling, all sparkled, sang songs of light, lived of a life which was scintillating and sweet, immaterial and bewitching; one would have thought it was the palace of the fairies.[9]

Lalique's 132ft-high fountain was an obelisk which sprayed water in gentle arcs of varying degrees, suggesting the shape of an evergreen tree with limbs gently bowed under frost. The fountain itself, whose 17 tiers were each punctuated by eight female statuettes, was constructed of frosted-glass panels and was called the *Source de la fontaine*. There were at least 15 versions of the female figure. One of the loveliest was of a vaguely Oriental-looking woman. She wore an elaborate veil over her bowed head, her feet were bare, and her flowing drapery was studded with what looked like beads or water droplets; in her left hand was a fish, its curling tail cupped in her right hand. The *Sources en masse* were in effect a monumental totem-pole-like personification of water. The 136 figures – especially with nocturnal illumination – must have been breathtaking. Maximilien Gauthier called the fountain a "graceful symbol of springs, or streams, and of rivers of this sweet country France . . . [The fountain] seems to become a vignette which, amazingly, stands for the sense of joint effort which Paris today embodies fully."[10]

Elsewhere at the exposition, many of Lalique's vases and lighting fixtures enhanced room settings by noted *ensembliers*, while the *parfumerie* section, near to the great fountain, displayed many of his bottles. Roger et Gallet, the perfumer, commissioned Lalique to design the firm's entire display; not only his bottles, but his furniture and display stands and cases, were on view.

Lalique also decorated a dining room in the Manufacture Nationale à Sèvres pavilion. A starkly, but stunningly, decorated room, it featured a grid of modernist Lalique lighting fixtures on the ceiling, marble walls with silvery ceramic inlay on which were depicted a forest scene (complete with wild boars pursued by a pack of hounds) and a table setting consisting, among other pieces, of Lalique decanters, goblets and candelabra. Gauthier wrote that Lalique seemed to have surpassed even himself with this *salle à manger*, and he quoted Gustave Geffroy's poetic reaction to the

8. Maria Oakey Dewing, "The Glass of René Lalique", *American Magazine of Art*, June 1919, 301.

9. Mourey, "A Great French Craftsman", 116.

10. Gauthier, "Le Maître Verrier René Lalique", 419 [authors' translation].

ravishingly decorated walls: "the kind of arboreous patterns with which winter frost decorates even the most humble of windows".[11]

Lalique's own pavilion, designed by him in collaboration with Marc Ducluzand, was a simple, flat-roofed building with two side extensions. Severely modernist, even mausoleum-like, the structure was on first glance more akin to those of Le Corbusier in the fair than to the ornate confections that were the Primavera, Pomone and Galeries Lafayette pavilions. The entrance, however, was a subtle masterpiece, with its silver-inlaid ceramic steps leading to the door, whose quasi-naturalistic decoration contained some 2,000 pieces of molded glass. A large assortment of *cire-perdue* glass was on view, as well as a dining-room display, a solitary example of the early gold-smithswork, and one-of-a-kind display pieces, including a huge, bellows-shaped vase, some 6½ft high. Lalique displayed additional production pieces at a small showroom on the Pont Alexandre III, where a temporary "Rue des Boutiques" was set up. Lalique exhibited lighting fixtures, cups, bowls, vases and other wares of opalescent, clear and frosted glass.

Without a doubt, Lalique was one of the stars of the Exposition. Not only did his exhibits "prove to the world the beauty of crafts-manship in glass",[12] they indisputably established Lalique as the *maître verrier* of France.

The 1925 Exposition was the best publicity a designer could hope for, but Lalique did not rest on his laurels. He continued to produce his glass at a feverish pace while his son, Marc, upgraded and im-proved their glassmaking facilities (as well as marketing and sales methods), and he continued to exhibit at salons and other fairs. One selling tool used by the Lalique firm was the catalogue, one of which, the extensive and important 1932 *Catalogue des Verreries de René Lalique,* has proved invaluable for the identifying of a great number of Lalique's pieces. Not only does every piece or line have a name – from the tiniest glass medallions (*Psyche, Narcisse debout*) and per-fume bottles (*Camille, Marquita*) to the largest vases (*Oran, Oranges*) and *surtouts* (*Caravelle, Tulipes*) – but there is also detailed infor-mation regarding dimensions, model numbers and price (color or enamel was always more expensive than clear or undecorated). The catalogue is a bible for anyone interested in Lalique, and fortunately it is available in facsimile version today. Some lamps, vases, lighting fixtures and small table accessories are not listed in the catalogue, but it is otherwise exhaustive.

Other retail establishments produced catalogues of Lalique glass, and their advertisements were often featured in art, design and other publications. The Breves' Lalique Galleries in London took out advertisements in *Autocar* and *The Studio Yearbook,* and also produced at least two catalogues of their own, the handsomely designed *The Art of René Lalique* and *Lalique Lights.* The copy written to sell the product was predictably poetic and at times hyperbolic, but it was nonetheless sensitive about the product, not at all like the "hype" with which we are familiar today:

Among all the famous artists in glass, there has never been such a consummate master as René Lalique. For Lalique not only pos-sesses a rich imagination and an unerring sense of form – he has an extraordinary faculty for exploiting the colour and texture of the glass itself. His versatility is astonishing. He can be delicate, fantastic, bizarre, or vigorous, yet his style always harmonises with his subjects, and the originality of the true artist marks all his work . . . Lalique, indeed, is the pioneer in the Age of Glass which is now at its beginning.[13]

Even the "hard sell" is subtle and refined:

Not the least of the attractions of Lalique Glass is the breadth of its appeal. There are pieces which immediately strike a responsive note with the connoisseur, the huntsman, the motorist, the artist, or the man or woman who loves beauty for its own sake. It is the supreme tribute to Lalique that he can appeal so intimately to such widely differing temperaments. At Breves' Lalique Galleries his work is to be seen in all its lavish variety. Here it is possible to acquire a single exquisite specimen to bestow upon a friend, a service of glass for the table, or a lovely bowl to adorn a room.[14]

In 1933 a very special exhibition was organized at the Pavillon de Marsan. It was not a salon display, but a special tribute to Lalique – the relentless innovator, yet constant upholder of French tradition. This retrospective, unprecedented in the 50-year history of the Musée des Arts Décoratifs, included examples of Lalique's most recent vases with *taillé*, or cut, decoration (many not actually cut, but molded with such sharp-edged designs that they looked like cut-glass), as well as a selection of jewelry, glassware and even tables. One highlight of the exhibition was a glass altar, whose rail was decorated with frosted-glass lilies and surmounted by a reredos depicting a sex-tet of molded angels. (Lalique had designed altars for a chapel in Normandy in 1930 and one in Jersey four years later, and altars similar to it had been shown at the 1930 Salon d'Automne and the 1931 Salon of the Société des Artistes Décorateurs.)

A spate of exhibitions and commissions in the United States fol-lowed in the wake of the Musée des Arts Décoratifs retrospective (interestingly, one of its immediate precursors was a 1932 exhibition in Japan). Nicholas Dawes wrote that "during the 1930s the Lalique Company found increasing commercial success in the United States, largely because of a concentrated sales campaign managed by Marc Lalique".[15] In 1935 Marc's aggressive marketing strategies – coupled with the expertise of Jacques Jugeat, his American distributor – re-sulted in a major showing of Lalique glass at B. Altman & Company in New York. Much of the glass had been in the Paris retrospective, but some was designed exclusively for the Fifth Avenue department store. In 1939 there was an exhibition at Saks Fifth Avenue, though it was considerably smaller and included mostly small boxes, bottles and other *garnitures de toilette.*

Lalique's last presence at a major exposition was in 1937, at the Exposition Internationale des Arts et Techniques, which was de-voted primarily to industrial design. Lalique contributed a com-memorative medallion of frosted glass with sepia *patine* – a stark, neoclassical design featuring two winged male nudes – as well as a simple fountain of hexagonal segments decorated with a motif of stylized bubbles. "The fountain," Dawes wrote, "represented Lalique's interpretation of industrial design, but the overall appear-ance was cold and sterile, lacking the subtlety of line which distin-guished the sophisticated designers."[16]

11. *Ibid.,* 417.
12. B. Altman and Company, *René Lalique, Sculptor in Glass.*
13. Breves' Lalique Galleries, *The Art of René Lalique,* London, undated, 2.
14. *Ibid.,* 15.
15. Dawes, *Lalique Glass,* 117.
16. *Ibid.,* 121.

55 Group of Lalique
perfume bottles, with
Pyramidale carafe at
rear left, 1930s,
carafe 12½in (31cm).
From left to right,
front flacons are: *Le
Provençal* atomizer for
Molinard, 7¼in
(18.5cm); *Madrigal*,
for Molinard, 6¾in
(17.5cm); *Fleurettes*,
6½in (16cm); *Iles
d'Or*, for Molinard,
4¾in (12cm), and
Calendal, for
Molinard, 4½in
(11.5cm). Rear right,
Imprudence, for
Worth, 8¼in (21cm).
Galerie Moderne.

THE FLACONS AND POWDER BOXES

6

56 *Ambre Antique*
flacon, for Coty, 1910,
6in (15cm). Collection
Mary Lou Utt, USA.

This was one of
Lalique's earliest
designs for Coty. It is
especially elegant with
its neoclassical female
figures in bas-relief,
highlighted with a
russet *patine*.

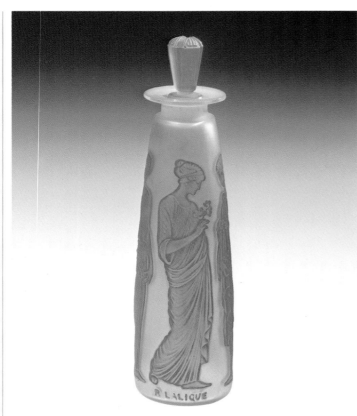

56

57 *Cigalia* flacon and
box, for Roget et
Gallet, *c.* 1910, 5in
(12.5cm). Collection
Mary Lou Utt, USA.
The four cicadas
clinging to the sides of
the perfume bottle are
echoed on the
pressed-wood box,
which was also
designed by Lalique.

*A*lthough they were among the smallest glass articles that Lalique created, the perfume bottles he manufactured for nearly 40 years – and which Cristal Lalique continues to produce today – represented the perfect marriage of the highest design standards and inexpensive mass production. Between the tiny teardrop of a *cire-perdue* scent bottle (*c.*1893), which Lalique painstakingly created in his Rue Thérèse studio, and the sophisticated flacon with blue-highlighted scalloping, which he designed for Worth's "Requête" in the late 1930s, came millions of perfume bottles of all shapes, sizes, colors and motifs.

The history of aromatic essences and their receptacles is almost as long as that of glass. Fragrances and unguents were concocted in ancient Egypt and classical Greece, and were stored in elaborate vessels of carved calcite (often incorrectly called alabaster), onyx and other fine stones. Glass perfume bottles and terra-cotta containers were used by the Romans for aromatic oils. But it was not until the 18th century that the rumblings of a perfume industry *per se* began to be heard – in France. During Louis XV's long reign, the porcelain, furniture, tapestries and silver produced were works with refined contours, lustrous surfaces and a light-hearted gaiety. Everything was made with a sensitive view to tones, textures and lines. Mme de Pompadour was a great tastemaker of the time, and the subtle style was in part due to her and to the increasing prominence of women in social and court life in general. In such a stylish environment Houbigant, Revillon and Lubin thrived as *parfumeurs* to the élite. Perfume containers in the rococo era were opulent designs of porcelain or, less frequently, cut-crystal, and they were often embellished with gold or silver mounts and enamel flowers or genre scenes à la Boucher or Fragonard. At the same time, Battersea-enamel perfume bottles were being produced, the transfer-printed and overpainted surfaces of which depicted landscapes, flowers, birds and the like in delicate hues on a white background. By the end of the 18th century a great many European factories were producing fragrance containers in enamel, porcelain and blown and cut glass, the latter material proving to be the most popular.

In the 19th century perfume bottles were made by major glass-making firms such as Baccarat and St. Louis in France, Stevens and Williams and Thomas Webb and Sons in Great Britain and various Bohemian glasshouses. Outstanding, often one-of-a-kind, perfume bottles were created by Art Nouveau designers later in the century, including Tiffany and Gallé. As the glass industry found itself becoming increasingly mechanized by the dawn of the new century, so too the manufacturers of perfume were able to produce more high-quality fragrances at relatively cheap prices, as Martin Battersby described in *The Decorative Twenties*:

> The recent discoveries of chemical ingredients which, to a great extent, could replace the rare and costly essences which had hitherto been necessary to fix scents, meant that perfumes could be produced in greater quantities and in a wider range of varieties.[1]

By the year 1900 scents were available in hand-made bottles (which were often costlier to produce than the liquids within) or they were economically packaged, and "it was common for individual druggists

1. Martin Battersby, *The Decorative Twenties*, London, 1971, 65.

to concoct their own scents and eau de cologne, offering them for sale in plain glass pharmaceutical bottles wrapped in waxed paper".[2]

Into this climate of fervid productivity, cheap materials and either too unimaginative or too expensive packaging (not to mention the nascent competition from couturiers-turned-*parfumeurs*) came François Coty and René Lalique. Together they made Coty's 1906 prediction, that he would manufacture the finest scent, present it in a very tasteful and simple container and sell it at a reasonable price,[3] come wondrously and profitably true.

The Corsican-born Coty, who established the House of Coty in 1904, came soon afterward to occupy premises near Lalique's on the fashionable Place Vendôme. Coty's first success was his "La Rose Jacqueminot" perfume, which had been packaged in bottles made by the long-established Baccarat firm. But if he was to fulfill his prophecy, he needed to find a more economical way of mass-producing the bottles for his scent. This is where Lalique came into the picture.

Gabriel Mourey dramatically described the state of glass design and Lalique's own mood when, in about 1905, Coty and he first made contact, Coty supposedly having seen some of Lalique's early flacons in a window display:

> With the exception of Gallé, very few [glass] artists had seen the part which could be played both industrially and artistically by this admirable material. But Lalique's fertile imagination saw all its decorative possibilities . . . to infinity. Was it not then a case of building up everything again – or rebuilding?
>
> He was in this state of mind when he was visited by the *parfumeur*, Coty, who came to ask him to make glass labels for the scent-bottles manufactured by the Cristalleries de Baccarat. First of all, Lalique refused. To design the whole bottle might interest him, but to add a decorative motive to an already existing bottle seemed to him puerile and supererogatory. If M. Coty would leave him free to do what he liked, he, Lalique, would be satisfied. So M. Coty gave in . . . [Lalique] was enamoured of the idea of making the scent-bottle a work of art, a precious vessel containing a precious essence.[4]

Whatever the exact circumstances of the first meeting, and whatever the deal that was struck, it is clear that the two men were seized by the possibilities of working together. Coupling Coty's popular scents and business acumen with Lalique's artistic sensibility and technical skill was bound to produce goods that would bring customers to their shops and the world of commerce to their feet. The days of the traditional, cylindrical vial were numbered. Lalique accepted Coty's commission with enthusiasm.

The first bottles that Lalique designed for Coty were actually produced elsewhere, at the glassworks of Legras and Company, the large firm in St.-Denis, near Paris, which was founded in 1864. These bottles were still quite simple and restrained in design – chiefly undecorated, rectangular or square flasks whose decorative stoppers and rather modern labels were also designed by Lalique. By 1909 Lalique was producing bottles at his rented Combs-la-Ville factory (probably concurrently with Legras bottles, at least for a short period of time), and Nicholas Dawes, comparing the Legras

glass to Lalique's own early bottles, remarks on the clarity and brightness of the Legras product, as well as its keener edges and crisper molding.[5] Lalique's glass (which was signed), though no less attractive, seems rougher-looking, its edges not so sharply defined nor its body free from bubbles and other impurities. This was due, in part, to the content of Lalique's glass. Unlike Legras', Lalique's glass was *demi-cristal,* not pure *cristal;* it contained about 12 per cent lead oxide as opposed to the 24 per cent for *cristal.* Also, each of these early Lalique bottles was molded at the base with the "extended L" signature, in which the first character of the word Lalique was drawn out to underscore and enclose the other six letters.

At first, Lalique employed somewhere between 50 and 100 workers at Combs-la-Ville, and the output of the factory consisted almost exclusively of commercial perfume bottles. The technology used for mass-produced bottles was partly borrowed from the manufacturers of French pharmaceutical and wine bottles, including molding processes developed by Claude Boucher at his wine-bottle and flacon factory in Cognac.[6] Boucher's technical improvements included the invention of the revolving mold and ring mold (*moule de bague*) and a more efficient procedure for inserting the still-molten glass into the mold. The introduction of the precision-cast metal mold at the turn of the century was a huge step forward in glass-making technology. A metal mold was costlier to use, but it resulted in a higher-quality product.

Two semi-automated, highly advanced techniques were employed in Lalique's factory for producing molded-glass scent bottles: *pressé soufflé,* in which the molten-glass mixture was blown either by mouth or bellows into a hinged double mold, and *aspiré soufflé,* in which the glass was sucked into a mold which automatically created a vacuum (this process had been developed in Great Britain in the late 1880s). All the simple Lalique perfume-bottle designs, and all those made in large quantities, were produced by automated means.

57

2. Dawes, *Lalique Glass,* 13.

3. Philippa Warburg, "Beginning with Lalique", *Hobbies,* September 1980, 52.

4. Gabriel Mourey, "Lalique's Glassware", *Commercial Art,* July 1926, 32, 34.

5. Dawes, *Lalique Glass,* 15.

6. *Ibid.*

By the time Lalique had purchased the Combs-la-Ville glassworks in 1910, his productivity level had substantially increased. Not only was he producing flacons for Coty, but he was also beginning to receive commissions from other *parfumeurs* and was making flacons, larger eau de cologne bottles and related powder boxes for sale at his own shop. Lalique's decorative flacons, into which perfumes from ordinary bottles could be decanted and then artfully arranged in madame's boudoir, were special: they were priced reasonably enough to appeal to a large number of buyers, and at the same time were beautiful enough to tempt even the most discerning and tasteful client.

Lalique's bottles – it could be said of them that the message was not in the bottle, but was the bottle itself – were, at first, flattened forms of clear glass. Molded in low or intaglio relief, they were often embellished with colored *patines*, and their separate stoppers were adapted to the necks of the bottles by applying carborundum powder to both them and the necks – the *bouchon à l'émeri* method, which imparts a frosted look to the glass and allows for both a tight fit and easy extraction. Both stopper and flacon were engraved with the same control numbers, though it is not known whether the numbers were put on before or after the stopper was properly fitted to the bottle. Such numbers are visible on most of Lalique's scent bottles, including the commercial models, and provide an excellent way to detect parts which were not originally of a piece.

Among the early empty bottles which Lalique produced and sold directly to the public was *Cigales (Cicadas)*. Dating from before 1912, it is an elegant creation whose basically square body is magically transformed by the closed-winged cicadas, their outlines highlighted with *patine*, which cling to the corners. The flattened-orb stopper depicts a daisy blossom, a floral design in sympathy with the insect motif of the bottle itself, and the whole concoction is quite Art Nouveau in feel. The stoppers on many other pieces are similarly in harmony with their bodies. The lovely *Telline* has its flattened body in the guise of two clamshells on their sides, and its stopper is in much the same shape, but smaller. Likewise, a bottle of plain, inverted-conical form (before 1912) is wondrously embellished by two wings and a stopper aswarm with small lizards. *Amphytrite* has a stopper in the form of the wife of Poseidon, which emerges from a flattened body with the cochleate outline of a whorled shell. There are a number of other designs whose stoppers take human form.

Lalique's perfume bottles, whether for his own shop or commissioned by others, are often impossible to date and, less often, to name. Perfume companies frequently market the same scent for 20 or 30 years, sometimes longer (Nina Ricci's "L'Air du Temps", with a bottle designed by Marc Lalique, is 40 years old), and therefore the exact date (or even decade) when it was first produced cannot always be pinpointed. Some of Lalique's empty bottles were, likewise, in production for a decade, even two decades. *Cigales*, for instance, appeared in an *Art et Décoration* article of 1912 (it is dated *c.*1910) and was still being offered for sale in Lalique's 1932 catalogue. The catalogue is invaluable for naming and dating to 1932 or earlier a good 60 scent bottles; but there were quite a few models – such as the lizard one – which were produced earlier and which appeared in the

Art et Décoration article without a name. Some pieces, indeed, appear not to have been given names until they were entered in the later catalogue, or perhaps displayed in the 1925 Paris Exposition.

Before concentrating on the bottles produced for specific *parfumeurs*, a survey of the motifs employed by Lalique is in order. Many of his early-20th-century bottles display the love of nature inherent in Art Nouveau. *Cigales* and the lizard bottle are two examples of Art Nouveau scent bottles; another is an oval flask of clear and frosted glass, whose body includes a writhing snake heightened with dark-gray *patine* and whose stopper is the open-jawed serpent's head. The bottle is closer in style to the earlier *Knot of Serpents* brooch in the Gulbenkian than it is to the stylized 1920s *Serpent* vase (in ruby-red and other hues). In the latter the form and color of the vase itself are dominant; in both the jewel and the perfume bottle it is the form of the snake itself that matters.

Nénuphar, with its squared body gently tapering toward the top, is adorned with the lilypad motif so beloved by Art Nouveau designers, especially those of the Ecole de Nancy. Like most of the floral forms on Lalique's bottles, however, it is less naturalistic and more ordered and stylized, indeed almost geometric in its regularity. Other stylized plant forms decorate the flacons called *Petites feuilles (Small Leaves)*, *Clamart*, *Epines (Thorns)*, *Amélie* and *Fleurs concaves*. Two lovely bottles, however, hark back to the *japonisme* of Lalique's hair combs: *Muguet* and *Clairefontaine*. Their bodies are of clear, undecorated glass, but the stoppers are luxuriant, naturalistic sprays of lifelike lilies-of-the-valley. Indeed, they appear to be bouquets of flowers emerging from water-filled vases, not simple flacons with tops.

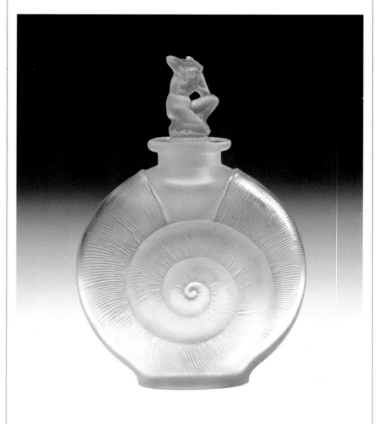

59

60

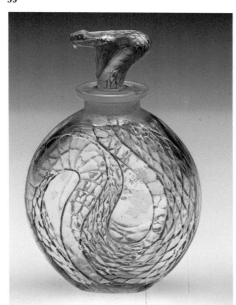

61

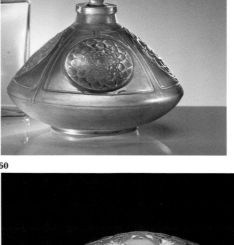

62

58 *Amphytrite* flacon,
c. 1925, 3¾in (9.5cm).
Collection Mary Lou
Utt, USA.

59 *Cigales* flacon,
c. 1912, 5¼in (13cm).
Collection Mary Lou
Utt, USA.

60 *4 Soleils* flacon,
c. 1910, 3in (7.5cm).
Collection Mary Lou
Utt, USA.

61 *Serpent* flacon,
c. 1920, 3½in (9cm).
Collection Mary Lou
Utt, USA.

62 *Fleurs concave*
flacon, 1920s, 4¾in
(12cm). Collection
Mary Lou Utt, USA.

63

63 *Lunaria* flacon,
c. 1910, 3¼in (8cm).
Collection Mary Lou
Utt, USA.

The bottles on these
two pages were all
sold empty and were
intended to hold
madame's fragrance
of choice. All are
shown in the 1932
catalogue.

Other flacons with glorious, cascading, crescent-like stoppers of bouquets were produced, and their overflowing sprays and branches were presented, not in the realistic detail of *Muguet* (which has more openwork and hence was more fragile and difficult to mold), but as more solid masses of limbs, stems, flowers and berries against solid-glass backgrounds (occasionally even these stoppers had bits of lacy openwork). These flacons were named after their *bouchons,* or stoppers – *Bouchon cassis, Bouchon fleurs de pommier, Bouchon eucalyptus* – and their bodies were generally cylindrically shaped, but gently tapered at both top and bottom to conform to the horseshoe shape of the stoppers. Some of Lalique's most successful *luminaires,* or table lamps, resembled outsized perfume bottles of this type.

Neoclassical motifs also appeared on Lalique's bottles and stoppers – stoppers embellished with acanthus and lotus, bodies of frolicking nude nymphs and satyrs or more subdued tunic-clad dancers, often amid floral garlands. Some of the figures ebb and flow, relating to their surroundings in a distinctly Art Nouveau manner. This can be seen in the *Sirènes* perfume burner, or *brûle parfum,* of *c.*1914, on which female nudes languorously twist their bodies, which end at the base, not in feet, but in a sweep of lotus-like plant tendrils. More restraint is shown in the frosted-glass flask (*c.*1924) whose pairs of female nude dancers convey a more understated, restrained eroticism characteristic of Art Déco. The same is true of Lalique's frosted-glass atomizer for Molinard's "Le Provençal", a cylinder depicting a frieze of noble female nudes amid lush floral garlands. A transitional piece is the bottle with crescent stopper designed in about 1914 for the "Leurs Ames" perfume by D'Orsay. Two sinuous female nudes, one at each side, cling to the branches of a squat flowering tree. The flora of this piece seem to hark back to the naturalism and *japonisme* of Lalique's Art Nouveau works, whereas the women are mannered maidens whose style falls somewhere between that of the *femmes fatales* of Art Nouveau and the classical nudes of Art Déco. The form of the piece, however, displays an unstinting purity of line. The outline is simple and uncluttered, the towering, mostly clear-glass crescent almost entirely framing the bottle and effecting a pure, circular harmony between the two elements.

64

64 *Leurs Ames* flacon, for D'Orsay, *c.* 1912, 5¼in (13cm). Galerie Moderne.

65 *Pan* flacon, *c.* 1912, 5in (12.7cm). Collection Mary Lou Utt, USA.

66 *Epines* flacon, *c.* 1920, 3¾in (9.5cm). Collection Mary Lou Utt, USA.

67 *Le Corail Rouge* flacon, for Forvil, *c.* 1925, 4in (10cm). Collection Léon Khachikian, Paris.

68 *Muguet* flacon, *c.* 1930, 4in (10cm). Collection Mary Lou Utt, USA.

69 *Clairfontaine* flacon, *c.* 1930, 4¾in (12cm). Collection Mary Lou Utt, USA.

Pan, Muguet and *Clairfontaine* all appear in Lalique's 1932 catalogue, as does *Epines (Thorns),* which was offered in four sizes as part of a ten-piece "garniture de toilette". *Leurs Ames* was produced for D'Orsay, but it was available with or without the name molded at the bottom, leading one to believe that Lalique (and his retailers) sold the bottle empty, without fragrance.

65

66

67

68

69

70 *Panier de roses* flacon, *c.* 1910, 4in (10cm). Collection Mary Lou Utt, USA.

71 *Clamart* flacon, *c.* 1929, 4½in (11cm). Collection Mary Lou Utt, USA.

71

70

72

72 *Telline* flacon, *c.* 1929, 4in (10cm). Collection Mary Lou Utt, USA.

73 *Nénuphar* flacon, *c.* 1913, 4¾in (12cm). Collection Mary Lou Utt, USA.

The waterlily, or *nénuphar*, was a popular motif in the Art Nouveau period, but Lalique has stylized and ordered the pads in a more Art Déco vein on this flacon, as he has the leaves on *Clamart*. Note how the stopper on *Telline* is a miniature scallop shell, echoing the shape of the bottle itself.

73

74

75

76

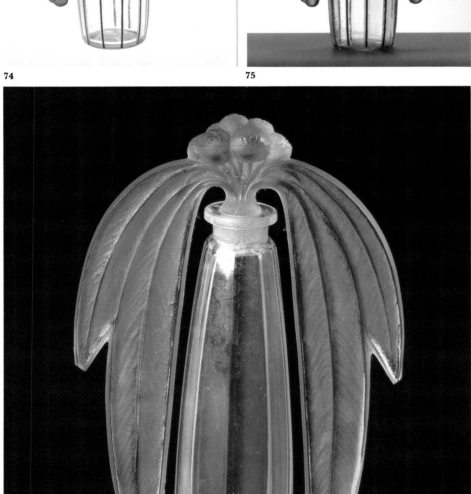

77

78

74 *Bouchon cassis*
flacon, *c.* 1929, 4½in
(11cm). Collection
Mr. and Mrs. V. James
Cole, New York.

75 *Bouchon cassis*
flacon, *c.* 1929, 4½in
(11cm). Collection
Mary Lou Utt, USA.

76 *Bouchon mures*
flacon, *c.* 1929, 4½in
(11cm). Galerie
Moderne.

77 *Bouchon eucalyptus*
flacon *c.* 1929, 5½in
(13.5cm). Private
collection, Paris.

78 *Bouchon fleurs de
pommier* flacon, c.
1929, 5½in (14cm).
Collection Mary Lou
Utt, USA.

These five bottles are
named after their
elaborate, crescent-
like stoppers (*bouchon*
means stopper). The
flacons themselves are
subtly tapered at the
top and bottom to
allow their
overflowing stoppers
to conform nicely to
their cylindrical
shapes.

LALIQUE

79 *Calendal* flacons for
Molinard, designed in
1929, produced
through 1960s, 4½in
(11.5cm). Galerie
Moderne.

80 *Petites feuilles*
flacon, *c.* 1929, 4in
(10.2cm). Collection
Mary Lou Utt, USA.

81 *Sirènes* brûle
parfum, *c.* 1922, 7¼in
(18cm). Galerie
Moderne.

82 Left, *Le Jade* flacon,
for Roger et Gallet, *c.*
1925, 3¼in (8cm);
right, *Amélie* flacon,
c. 1925, 3¾in (9.3cm).
Collection Mary Lou
Utt, USA.

The colors on
Lalique's perfume
bottles varied from
lightly applied *patines*
in pastel hues, as seen
in the trio, top, and
the *brûle parfum*, left,
to deep, vivid hues,
like the green glass of
the two flacons below.

79

81

80

82

An oval flacon (of before 1912) with an antique bas-relief pattern is described by Gustave Kahn as a gem which "the great designers of the 18th century would have loved":[7]

> A young Greek and his lover, their feet off the ground, are going to their wedding, are flying towards love. Full of grace and mirth, caught up in the rhythm of their passion; two limbs trimmed with ribbons extend above their heads like a triumphal arch, very light, very subtle, and it seems not only to frame them with its beauty and its scent, but to become a part of them. They seem to be hurling themselves up to the triumphal arch, through a series of flowered hoops, thick and shady towards the edges of both the sun and the brink of happiness.[8]

By the 1920s Lalique was designing perfume bottles (and often the boxes) for at least 30 *parfumeurs* besides Coty. The House of Worth was his biggest client, and D'Orsay, Houbigant and Roger et Gallet (whose display Lalique designed at the 1925 Paris Exposition) also provided him with commissions. He designed on a smaller scale for D'Heraud, Forvil, Molinard, Jay Thorpe, Arys, Corday, Morabito, Raphael, Godet and Vigny. He also produced powder boxes and other *garnitures de toilette* for perfume companies, as well as for sale in his own shop. One of his most famous and long-lasting designs is *Houppes (Powder Puffs)*, produced as a powder box of frosted, opalescent and clear glass for his own retailing and as a cardboard container for Coty's Airspun powder; the box, its white puffs heightened with gold, black and orange hues, is back in production today.[9] There was even a 9in-high version of *Houppes* (with an inverted funnel-shaped lid), which was presented at the 1925 Paris Exposition as a *grande boîte à poudre*. Another most interesting powder box for Coty was very much in the Art Nouveau style, its lid molded with embracing maidens in flowery dress, its bottom covered with swirling ribbons and flowers, and overall a highlight of sienna *patine*.

Over the years, Lalique must have produced thousands of scent bottles and powder boxes for Coty. According to Glenn and Mary Lou Utt, foremost experts on Lalique perfume bottles, the 4⅜in-high bottle for "L'Effleurt de Coty" (unsigned; 1908–10) was probably the first one produced for Coty. Its plain rectangular body is molded on the front with a frosted and brown-stained panel that depicts a sinuous female nude who emerges, genie-like, from a serpentine flower blossom into a billowy sky; its tall stopper is molded with a stylized-insect motif. Among the other early Coty commissions was "Ambre Antique", at first a plain square bottle with floriate stopper, but later a tapering cylinder molded in shallow relief with female figures in Grecian costume, with a brown stain and stylized flower-blossom stopper. One of the "Le Cyclamen" bottles was a slightly angled cylinder, tapering at the top; it depicted tiny, fluttering nudes whose protracted wings, twice the length of their bodies, reached to the bottom of the bottle. Over the years, it was not unusual to have two or more bottles of different design containing the same scent, nor to have two different fragrances bottled in the same design (not, of course, at the same time). Identification of the bottles is therefore made quite difficult at times, unless the labels are still attached or, more unlikely, the original cardboard boxes intact. Coty was the first to use cardboard containers for perfumes (before 1910) and Lalique came to design quite a few of the matching boxes. One of the most stunning was for Roger et Gallet's *Le Jade* fragrance of *c*.1925 (the best-quality flacons were made for this still-existing firm). The vial is in the shape of a Chinese snuff bottle, and both the jade-green glass body and the stopper are decorated with interlacing leaf and tropical bird forms. The box is in dramatic black, green and gold hues, and the embossed, gold label is a roundel with two stylized birds encircling the name of the fragrance and its maker.

For D'Orsay Lalique designed a variety of scent bottles, mostly in the 1920s, including the crescent-stoppered "Leurs Ames" (*c*.1914) and "Fleur de France", "Rose", and "Chevalier" (a trio of these was available in a silk-lined, burgundy-leather case, the simple square bottles edged with beading and topped with lush floral stoppers highlighted with a sienna *patine*). D'Orsay's "Le Lys" fragrance came in a rounded bottle studded with jaunty flower blossoms whose stamens and leaves were highlighted in a reddish *patine*. Its stopper was a more mannered version of the same flower head, but neatly adapted to the perfectly round shape. This model was made in three sizes and usually had the perfume's name on the stopper. Very similar in design was *Emiliane*, a round frosted and stained glass box whose top was covered with stylized blossoms on a red-stained ground. The box exists with *D'Orsay* molded on the rim but, interestingly enough, it also appears in Lalique's 1932 catalogue, without the color, lending credence to the argument that some of the empty containers which Lalique sold himself were also designs sold to *parfumeurs*. Copyright regulations would almost certainly prohibit such an arrangement today, but so renowned was Lalique that D'Orsay was probably quite amenable to whatever terms he imposed.

Lalique's design for Worth's fragrance, "Dans la Nuit", was a stunning spherical bottle in, among other colors, rich blue, peppered with bas-relief stars and sometimes topped by a disc stopper whose crystal side, when turned, resembled a crescent moon. A powder box was also produced in this shape. Worth also commissioned Lalique to design bottles for their "Imprudence", "Je Reviens" and "Sans Adieu" scents. Indeed, the House of Worth produced perfume on a huge scale and Lalique made bottles to match their demand, though many of them were quite simple colored forms and different scents were often sold in the same bottle. Worth, incidentally, was one of the many fashion houses which began to produce "designer perfumes" in the 1920s, a foretaste of today's fashion world, in which it seems that every designer worth his weight – and those who want desperately to be – has a scent or two with his name affixed to it.

Many of Lalique's scent bottles are distinctly Art Déco, whether in their bold geometric designs or their stylized flowers and leaves or other more unusual motifs. Corday's "Tzigane" scent came in a bottle whose basic cylindrical shape was molded with a stylized relief pattern of spiraling zig-zags, with a stopper to match. The popular *Cactus* bottle, a compressed sphere with stopper, was decorated all over with black enamel-tinged bosses, which are without a doubt the plant's prickles, but stunningly stylized à la Art Déco (this bottle is still in production). Worth's "Imprudence" was available in a starkly

7. Gustave Kahn, "Laliques Verrier", *Art et Décoration*, XXXI (January–June 1912), 155 [authors' translation].

8. *Ibid.*

9. There is some confusion as to who the designer of the cardboard powder box was. In a 1980s press release, the Coty firm states that Leon Bakst, best known for his depictions of the Ballets Russes, created the design, whereas other sources name Lalique its creator. Since without a doubt Lalique designed the very similar *Houppes*, there would seem to be a stronger case for the Lalique attribution.

LALIQUE

83

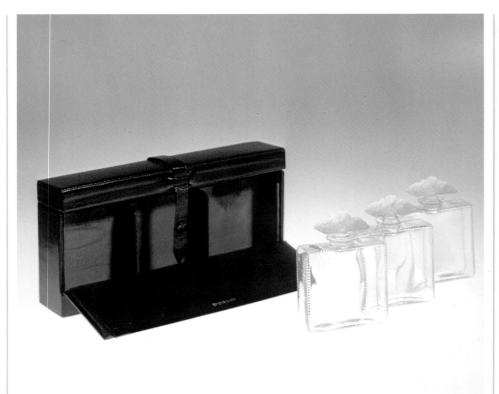

modern, clear-glass bottle consisting of a set of graduated discs and ending in a matching stopper. Another bottle for Worth, in green glass, had a plain cylindrical body with a stopper made up of such discs. *Palerme*, a clear-glass bottle, has a tapering cylindrical body embellished with garlands of "pearls", a simple yet luxuriant motif that is often found on pieces of ceramic and furniture by other Art Déco designers. A dizzying mass of beaded spirals appears on another clear-glass scent bottle, this one flask-shaped.

A quite unusual bottle of blue and frosted glass for the scent, "Canarina", has a simple, square shape with square flat stopper, but molded on one side are 11 stylized eyes. The same Egyptian-style eyes appear on the perfume's box. A rare black-glass bottle for D'Orsay has an almost square shape, a narrow neck and a stopper decorated with stylized lizards. This bottle was commissioned for the scent, "Mystère by D'Orsay", but may have been used for other D'Orsay fragrances as well.

A rare enameled and frosted-glass bottle, designed for the couturier, Lucien Lelong, and intended for the American market, has a pattern of overlapping scales, a bit like the garlands of *Palerme*, but heightened with black enamel, not pearls. An elegant chromed and enameled metal case, black with silvery scales, held this exquisite, almost architectonic bottle.

The stylized leaf pattern on *Marquita* could almost be an upside-down variation on the scales of the Lucien Lelong bottle, except for the fact that the leaves bear a resemblance to natural forms, perhaps the scaly skin of an artichoke. *Clamart*, with its overlapping-leaf de-

sign, and *Epines,* with its interlocking thorny tendrils (this design also covered a vase), both look to nature for their inspiration, but Lalique stylizes both motifs – not beyond recognition, but certainly far more than he did with his early *cire-perdue* glass.

Perles (in polished and satin glass) and *Epines* (in clear and enameled glass), as well as *Fleurettes* (with its simple friezes of flowers on its edges), were patterns in which a complete *garniture de toilette* was available. Scent and cologne bottles, powder and pomade boxes, pin trays and such could be purchased by women of distinction and impeccable taste. Even mirrors and picture frames were made to match – in short, a dressing-table of coordinated accessories.

Another related object created by Lalique was the perfume burner, or *brûle parfum*, an adaptation of the cassolette, a small brazier in which either liquid perfumes were evaporated or aromatic pastilles were burned. These vintage "air-fresheners" or "room deodorizers" had for centuries been made of assorted materials – silver, marble, lacquer and porcelain among them – and Lalique created some lovely *brûles parfums*, mostly in frosted or opalescent glass. *Sirènes* was one such opalescent *brûle parfum*, and there was also *Carousel*, with four sparrows, their tails upraised, topping its plain base. *Papillons*, with an elongated dome cover, was decorated with a swarm of overlapping butterflies, and *Faune* had one of the mythical creatures surmounting a cylindrical vessel whose lower half was molded with vertical ribs topped by three rows of florid bosses. Another lovely frosted-glass example, *Hygénie*, was bullet-shaped and its surface was molded and pierced with an array of wild flowers and leaves.

87

86

D'Orsay and Worth were, along with Coty, Lalique's biggest *parfumeur* clients.

84 Three flacons for D'Orsay in blue leatherette traveling case, lined with silk, *c.* 1910; height of bottles, 3½in (8.5cm). Collection Mary Lou Utt, USA.

85 *Poesie D'Orsay* flacon, 1914, 5½in (14cm). Collection Mary Lou Utt, USA.

86 *Je Reviens* flacon, for Worth, 1932, 11¼in (28cm). Private collection, Paris.

87 *Imprudence* flacon, for Worth, 1938, 4in (10cm). Collection Mary Lou Utt, USA.

The designs on the D'Orsay flacons and stoppers are quite florid and decorative compared to the geometric, even architectonic, Worth bottles. The large blue one would have been used for display purposes, hence the metallic base.

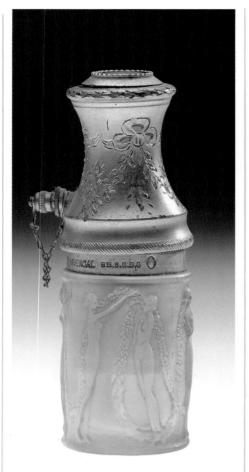

88

88 Atomizer for *Le Provençal* fragrance, by Molinard, 1920s, 7¼in (18.5cm). Galerie Moderne.

89

90

91

89 *Papillons* brûle parfum, *c.* 1920, 7½in (19cm). Galerie Moderne.

90 *Perles* garniture de toilette, *c.* 1928: three trays, 9¼, 4½, 5¼in (23, 11.3, 13cm) long. Galerie Moderne.

91 *Perles* box and cover, *c.* 1928, 2½in (6cm). Galerie Moderne.

92 *Au Coeur des Calices* flacon, for Coty, *c.* 1912, 2¾in (7cm). Galerie Moderne.

93 *Canarina* flacon, with box, 1920s, 2in (5cm). Collection Mary Lou Utt, USA.

94 *Cactus* flacon, *c.* 1929, 4in (9.8cm). Collection Mary Lou Utt, USA.

95 *Phalene* flacon, for D'Heraud, 1923, 3½in (9cm). Galerie Moderne.

92

93

94

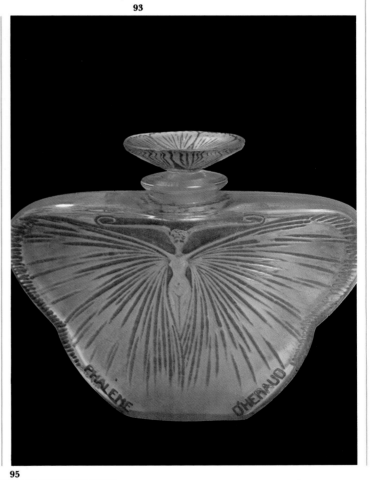

95

96 Flacon for Houbigant, part of presentation set, *c.* 1928–30, approx. 2½in (6.3cm). Collection Mary Lou Utt, USA.

97 Box and four scent bottles, presentation set for Houbigant, *c.* 1928–30. Collection Mary Lou Utt, USA; photo courtesy Bonhams Auctioneers, London.

96

97

Like the perfume bottles, the powder boxes created by Lalique were decorated with a plethora of neoclassical, organic, stylized and, to a lesser extent, geometric designs. Often the same patterns could be found on boxes and bottles, although they were not necessarily a pair, or part of the same *garniture de toilette*. One of the first was the black-glass *Coq* (*c.*1910), which was likened to a Japanese woodcut for its bold design and execution. The same design was offered in frosted and clear glass in Lalique's 1932 catalogue, as were a great many other avian motifs, from two nesting doves and a flowing-tailed peacock to a very *japoniste* pair of cranes (he called this *Rambouillet*, after the town), a flock of swans in water and a sextet of blue tits, *Mésanges*, whose open right wings met at the center to form a star-like design. Flowers, fish, insects, cherubs, maidens, shells – all these motifs and more could be found on Lalique's round boxes, which were available in a variety of colors and finishes. Two Art Déco designs were *Tokio*, a stunning floral box with a burst of bubbles like fireworks on its lid, and *Chantilly*, which depicted on separate panels six different stylized deer or gazelles amid foliage. The French term for such creatures – deer, gazelles and antelopes, whose grace and elegance made them popular subjects for Art Déco designers – is *les biches*.

It is sometimes difficult to discern whether a Lalique box was intended for powder, sweets or trinkets. If a box is part of a *garniture de toilette*, we know that it was intended for powder or some other cosmetic. But many boxes were sold separately and presumably their owners used them for whatever purpose they saw fit.

The 1925 Paris Exposition was a showcase for the French perfume industry, which had grown by leaps and bounds in the last quarter of a century to lead the world in production and to set the highest standards for both the essences themselves and their containers. The perfume section of the fair, situated in the Grand Palais, was rife – one could say heady – with Lalique scent bottles, and Roger et Gallet commissioned Lalique to design its whole display – furniture, cases, vitrines and, of course, containers.

The general report of the 1925 fair, published later that year, outlined the progress that the perfume industry had made:

> The taste for perfume has spread throughout every social class. Decorative bottles and boxes are no longer found exclusively in de luxe shops; they can be seen in innumerable storefronts in Paris and the provinces and appear in the most modest households. Designs by French artists are everywhere, at home and abroad, where the perfume industry is but a vehicle to aid the spread of French taste.[11]

Lalique's designs were instrumental in France's attaining the premier position it held in the international perfume market. Coty and his fellow *parfumeurs* all adhered to the "fine perfume in a handsome container at an attractive price" canon, and, as Coty had prophesied, "the world of commerce [was] at his feet". As Nicholas Dawes remarked, "by the 1920s *parfumerie* was considered an admirable and respectable branch of the decorative arts".[12] Hence its high visibility at the 1925 Exposition.

In the *parfumerie* pavilion Lalique also designed the huge centerpiece, a stylized *Fontaine des parfums* whose theme echoed that of his

98

99

98 *Tokio* box and cover, *c.* 1928, 6¾in (17cm) dia. Galerie Moderne.

99 Powder box and cover, with fish design, *c.* 1910, 3¼in (8cm) dia. Courtesy Christopher Vane Percy.

Round boxes such as these were intended for loose powder, trinkets, candy or whatever the owner desired. Some boxes were parts of *garnitures de toilette*, but others, like those above, were sold separately.

10. The authors would like to thank Glenn and Mary Lou Utt for sharing with them this and other information on Lalique perfume bottles. The valuable data the Utts have assembled on the subject will soon be published in their *catalogue raisonné* of Lalique fragrance bottles.

11. Quoted in Dawes, *Lalique Glass*, 60.

12. *Ibid.*, 17.

100 *Arrow Head* scent pendant, *c.* 1912, approx. 1½in (4cm). Courtesy Christopher Vane Percy.

101 *Eucalyptus* scent pendant, *c.* 1912, approx. 1½in (4cm). Collection Mary Lou Utt, USA.

Scent pendants were an interesting sideline to Lalique's perfume-bottle production. For some reason, such pendants did not prove successful with Lalique's clients, so their production was cut down, thus making them rarities with collectors today.

100

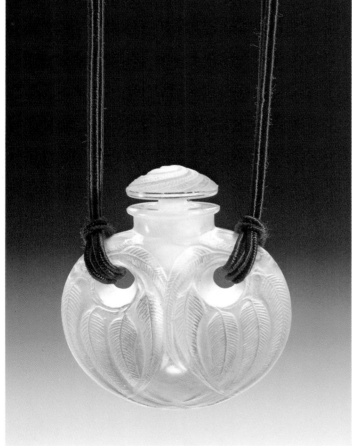

101

large outdoor fountain. It was much admired by Maximilien Gauthier:

> Here, in the Grand Palais, is the central motif of the hall of section 23, the *Fountain of Perfumes* – not spurting out in actuality, but symbolically; a huge flower of blown and engraved glass, a masterpiece of painstaking technical prowess and of subtle coloring.[13]

Gauthier called the Roger et Gallet stand a "refuge of tranquillity and discreet luxury, where there rules the mystery of a sweet brightness which is amenable to the infinite expansion of the scents".[14] A spray of glass flowers hung over the display and the floor was of precious wood encrusted with glass. The furniture, of "simple lines and somber tones", according to Gauthier, allowed all the light to shine on the four vitrines, where "one sees the impeccable perfume bottles aglow".[15]

After the 1925 Exposition Lalique continued to hold his premier position in the world of *flaconnage artistique*. Imitators came and went in great numbers, but Lalique reigned supreme, despite at one time threatening to "throw up glass as I once threw up goldsmith's work".[16] In response to the inferior scent bottles which every glass factory now seemed to include in its inventory, Lalique raised his standards even higher, thus making his bottles both more difficult to copy and more desirable among his clients.

An interesting "sideline" of Lalique's was the production of glass scent pendants. Rarities now, such pendants were not terribly popular when they were first marketed. One of Lalique's earliest such pendants was the tiny, four-sided *Arrow Head*. On each of its sides was depicted a head with flowing tresses, and its minute stopper was signed and stained with a brown *patine*. Two other pendants were *Eucalyptus* and the much-later *Replique*. The latter was a special commission for the *parfumeur*, Raphael. It was made of frosted glass and sported a gilt screw-top metal cap, complete with a hole through which to thread a silk cord. These pendants did not prove to be a success with the ladies, and Lalique cut down on their production.

After Lalique's death, production of many of his perfume bottles continued and a posthumous design was introduced in about 1946 for Worth's "*Requète*" scent. With blue-enamel scalloping around its circumference and touches of blue around its stopper, it is a simple yet stunning and thoroughly modern design. Marc Lalique created new bottles for many years (especially for Nina Ricci) and also modified some of his father's designs. Today Marc's creations are still being produced, notably Nina Ricci's "L'Air du Temps".

Some 50 years ago Gabriel Mourey wrote most prophetically of Lalique's bottles:

> Some of the scent-bottles drawn and modelled by Lalique . . . deserve to be treasured up and will certainly be kept in public and private collections as genuine works of art.[17]

One wonders whether Lalique ever envisioned such lofty resting places for some of his finer fragrance containers, or whether he realized what a pioneer he would be considered in a sparkling new industry. No one of his vast talent and vision came before, and no one since has eclipsed him. His position as the leading light of the modern, artistic scent-bottle industry will never be overshadowed.

13. Gauthier, "Le Maître Verrier René Lalique", 415 [authors' translation].

14. *Ibid.*

15. *Ibid.*

16. Gordon-Stables, "Lalique", 33.

17. Mourey, "A Great French Craftsman", 107.

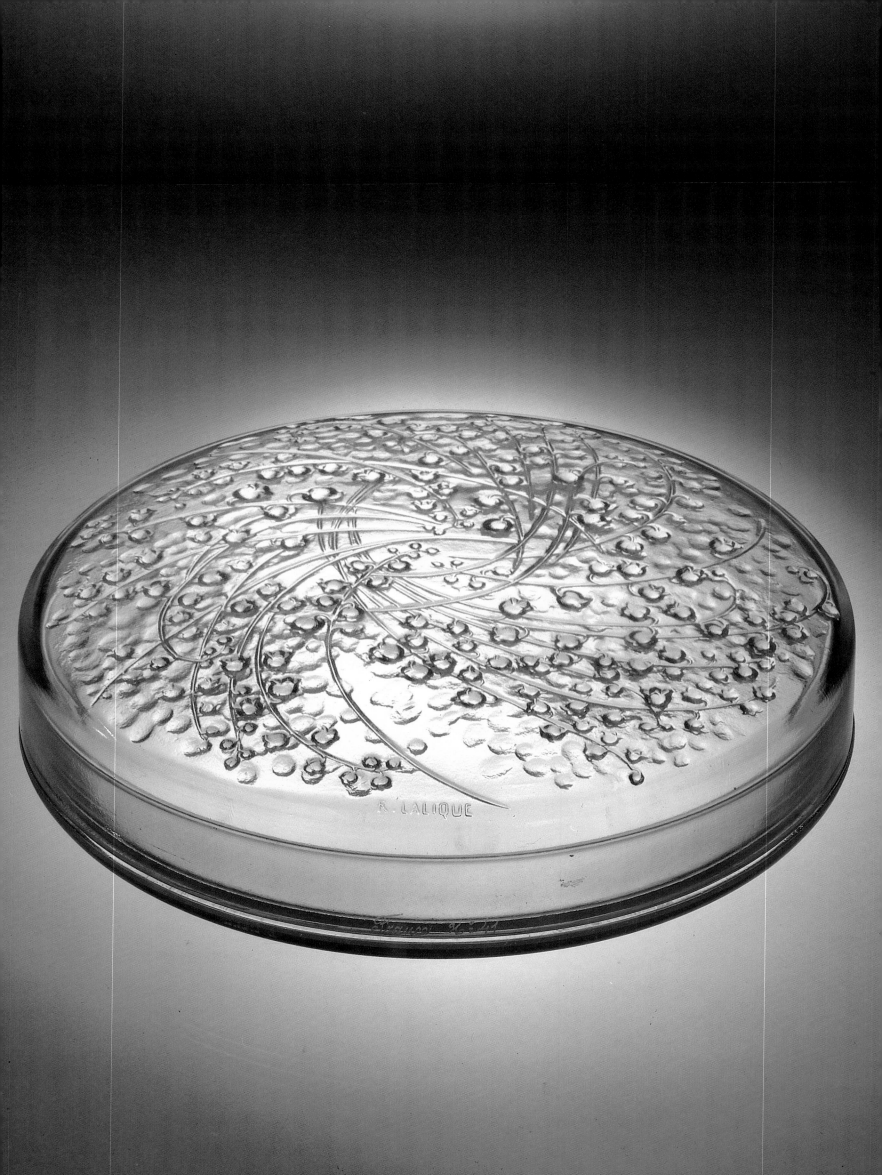

102 *Grande muguets* box
and cover, *c.* 1925,
10¼in (25.5cm) dia.
Galerie Moderne.

BOXES
AND
DESK
ACCESSORIES

7

*I*n the 1932 *Catalogue des Verreries de René Lalique* only the designer's vases outnumber the array of boxes which were available to his discerning clients. They came in clear, frosted or opalescent glass, or combinations of the three; they were highlighted with earthy *patines* or, less commonly, molded in brightly colored glass; they were circular, rectangular, square, even egg-shaped, and they were decorated with bas-relief or three-dimensional motifs running the gamut of Lalique's design repertory. The 70 boxes or so illustrated in the catalogue – and the many others which were made earlier or later – held powder, pomades, cigars, cigarettes, candy or trinkets, and, humble as they may seem, they followed in a long tradition of decorative little boxes.

Small covered containers had long been made of precious or ordinary materials to hold everything from patches and pills to sewing implements and snuff. What could be more common and practical than a square or round box to contain the bits and pieces men and women used for amusement, for adornment, for relaxation or for nourishment? What could be nicer than to decorate such a container and make it attractive whatever its contents? Why not make these little boxes works of art, something to show off, to display amid a lady's or gentleman's possessions, to coordinate with their wardrobe or room decor?

Such decorative boxes had come into use centuries earlier. Lovely celadon boxes were made in China as early as the Sung Dynasty (11th–12th century), ivory caskets carved with scenes of royalty and knighthood were used in the early Middle Ages, and elaborate lacquer *inrō* (a wooden box to hold a man's personal seal and/or ink pad, worn suspended from his belt) date to the Momoyama period (1573–1614) in Japan. Eighteenth-century Europe witnessed the efflorescence of the use of such containers in the guise of *bonbonnières* (for sweets), *étuis* (for ladies' sewing accessories), patch boxes (for fashionable fake beauty marks), snuff-boxes (almost exclusively for men) and other "toys", as they were collectively termed in English, or *galanterie*, as the French called them.

At first items of little value, many of these "toys" were transformed into precious *objets de vertu*, especially in the Paris of Louis XV and Louis XVI. The jewelers of the day used gold, enamel and rare gems to create small masterpieces that at times rivaled the *ébénisterie* produced by the likes of André-Charles Boulle and Charles Cressent. (Some furniture makers tried their hand at producing small caskets in wood with gilt-bronze mounts, mini-versions of their commodes and cabinets.) Other Continental and British goldsmiths followed suit. Some of the loveliest boxes were made in Switzerland and incorporated musical works, automata and watches. Cheaper, but still handsome, containers were also created, for example Battersea enamel boxes in Great Britain.

In the 19th century goldsmiths and silversmiths followed in the footsteps of their predecessors, producing snuff-boxes, writing sets (*écritoires*), card cases, vesta boxes, smelling-salt containers, vinaigrettes, tobacco boxes, cigar and cigarette cases, toothpick boxes and jewel caskets in every shape and material imaginable. The large variety of such containers and their similar forms and motifs often make it difficult to identify the original use of a box, as Margaret Holland writes in the *Phaidon Guide to Silver*:

> Authorities such as the Victoria and Albert Museum never differentiate between boxes, yet their original functions often differ and in many cases their form is recognizable. In others it is not. Unspecified boxes . . . appear from virtually every country, from the late 17th century onwards . . . Many [are] undoubted novelties, fulfilling a short-lived purpose; others described variously as cachou, pill, tinder, pounce, counter, coin boxes or something else, all lacking proof of identity.[1]

Small and medium-sized boxes for countless purposes were produced in the Arts and Crafts and Art Nouveau styles. Some of the most beautiful are of blue and green enamel on silver and were designed by Archibald Knox and C. R. Ashbee in Great Britain. Josef Hoffmann, Dagobert Peche, Koloman Moser and other Wiener Werkstätte figures designed proto-modern boxes in metal and wood. In America, Louis Comfort Tiffany made vivid Art Nouveau confections in Favrile glass, wood and enameled metal; in France, Georges de Feure produced luscious porcelain *bonbonnières* in pastel hues and Emile Gallé fashioned assorted *boîtes* in cameo glass. And for every one-of-a-kind or limited-edition, artist-designed box, there must have been tens of thousands of mass-produced containers in metal, wood, ceramic and, of course, glass.

So it was that when Lalique began to mass-produce his glass boxes he was not filling a void, as he was with his perfume bottles. The market was already inundated with powder boxes and candy containers of every imaginable type and some of them were quite nicely made. They did not, however, bear the Lalique name, the name which, thanks in part to the opportunities provided for Lalique by François Coty and others, was a major selling point on any article, no matter how many hundreds of similar products were already available.

Lalique designed at least a dozen boxes in his goldsmithing years including a lovely circular box of ivory, enamel and gold (*c.*1896). The trinket box, 4½in in diameter, is studded on its plain ivory lid with a central boss in translucent opalescent enamel with foil inclusions, and the boss is decorated in wired *cloisonné* enamel, enclosing bees alternating with berried tendrils and having a brilliant cabochon blue stone at its center. A deep yellow enamel band forms the roundel's border. Apart from the one precious stone and the gold *cloisonné* veins, which give the design its form, the remaining effect – from the yellow surround and the blue berries to the rings on the bees' waists and the shimmering luminescence at the tips of their wings – is stunningly achieved by the expert enameling. Bees and other flying insects are found on many of Lalique's Art Nouveau pieces, but these three are especially lovely, perfectly ordered and symmetrical, yet vibrant with color.

Lalique also designed a small number of boxes in silver, copper, ivory and other jeweler's materials. Such *boîtes* or *coffres* are mentioned in turn-of-the-century periodicals, but few are known to exist today. Three such early boxes are in the Gulbenkian Collection. *The Kiss* (*c.*1900–02) is an oval metal box whose subject – a couple kissing amid a frame of leafy branches – was also depicted on a gold, enamel

---

1. Margaret Holland, *Phaidon Guide to Silver*, Oxford, 1978, 230.

and ivory brooch of the same period (also in the Lisbon museum). *Two Owls* (*c*.1900–01) is a circular box of silver, enamel and horn; on its lid the birds perch on branches, and the tree-limb motif continues around part of the box's border. (This box is pictured in *The Studio* for August 1905, in a review of the Lalique exhibition at Agnew & Sons in London, in which it was displayed.) The oval box, *Snakes*, is executed in gilt-copper and enamel, and the two intertwining serpents on its lid are another superb representation of one of Lalique's most dramatic Art Nouveau subjects.

An interesting rectangular box (*c*.1905–07) in the collection of the Paris Musée National de l'Art Moderne, is called *Elf* and depicts on its lid a quintet of fantasy figures carved in rock crystal. In the middle a luminous nude female, highlighted in green enamel, spreads her winged arms in a bountiful gesture, and on both sides a pair of carved young nudes falls back, seemingly charmed or stunned by her radiance. The subject is at once classical and Art Nouveau, and it resembles many of the diaphanous, quasi-classical figures found on many of Lalique's later glass boxes.

Such boxes as the ivory ones, those in the Gulbenkian and the one in Paris had as direct precursors the *bonbonnières* and other French boxes of the 18th century. Although only the one was fashioned in gold, they were all jeweler's creations, *objets de vertu* which fit naturally into Lalique's first career.

A transitional box (*c*.1910–15) – a very special model made in a limited edition of probably no more than ten – was a *coffre* of dark green or black molded glass, with silver-plated metal hinges and clasps. It was most likely for jewels (its dimensions are 3in × 7in × 4⅛in) and depicted a swirling mass of thorny thistle branches on which stylized scarab beetles act as the hinge and clasps. The motif is certainly an Art Nouveau one, especially the asymmetry of the prickly tendrils, but the geometric, almost hieroglyphic, motifs engraved on the insect's shell and head link it to Art Déco as well. One of these boxes is in the collection of the Corning Museum of Glass in New York and another is in the Hessisches Landesmuseum in Darmstadt.

Another interesting casket (5½in × 12¾in × 7½in) has several motifs. All these transitional boxes are rectangular in shape, with wooden carcasses and trim and metal hinges, keyholes and keys. Bombé molded-glass panels, to whose backs silver foil has been affixed, are set into the wood at the top and sides of these caskets, which are almost certainly jewelry boxes (though some have identified them as humidors). The subjects depicted on the boxes (as listed in the 1932 catalogue) are butterflies, figures and *monnaie du pape* (or honesty plant, with its decorative, flattened silvery rods, a favorite plant motif of Lalique). According to the catalogue, the *coffre* was available in the large size in those three subjects, but it also came in a smaller size – in *Papillons*, *Monnaie du pape* and *Chrysanthèmes* – which had glass panels only on the top and around the keyhole. One such *coffre*, with *monnaie du pape* glass panels and amaranth-wood trim, is in the collection of the Metropolitan Museum of Art in New York. It was purchased by the museum in 1924.

These one-of-a-kind or limited-production boxes by Lalique were products of Lalique the goldsmith, even though they frequently had a high glass content. Lalique the glassmaker produced boxes of quite

103

103 *Papillons* box, *c*. 1920, 3¾ × 12¼ × 7½in (9.5 × 31 × 19cm). Private collection, London.

This casket, of exotic wood inlaid with a large molded-glass panel on the top and a small circular one around the keyhole, was also available with honesty-plant and chrysanthemum designs. A slightly larger version had glass panels covering its four sides as well as the top.

104

105

These three boxes well illustrate the variety of containers Lalique produced in his career. The ivory and enamel trinket box is an early Art Nouveau creation, whereas the others are from the Art Déco period. Interestingly, all three sport central motifs – namely, the enamel roundel on the ivory box, the glass boss on *Sainte-Nectaire* and the nude female figure on *Sultane*.

104 Trinket box and cover, *c.* 1896, ivory, gold, enamel, foil, 4½in (11cm) dia. Kagan Collection, USA.

Lalique designed at least a dozen boxes in his goldsmithing years, and this is one of the loveliest. As with many of his Art Nouveau creations, the box is decorated with insects, here, three bees. A trail of gold outlines the vibrantly colored enamel bodies and wings of the insects.

105 *Saint-Nectaire* box and cover, *c.* 1924, 3½in (8.5cm) dia. Galerie Moderne.

106 *Sultane* cigarette box and cover, *c.* 1922, 5½in (14cm) long. Collection Mary Lou Utt, USA.

106

107 *Myosotis* flacon,
c. 1920, 9¼in (23cm).
Collection Mary Lou
Utt, USA.

108 *Degas* box and cover
c. 1922, 3¼in (8cm)
dia. Galerie Moderne.

109 *Amour Assis* box and
cover, *c.* 1920, 5¾in
(14.5cm). Galerie
Moderne.

Many of Lalique's
boxes had small
figural knobs – or in
the case of *Amour
Assis*, finely molded
sculptures – on their
lids. These finials
echoed the figural
stoppers often found
on Lalique flacons,
such as the woman on
Myosotis, pictured.

a different sort – in fact, every sort of glass *boîte* imaginable. Sometimes they were parts of his *garnitures de toilette*, such as those in the *Perles, Epines, Myosotis (Forget-Me-Not)* or *Fleurettes* patterns, but mostly they were boxes sold individually; generally, though not always, they were circular in shape.

Two cigar boxes, *Roméo* and *Corona*, are rectangular and rather restrained, some might say masculine, in design. *Roméo* is molded all around with plain vertical ribs; its frosted-glass top, which slides off lengthwise, had a *demilune* knob set on a stepped panel and the entire top bears a stylized-leaf design. *Corona* is even simpler, sporting an overlapping-leaf design all over its bottom and slightly bombé top. *Sultane*, a square box (probably for cigarettes, at 5½in in length) of frosted and clear glass, has a base of overlapping leaf forms in an abstract diamond pattern throughout; its lid is arresting – a glass cushion in whose center sits a sensuous female nude in the lotus position, back arched and hands clasped behind her thrown-back head.

Two cigarette boxes in clear and frosted glass are *Hirondelles*, on whose lid is a flurry of overlapping swallows and whose sides are molded with a geometric motif, and *Zinnias*, also with a geometric design on its sides and the top molded with showy blossoms amid spade-shaped leaves. An interesting hexagonal box is *Saint-Nectaire*, on which whirling fern leaves form a vortex centering on a clear cabochon. All three boxes are listed in the 1932[2] catalogue as being available in *blanc* (meaning frosted or clear glass, not color); *Saint-Nectaire*, however, perhaps of a later vintage, has strong black enameling in its recesses. Another cigarette box, *Khedive*, is offered in Breves' Galleries catalogue,[3] but not in Lalique's 1932 list. This stunning container – its winged sun disc motif was the symbol of protection often seen on the lintels of Egyptian temples – is an example of the Egyptomania which swept Europe after Howard Carter's discovery of Tutankhamen's tomb in 1922. "Khedive", from the Turkish word for prince, was the title given to the viceroy of Egypt under Ottoman suzerainty (1867–1914).

Some of the most unusual and attractive boxes are those which, like *Sultane*, have figural knobs or finials on their lids. *Myosotis*, a *garniture de toilette*, includes a powder box on whose domed cover sits a nude surrounded by tiny blossoms. The other three components of this *garniture* (for eau de cologne, toilet water, etc.) have kneeling nudes as stoppers, similarly bedecked in floral garlands. The forget-me-not motif is repeated in vertical bands down the sides of all four pieces. *Degas*, named after the artist who loved to paint (and sculpt) ballerinas in a variety of poses, is a frosted-glass circular powder box (some have a vestigial blue *patine*) whose knob is the torso of a dancer. Her long skirt flows around her, forming the lid of the box. Another frosted-glass box, with hints of sienna *patine*, has a stunning top consisting of a woman whose voluminous pleated gown extends around her, continuing along the ribbed sides of the rounded, triangular bottom section of the box. The grace and lyricism of these two figural-finial boxes are in marked contrast to the levity and charm of *Amour Assis*, a circular box with cover of clear and frosted glass whose chubby molded Cupid finial is taller than the box itself. The impish look on his face and his childish pose, coupled with his curly ringlets

2. "The Lalique Collection", 130.
3. Breves' Lalique Galleries, *The Art of René Lalique*, plate 32, no. 55.

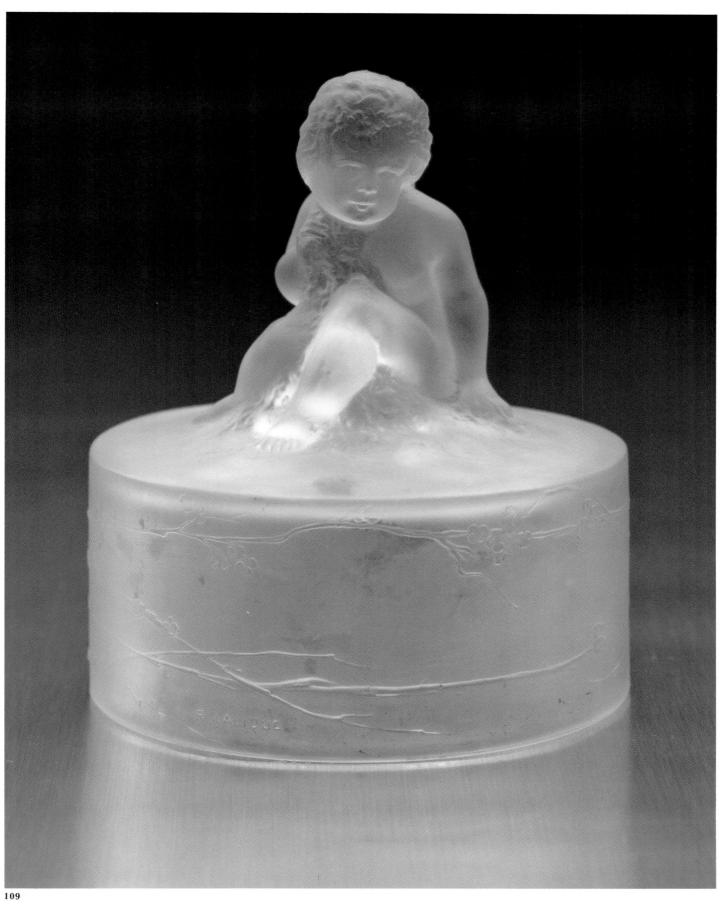

109

and the flower-strewn ground on which he sits, appear almost incongruous with the sparse, delicately patterned prunus design on the sides of the box.

Decorative, non-figurative finials appear on the circular boxes, *Primavères*, *Vallauris* and *Cheveux de Vénus (Seaweed)*. Each has a floral motif, though the last of them, dating as far back as 1912, is quite naturalistic in appearance compared to the stylization of the other two. A charming round box, available as a flacon with stopper and atomizer as well, is *Enfants*. The frosted-glass base is a frieze of pudgy cherub-like children, their arms raised up as if to hold the tiered canopy top decorated with five concentric floral garlands. These charming little figures are reminiscent of the colorful, flower-bedecked putti represented in ceramic by the turn-of-the-century Austrian designer, Michael Powolny, and other Wiener Werkstätte ceramicists.

The inverted-funnel finial of the 9in-high *Houppes (Powder Puffs)* box, displayed as a *grande boîte à poudre* at the 1925 Paris Exposition, and later transformed into a paper powder box, is echoed in *Eglantines*, whose base is awash with overlapping blossoms and whose lid is molded with their radiating stems, rising to a fruitstem-like finial in the middle. The lid of another box is similar, except that its flowers continue on to half of the lid, the other half being stems and finial. An unusual frosted-glass circular box, with traces of sienna staining, has a large, semicircular finial-handle showing three finches amid a thicket of ferns which drapes down the sides of the box. Such a *demilune* handle is rarely seen on boxes – its shape is more likely to be that of a *luminaire* or *surtout* (or seen on small ashtrays and seals).

The vast majority of Lalique's boxes are circular, of frosted and clear glass, with flat or slightly bombé lids molded in any number of figural, floral and faunal motifs, some more stylized than others. One of the early figural ones, which was illustrated in *Art et Décoration* in 1912,[4] is *Angels and Perfume Burner*, as Breves' catalogue, *The Art of René Lalique*, calls it. Such sensuous, elongated nudes are unlikely to be conventional angels; more likely, they are winged handmaidens of Venus, taking sustenance from the aromatic essences rising up in an Art Nouveau swirl of smoke from the nicely detailed cassolette between them. The box, which has a 3¼in diameter and may be as early as 1905–10, is stained overall with a sienna *patine*, and its base is molded with lovely flowers and tendrils, as is the side of its ½in-high lid. The elegant women, their wings gently conforming to the round shape of the box, seem to be tiptoeing, or floating, in an olfactory ritual.

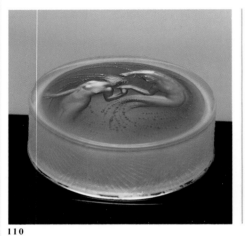

110

111

112

113

110 Box and cover with two nymphs, *c.* 1925, 3½in (8.5cm) dia. Galerie Moderne.

111 Box and cover with three dancing maidens, for Coty, *c.* 1910, 3¾in (9.5cm) dia. Galerie Moderne.

112 Powder box and cover with two dancers, for Coty, *c.* 1910, 2¾in (7cm) dia. Galerie Moderne.

113 *Primavères* box and cover, *c.* 1922, 6½in (16cm) dia. Galerie Moderne.

4. Kahn, "Lalique Verrier", 149.

114

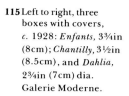

114 Box and cover, with figural finial, *c.* 1920, 4in (10cm). Collection Mary Lou Utt, USA.

115 Left to right, three boxes with covers, *c.* 1928: *Enfants*, 3¾in (8cm); *Chantilly*, 3½in (8.5cm), and *Dahlia*, 2¾in (7cm) dia. Galerie Moderne.

115

116

117

116 *Angels and Perfume Burner* box and cover, *c.* 1912, 3¼in (8.3cm) dia. Private collection, London; photo by Zeljan Pavicevic.

117 *Roger* box and cover, *c.* 1925, 5½in (13.8cm) dia. Galerie Moderne.

118 Left, *Cléones* box and cover, *c.* 1925, 6¾in (17cm) dia.; right, *Houppes* box and cover, *c.* 1920, 5½in (14cm) dia. Collection Mary Lou Utt, USA.

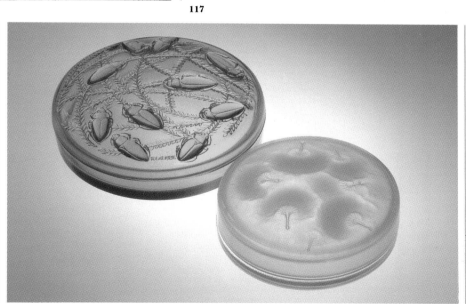

118

79

119

120

121

122

119 Box and cover with baby pierrots, *c.* 1926, 3½in (9cm) dia. Galerie Moderne.

120 *Oeuf pervenches* box and cover, *c.* 1930, 4½in (11.5cm) long. Galerie Moderne.

121 *Oeuf poussins* box and cover, *c.* 1930, 4½in (11.5cm) longer. Galerie Moderne.

122 *Grande cyprins* box and cover, *c,* 1925, 10¼in (25.5cm) dia. Galerie Moderne.

123 *Grande cyprins* box and cover, *c.* 1925, 10¼in (25.5cm) dia. Collection Glenn and Mary Lou Utt, USA.

124 Box and cover with knot design, *c.* 1922, 3¾in (8cm) square. Galerie Moderne.

125 *4 Scarabées* box and cover, *c.* 1912, 3½in (8.5cm). Collection Laurie and Joel Shapiro, Detroit.

123

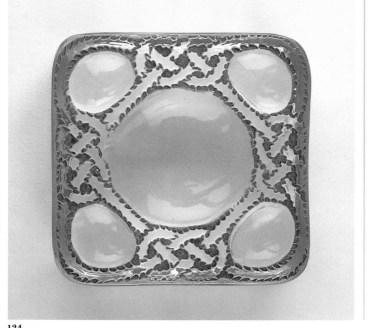

124

125

Other figural boxes were also done in an Art Nouveau manner. Among them is an untitled Coty box with two swirling maidens dancing on the lid, and similar ribbon or leaf motifs unfurled on the sides. There is also *2 Figurines*, which features a pair of attenuated nude females standing amid a shower of blooming tree boughs. One of the few figural boxes available in color was *2 Sirènes*. It was very large, over 10in in diameter, whereas most boxes ranged from 2½ to 4in in diameter. Two ocean nymphs, their fins gently articulated and the stylized beads of their hair metamorphosing into swirling arcs of water all around them, cavort on the lid; the subject is faintly erotic, not unlike that found on other representations of two women in Lalique's design repertory (and those of other Art Nouveau and Art Déco artists). This box was available in vivid "amber and opal-blue", according to Breves' catalogue, as well as in opalescent glass. Strangely, it was advertised as a "sandwich box" (probably because of the way in which the top fits on to the bottom). Sirens appear singly, in pairs or in groups on other Lalique pieces, including inkwells, platters and plaques.

Other figural boxes are not so overtly Art Nouveau, although the flimsily robed neoclassical dancers on *Louveciennes*, the nude dancing females on *Fontenay*, *figurine et raisins*, *2 Figurines et branches* and *Figurine et bouquets*, and the water-bearer on *Ermenonville* all fit the mode, as do the swirling floral garlands on all of them but *Ermenonville*.

Two charming ballerinas, each on point and with a leg raised, remind one of the *Degas* box. Called *2 Danseuses*, it is a lovely, impressionistic image translated to glass in a style of its own, neither Art Nouveau nor Art Déco. Nothing could be farther removed from it than *Victoire*, which also seems to be in a class by itself. A muscular, winged Nike, brandishing a sword and wearing a helmet, is presented as a sturdy, almost Amazonian, nude.

Three interesting boxes bear a resemblance to the earlier-mentioned *Enfants*. One, *Amours*, is molded with a group of frolicking putti; another, *Anges*, shows these creatures in Christian guise as a cluster of winged children's heads. A very rare and unusual frosted-glass box in quite shallow relief depicts a group of what look like baby pierrots or harlequin puppets playing under a shower of stars. In a similar vein, *Masques* presents a party of face masks amid bouquets and blossoms.

As for animal motifs, many of the creatures which graced Lalique's goldsmithswork appear in relief on his containers (as they do on his vases). The peacock in all his resplendent, tail-feathered glory is seen on the box, *Paon*, a trio of strutting birds adorns *3 Paons*, and three more, this time quite stylized, peacocks appear on *Isabelle*. Two exotic birds decorate *Rambouillet*, elegant swans glide on *Cygnes*, and *Coq* represents a majestic example of that fowl in an interesting off-center image. This box was also available in black glass and in that guise has been compared to Japanese woodcuts; the cock is a common Oriental subject, and it is not surprising that it should appear on this *japoniste* box of *c.*1910. Not so popular during the Art Nouveau period were more common, less showy birds, but Lalique managed to stylize them or their settings to make them almost exotic. He did so on the large (over 10in in diameter) box,

Saint-Marc, on which two plump doves nest on the lid, their upraised wings and tail feathers almost an exercise in geometry. Likewise, *Mésanges* presents a flock of six blue tits flying in a perfect circle, their wings resembling a child's pinwheel toy (this box was available in a shimmering gold or opalescent, among other hues). *Geneviève* depicts two pigeons within a triangle, centering a very stylized spiral, or perhaps palmette, design.

One of Lalique's most famous boxes is *Roger*, of clear, frosted and, usually, rich black-enameled glass (color and opalescent examples exist, but they are rare). The top has a radial design of 10 clear-glass cabochons; amid and around these bosses are stylized fruiting vines and, at the outer edge, five exotic birds. The individual panels on the sides of the box sport additional vines and grape designs. The manner in which the enamel is sparsely applied to the glass is almost calligraphic, another nod – albeit a late one – by Lalique to *japonisme*.

Flying insects proliferate on Lalique's boxes, nowhere better than on the large opalescent and colored creations. Three shimmering dragonflies flutter on the lid of *Georgette* and a trio of moths on *Libellules* (despite its name, which means dragonflies); the opalescent examples of the two convey the translucence of these creatures' wings. *Cléones* depicts 10 beetles in a swarm of leafy thickets, quite naturalistically if compared to *Cigales*, whose 12 cicadas form a geometric pattern, six pairs neatly patterning six triangles. The box, *4 Papillons*, each butterfly forming a near-perfect triangle, is similar in concept to *Cigales*; and *4 Scarabées*, with a quartet of beetles arranged around a rose blossom, is also stunning. These last two boxes (*Papillons* and *Scarabées*) were available in plain and colored glass; they are illustrated in the 1912 *Art et Décoration* article.[5]

Lalique's menagerie did not end with birds and insects. A shoal of luminescent fish appears on *Grande cyprins*, a large box which was available in colored or opalescent glass; drawn directly from Japanese sources, such fish appeared frequently on Lalique's platters. A circle of running hare enclosing birds perched in bushes decorates *Fontainebleau*, as graceful and stylized an Art Déco box as *Chantilly*, with its six gazelles occupying floriate panels.

Floral forms, both representational and abstract, appear on Lalique's boxes. An interesting trio – *Grand vase*, *Vases* and *Panier de roses* – are miniature still-lifes in glass of blossoms in vases, the first two with very Oriental-looking vessels of spherical shape. *Dinard*, with its stylized roses and leaves, anticipates the plant designs on his rare creations in bakelite (this dark red box was made in both circular and square shapes; unfortunately, Lalique did not seem to produce any other objects in this brand-new medium). The overlapping blossoms on *Marguerites* and *Emiliane* (both available with a number of colored *patines*) are similarly stylized. An unusual egg-shaped box, *Oeuf pervenches*, is covered all over with a burst of periwinkles; *Oeufs poussins*, similarly shaped, depicts a flock of tiny, fully formed chicks still enclosed in their shells. The large opalescent box, *Tokio*, is a stylized flowerburst of bubbles which resembles a fireworks display (it originally held a satin box containing four tiny perfume bottles), and *Grande muguets* shows a similar florid explosion of lilies-of-the-valley with radiating stems.

5. *Ibid.*, 149, 158.

126

Some of Lalique's floral patterns could be quite classical – on the *Roses en relief* oval box and *Pommier du Japon (Japanese Apple Tree)*, for example, as well as on the two large boxes, *6 Dahlias* and *3 Dahlias*. *Gui* depicts branches of mistletoe similar to those on the 1912 glass-roundel invitation to Lalique's first *verrerie* display. *Véronique* is a handsome black-glass box whose lid displays two beribboned bouquets of the speedwell plant (one such box is in the Metropolitan Museum of Art in New York).

Two unusual boxes depict shells in quite opposite ways. *Coquilles* is a round confection whose eight angular shells resemble stylized classical anthemions; *Trésor de la mer*, in the shape of a clamshell on the surface of frothy waves, is quite realistic, especially considering its late date (*c.*1939); it was especially made for the Saks Fifth Avenue department store and contained a pearl of sorts within it: a small bottle of perfume.

DESK ACCESSORIES

Lalique produced a whole range of writing supplies and related articles, inkwells, blotters, seals, ashtrays, bookends and paper-weights among them.

127

The lid on the inkwell of *Colbert* almost resembles that on one of Lalique's Art Déco boxes, only here the stylized bird-and-berry motif also overflows onto the rectangular base. The design on the *3 Dahlias* box is quite naturalistic in comparison.
126 *Colbert* inkwell, *c.* 1931, 10¼in (25.7cm) long. Collection Laurie and Joel Shapiro, Detroit.

127 *3 Dahlias* box and cover, *c.* 1925, 8½in (21cm) dia. Galerie Moderne.

INKWELLS

Inkwells had of course been in existence for centuries before Lalique came to make them in glass (he made one earlier example, the elaborate silver and glass *Nessus and Deianira; c.* 1903–05; Gulbenkian Collection). Bronze ink containers were found at Pompeii; Georgian silversmiths created especially lavish inkstands, or standishes; and the 19th century witnessed the efflorescence of the inkwell – in porcelain, in silver and other metals, in wood, sometimes painstakingly carved or molded creations taking the shapes of teapots, human figures, flowers and even, in the hands of Louis Comfort Tiffany, crabs and mushrooms. Lalique's client and friend, Sarah Bernhardt, designed a bronze inkwell in her own "divine" image (today one example is in the Museum of Fine Arts in Boston). But by far the most common and cheapest material for inkwells was glass. By the time that Lalique began to mass-produce them, inkwells were nearly obsolete. He and other designers made them throughout the 1930s, though rarely after that, since by then the average writer had abandoned the ritual of pen-dipping in favor of new, no-fuss writing implements.

The 1932 catalogue illustrates 14 inkwells and there were several more created; but together they make a small number compared to his boxes and vases. Their variety is nonetheless impressive. The most stunning is probably the early *Biches*, a square box with a smaller square lid and a trough all around. The four sides of the well depict four different graceful deer standing amid stylized trees and foliage (one side has a doe and fawn). It is an elegant Art Déco creation, as is *Myrtilles (Bilberries)*, a flattened circular well with a stylized-bud lid, its frosted glass enhanced all over with rich black enamel. *Myrtilles* is quite large (8¼in in diameter) compared to the other round wells, such as *Serpents*, with its horrific intertwining snakes, *Escargots, Mures (Mulberries)* and *4 Sirènes*, each with a 6in-diameter (*4 Sirènes* also exists in a large 10in-diameter version). They

were available in opalescent as well as clear glass and their designs were all molded on the underside. *Nénuphar* is a tiny inkwell, slightly over 3in in diameter, and *3 Papillons*, with its shape conforming to that of the three butterflies surrounding the well, is less than an inch bigger.

Lalique also made large rectangular inkwells. One, *Colbert*, is described (but not named) by Breves' Galleries as "a design . . . specially made for M. Poincaré" (who was the French Minister of Culture). The caption continued:

> This is one of Lalique's most exclusive creations, the "edition" being limited to twenty, of which M. Poincaré acquired No. 1, the example shown . . . being No. 2.[6]

Since the inkwell is illustrated in Lalique's 1932 catalogue as having a limited edition of 50, it is likely that 20 of the 50 went to Brèves'. The inkwell is a lovely Art Déco creation, its front trough decorated at the left and right sides with stylized bird and berry designs, which also adorn the round lid of the well behind the trough. A very unusual design is *Sully*, made of frosted glass with rare black-enamel highlighting. Its overall motif is a geometric sawtooth, not unlike that seen on other Art Déco objects and quite akin to ancient Aztec and Mayan art, which inspired designers in the 1920s.

6. Breves' Lalique Galleries, *The Art of René Lalique*, 14.

BLOTTERS

In contrast to the geometric motifs on *Sully* are the much more organic, nature-inspired subjects which adorn Lalique's glass blotters, or *buvards*. Perhaps their waisted, bow-like shapes conformed better to interlacing fruit and floral, as well as figural, designs. Blackberries, artichoke leaves, cherries and snails were molded in relief on the frosted-glass outsides of five of the blotters; three others depicted *Sirènes enlacées assises (Seated, Intertwined Sirens)*, a faun and nymph, and two sirens reclining in an unmistakably erotic pose.

SEALS

The wide variety of seals (or *cachets*) created by Lalique run the gamut of his motifs. These tiny molded sculptures or relief panels[7] (from 1½in long to slightly more than 4in) had floral, faunal and figural subjects, and included a menagerie of charming animals which were often made larger on other Lalique creations such as paperweights and bookends. A turkey, duck, dog, rabbit, fox, mouse or fish – all could be purchased in plain or colored glass, with an extra charge for monogram engraving (one letter, 40 francs; two, 65 francs; and three, 100 francs). Another type of seal was one topped by a round or oval plaque, representing mostly human or mythological figures (sirens, faun, naiad, dancers), but also available with two budgerigars perched on flowery limbs, with blossoming fuchsia, with butterflies or with an elaborate sailing ship (*Caravelle*). There was also one patriotic plaque on which were molded the arms of England.

A half-dozen elongated, almost squared-off, figural and animal seals were designed as an eagle's head, a whole eagle, a draped female figure, a fly, two mice and two pigeons. Two elaborate seals represented a butterfly with its wings closed (*Papillon ailes fermées*) and one with them open (*Papillon ailes ouvertes*). A ring of lizards (*Anneau lézards*) made another unusual seal, and *Vase fleurs*, with its crescent-like overflow of flowers from the vase, was directly related to the scent bottles of the same type.

130

131

130 *Biches* inkwell, *c.* 1910, 6in (15cm) square, at base. Collection Laurie and Joel Shapiro, Detroit.

131 *Tête d'aigle* seal, *c.* 1908, 3in (7.8cm). Kagan Collection, USA.

The elegant deer adorning the square inkwell are fine examples of the graceful creatures who, along with gazelles and the like, appear in many Art Déco creations, and which are often characterized *en masse* as *les biches*. The eagle presents a contrasting animal image, yet is nonetheless Art Déco.

7. Around the turn of the century, Lalique also produced several seals of *cire-perdue* glass.

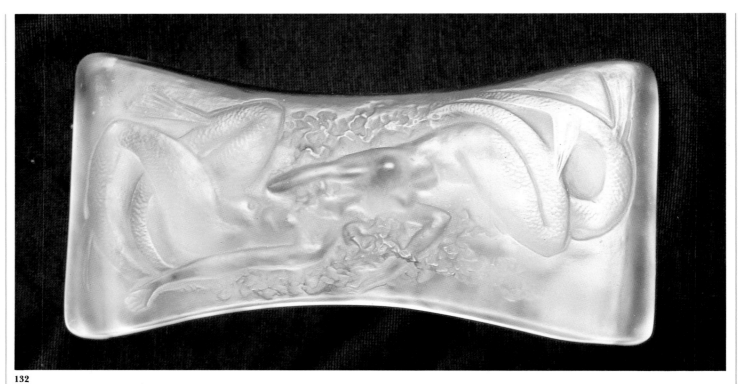

132

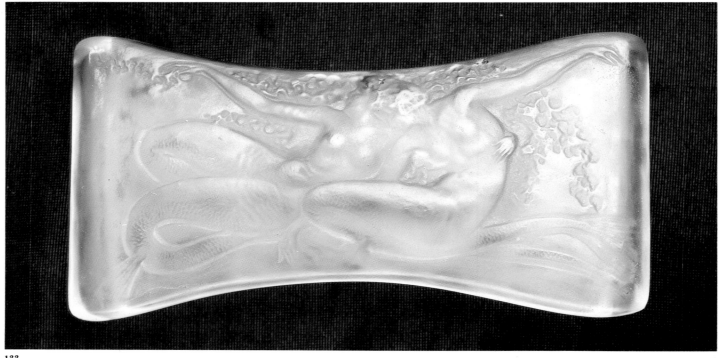

133

132 *2 Sirènes face à face couchées* blotter, *c.* 1910, 6½in (16cm) long. Collection J. Havard, London.

133 *Sirènes enlacées assises* blotter, *c.* 1910, 6½in (16cm) long. Collection J. Havard, London.

The waisted, bow-like shapes of these blotters, or *buvards*, seems ideal for the subjects they depict – sinuous nymphs, sensuously interlaced. Other blotters Lalique designed depicted decidedly unerotic snails, leaves and fruits.

ASHTRAYS

Ashtrays (*cendriers*) could be circular, oval, rectangular or octagonal; they were made of frosted, clear, opalescent or colored glass; they could have molded bas-relief borders or, as with the seals, they could be centered on round or ovoid plaques with intaglio or relief designs or with small sculptural figures or animals placed in the middle of a simple, round dish (a few of this type were made in *cire-perdue* glass).

Among the loveliest ashtrays are round, oval or polygonal ones edged with stylized floral designs or classical figures. *Médicis* is an oval ashtray on whose wide, garlanded borders sit four nymphs, each in a different state of repose. *Cuba* is incised with stylized tobacco leaves which alternate with recessed clear sections. *Jamaïque* has a scalloped edge of leafy shapes. Several ashtrays of this border type – primarily those with bold, stylized designs – have the names of exotic places which supplied tobacco to Europe: Cuba, Sumatra, Martinique, Tobago, Jamaica and Granada. Judging by their strong, almost masculine, motifs, they were probably intended for male customers, whereas those ashtrays called *Berthe, Alice, Irène, Louise, Nicole* and *Simone* have softer, prettier, mostly floral, designs. The 1920s saw the emergence of the "flappers" – women who smoked, applied their makeup in public places, and wore short skirts and trousers – thus providing a market for decorative cigarette cases, ashtrays and powder compacts. Several of Lalique's ashtrays have huge single blossoms centered on tiny raised stamens – excellent for stubbing out cigarettes, perhaps (he also designed tiny cigarette extinguishers, upright glass cylinders with decorative side handles). An especially lovely and unusual ashtray, *Dahlia et papillon*, depicts a butterfly alighting on an edge of the floral tray. It looks as if the piece might topple over with the weight of the winged creature, but obviously Lalique has achieved a perfect balance between the two parts. Ashtrays came in a wide range of colors, from the subtlest blues and ambers to the deepest greens and oranges.

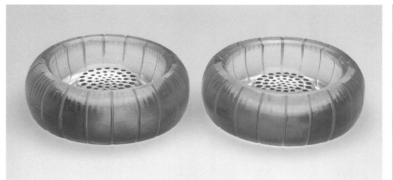

135

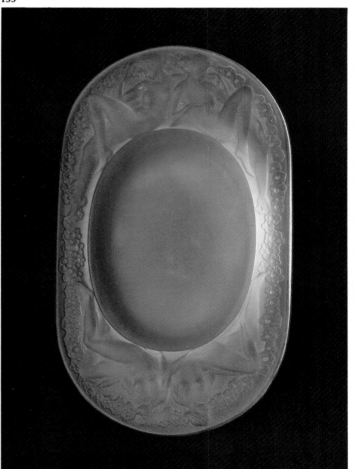

136

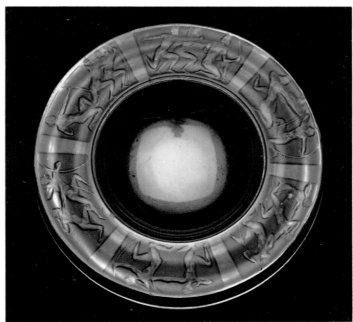

134

134 *Archers* ashtray, *c.* 1920, 4½in (11cm) dia. Galerie Moderne.

135 Pair of *Berthe* ashtrays, *c.* 1930, 3in (7.3cm). Galerie Moderne.

136 *Médicis* ashtray, *c.* 1920, 5¾in (14.5cm) long. Galerie Moderne.

The two figural ashtrays, or *cendriers*, are decorated with classical nudes, male athletes on *Archers*, garland-surrounded females on *Médicis*. The stylized flowerhead comprising *Berthe* is a marked contrast to the other two pieces, much more Art Déco in its stark regularity.

137

138

LALIQUE

137 *Simone* ashtray,
c. 1928, 4in (9.8cm)
dia. Galerie Moderne.

138 *Alice* ashtray, *c.* 1925,
4½in (11cm) long.
Galerie Moderne.

139

140

139 Pendant, woman with
doves, *c.* 1920, glass
with silk cord, 1½in
(4cm). Courtesy
Christopher Vane
Percy.

140 Oval pendant with
wasps, *c.* 1920, glass
with silk cord, 2¼in
(5.5cm). Galerie
Moderne.

141 Necklace with
Javanese fighting
roosters, *c.* 1900,
copper-backed glass
(*pâte-de-verre?*)/
enamel(?), baroque
pearl, gold, 4½in
(11.4cm) wide, chain
20in (50.8cm) long
unsigned. Collection
Glenn and Mary Lou
Utt, USA.

142 Circular pendant with
leaves, *c.* 1920, glass
with silk cord, 2in
(5cm) dia. Courtesy
Christopher Vane
Percy.

143 Buckle/clasp with
grazing stag, with
original box, *c.* 1908–
14, glass and metal,
4½ × 1½in (11 ×
4cm). Collection Mr.
and Mrs. V. James
Cole, New York.

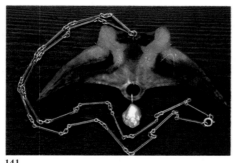

141

142

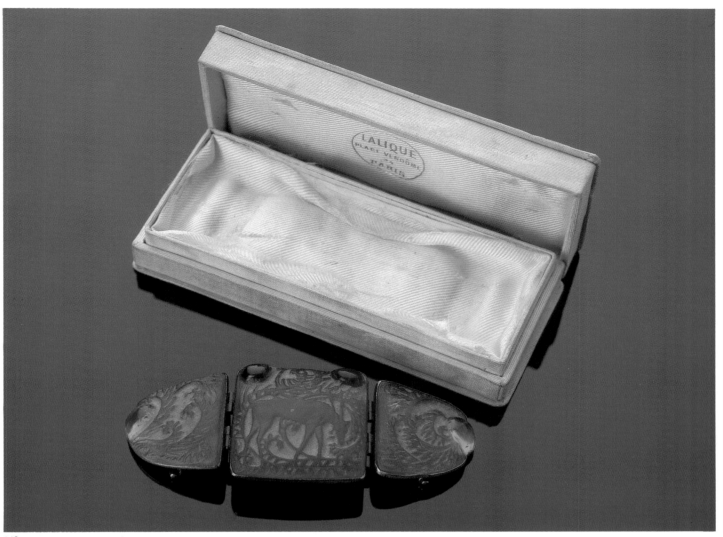

143

144

145

144 Brooch with monstrous dog's head, *c.* 1920, glass, metal, foil inclusions, 1¾in (4.5cm) dia. Courtesy Christopher Vane Percy.

145 Brooch with satyr's head, 1916, glass and gilt-metal, 1 × 1¾in (2.5 × 4.4cm). Courtesy Christopher Vane Percy.

146 Pendant with two dragonflies, *c.* 1920, glass with silk cord, 1½in (4cm). Galerie Moderne.

147 Pendant with two dragonflies, *c.* 1920, glass with silk cord, 1½in (4cm). Courtesy Christopher Vane Percy.

146

147

GLASS JEWELRY

Lalique produced all-glass jewelry more than a decade after he had stopped making jewels in gold, stones and other materials (though many transitional metal-mounted glass pieces were made in the 1910s, some even earlier), but this represented neither a return to his old career nor a concession to anyone who lamented the loss of his genius as a goldsmith. When the master began to apply his encyclopedic knowledge of glass-production methods to jewelry, the results were vibrant, chic, affordable, exquisitely made and, in contrast to many of his bejeweled fantasies, eminently wearable. Here is what one critic wrote in 1927:

> [René Lalique] likes nothing better than to produce things for use, beautiful things that may be employed every day in every type of household – lamps and vases, fruit-bowls, table glass, yes, and even inexpensive ornaments to hang round one's neck or pin in one's hat.[8]

In marked contrast was the earlier comment of another writer on the products of Lalique's goldsmith days:

> He was making necklaces, brooches, tiaras, combs, bracelets, and pendants, all most original in shape and colour, all most daring, unexpected, and fairy-like, and all destined for a few privileged ones such as real princesses, queens of the footlights, empresses of Fashion or of Banking, or perhaps of both.[9]

Lalique's late jewelry was not, of course, totally removed from his early pieces, many of which consisted of sections of molded glass – faces, plaques, medallions and the like. It was his nascent work with rock crystal (which resembles glass), enamels and glass while making the jewels which led him to explore more deeply the techniques of working with vitreous materials, and put him on the road to glass-making.

Some of Lalique's early *bijouterie* incorporated glass, and the next step he took in glass jewelry was to make glass brooches and buttons – usually circular or elongated "bar pins" – of molded glass affixed to metal (mostly copper) backings. Colored foil was frequently placed between the backing and the clear or colored glass. These glass jewels were first produced at Combs-la-Ville just before World War I, and were continued until the mid-1920s. The bas-relief roundels, attenuated ovals and rectangles, and other shaped jewels came in bright pinks, blues and greens, jewel-like reds, topazes and amethysts, and speckled hybrids or opalescent shades. Growling dog's heads, floral forms, fluttering insects, nude and draped figures, *les biches*, birds of various feathers and coiled serpents appeared on them.

The colorful mounted brooches and buttons were in marked contrast to those clear pendants – usually oval or circular, sometimes heart-shaped – whose underside-molded motifs tended to be very feminine female figures or floral designs, with a selection of pretty birds and butterflies, all reminiscent of carved rock crystal. The pendants usually came attached to a long silk cord, which went through a tiny, unobtrusive hole at the very top. There were also glass beads, strung on extensive lengths of silk in such a way as to leave much of the ribbon exposed and molded in the shapes of, among other things, lily-of-the-valley bells and ivy leaves, sometimes in colors and sometimes with central pendants of another design. The *Lierre (Ivy)* necklace had 10 beads of emerald-green-glass leaves surrounding a central glass roundel decorated with a large floret, all on a grey silk cord. Another necklace had nine berry clusters of bright blue glass, yet another seven barrel-shaped beads of stylized daisy and leaf design.

Necklaces worn closer to the neck, called *colliers*, were made of beads which were contiguous. They were often unusually shaped. One, for instance, at 1500 francs the costliest jewel in the 1932 catalogue, had 30 carved birds of clear and frosted glass perched on rectangular sections; another was a veritable garden of dahlia blos-

8. Gordon-Stables, "Lalique", 34.

9. Mourey, "Lalique's Glassware", 32.

soms, yet another a forest of stylized ferns carved on to 20 angular spheres. These *colliers* came in a variety of clear and colored glass, as did the wonderful expandable bracelets with elastic cords. One, called *Zig-zag*, had interlocking jagged beads (or *rondelles*), sometimes of two alternating colors. Others consisted of rectangular panels whose subjects were as diverse as sparrows, cocks, griffins, lilies-of-the-valley, palmettes and cherry trees.

Immensely popular after World War I with stylish young women, Lalique's glass jewels were on the whole moderately priced, but, according to Christopher Vane Percy, "although they were surprisingly resilient they were usually regarded as expendable".[10] Consequently, they are not so numerous today as one would expect, especially those multi-part bracelets and necklaces which may have lost a bead or panel and were not repaired.

An unusual trio of frosted-glass floral brooches – identified as being made of "*cristal, émail et brillants*" in a 1923 *Art et Décoration* article[11] – take on the characteristics of many of Lalique's boxes, with their exaggerated flowerheads and perfectly formed petals. The diamonds are an unusual element at this stage in the development of Lalique's jewelry.

The most handsome examples of Lalique's glass jewelry are those pendants strung singly on silk cords. Of colored, opalescent or frosted glass, sometimes highlighted with enamel, they come in a wide variety of shapes and colors, and depict sand dollars, flying cranes, lizards, berries, flowers and even crosses. Two trailing lilies adorn an amber-colored triangle, four pairs of wasps appear on a bright-blue oval, and a swarm of hornets is molded on an arresting oval in black and frosted glass. The oval was suspended from silk cord and it also had hanging from it the two fluffy ends of a cord knotted at a hole at the pendant's bottom. A bright, blue hoop-like pendant was simply molded with leafy veining, and a vaguely T-shaped pendant, molded with two overlapping dragonflies, was available in a bright green. An interesting orange-glass pendant of rectangular shape depicts a woman's head at the left. On her right hand perches a dove, while another bird flaps his wings and takes on a vertical shape at the right. One of the most exquisite pendants was a frosted mass of glass resembling a baroque pearl, across whose uneven surface glides a school of diagonally swimming fish in blue enamel (it also came with black-enamel fish).

Lalique also produced a small number of scent-bottle pendants, among them *Replique*, commissioned by the *parfumeur*, Raphael. It was in the shape of a frosted-glass acorn, with a gilt-metal screw-top cap at the top continuing the scale-like patterning of the glass body. It, too, was suspended from a silk cord (such cords were frequently in the same color as the pendants).

Nicholas Dawes has noted that the pressed shapes and motifs of many of these flattish pendants are those of *tsuba*, or Japanese sword guards.[12] Like many of Lalique's pendants, these metal sword guards have two holes (housing a small dagger and a kind of bodkin through which to tie the cord). Finely articulated animals, including snakes and lizards, as well as petal forms were common *tsuba* motifs, and there is no doubt that Lalique's pendants, like so many of the pieces throughout his career, are tinged with *japonisme*.

148

148 Pendant with fish, *c.* 1925, frosted glass with enamel, 2in (5cm). Galerie Moderne.

The irregular shape of the glass gives it the appearance of a giant baroque pearl, or a chunk of rock crystal.

10. Christopher Vane Percy, *The Glass of Lalique, A Collector's Guide*, London, 1977, 132–33.

11. "Des Bijoux Nouveaux", *Art et Décoration*, May 1923, 151.

12. Dawes, *Lalique Glass*, 65.

SCULPTURE

8

The glass figurines produced by René Lalique – generally beginning in about 1920, although *cire-perdue* statuettes were made as early as 1900 – comprise some of his most dramatic and finest works of art. From his statuettes of nude women – progressing from sinuous Art Nouveau silhouettes to geometric Art Déco stylizations – to his representations of all types of birds and beasts and his rare non-animal creations, these figurines, bookends, paperweights and automobile mascots are evidence of Lalique's high craftsmanship as a sculptor. Many of the figures were mass-produced, but they were nonetheless expertly executed, three-dimensional works of art.

At the age of 20, Lalique had studied bronze sculpting at the Ecole Bernard Palissy in Paris (the school bore the name of a 16th-century French potter and naturalist who produced so-called "rustic ware", pond-shaped dishes inhabited by realistically modeled snakes, snails, insects and lizards) and during the next decade he mastered the technique of *cire-perdue* bronze sculpture and glass-making, producing handsome relief plaques, including a lovely bronze of his wife in profile (a tiny copper relief of Mme Lalique also exists). He also made small *cire-perdue* figures, such as seals, perhaps dating as far back as 1895; these were most likely Lalique's answer to the bronze figural seals which prevailed at the turn of the century.

Lalique was at his height as a goldsmith when he began to experiment with glass in the 1890s. Some of his diverse sculptural creations from this decade and the one following are worth mentioning, including lovely three-dimensional silver, bronze and ivory figures and figural groups which show, on a larger scale than the figures on the jewels, how accomplished a sculptor Lalique was. Two silver centerpieces of *c.*1903–05 are excellent examples of his early sculpture. One (private collection, Paris) depicts a vortical mass of nine writhing nudes and is Rodinesque in its energy and drama; it is not large as sculpture goes, but it is monumental when compared to his tiny goldsmithswork figures. The other (Gulbenkian Collection) is a more restrained and romantic piece in the form of a small fountain, in the middle of which a tall, flower-bedecked water maiden perches on an open blossom. She stands amid a lilypad-covered pond dotted with four naiad and dolphin pairs half-emergent from the base; streams of glass pour out of the dolphins' mouths and glass water can be seen underneath and around the lilypads.

Lalique also produced a number of chalices and goblets in silver, glass, enamel and ivory, all of which were probably decorative and never intended to be used. Many of these monumental vessels incorporate carved figures, such as a wine goblet (*c.*1899–1901; Gulbenkian Collection) whose stem just under the cup is covered with a knob of four contorted *cire-perdue* glass figures. An especially charming chalice of gold, enamel and ivory, *Apostles* (*c.*1903–05; private collection, Paris), includes a circle of nine carved figures sitting on a bench just above the decorated circular base.

Three carved ivory paperweights (*c.*1902–04; Gulbenkian Collection) rank with any of the small sculptures produced by other turn-of-the-century romantic sculptors, such as the Englishman, Arthur Gilbert. One shows the ivory torsos of an embracing couple, their heads crowned with bronze and pearl-studded diadems in the

150 Chalice, *c.* 1904, silver and hand-blown opalescent glass, 8in (20cm). Collection Glenn and Mary Lou Utt, USA.

This chalice is one of a series, as many as three dozen may have been created.

150

shapes of fantastic birds and animals. *Medusa* depicts the Gorgon's head with a crown and collar of writhing bronze snakes, and *Fight* represents two male half-figures in combat, one with his hands around the neck of his gasping enemy.

Very soon after these silver and ivory masterpieces were produced, or perhaps even simultaneously, Lalique created *cire-perdue* glass statuettes, including the lovely, lyrical group, *Maiden on a Dolphin* (*c.*1907–09; Gulbenkian Collection), in *cire-perdue* glass, and *Pan*, the impish god perched on a tree trunk playing his pipes (*c.*1907–09; Gulbenkian Collection). Another of these rare early figures, highlighted in a sepia *patine*, is a seated wood nymph encircled by trailing flower garlands, yet another is a Symbolist (17in-high) standing woman whose nude form is partly covered with leaves, Daphne-like (this figure, from a South American collection, sold at auction in New York in late 1987 for $148,000). A superb *cire-perdue* animal figure, inscribed "25–19" and therefore dated to 1919, is that of a growling cougar crouched on a rock. Its matt, pitted surface is highlighted all over with a yellowish stain and its modeling is bold and assured. This figure is from the second phase of Lalique's work in *cire-perdue* glass. The first group of vases and figures dates from the early years of the century; the later, more numerous, ones were produced after 1919 and are marked and dated like the cougar. Vases comprised the majority of these later pieces, although there are other figural examples, such as ashtrays with little animals in their centers.

Lalique's sculptures in the 1920s were made in Wingen and were mostly mass-produced figural ones, the *cire-perdue* method proving too time-consuming and expensive when quantity was important.

The molded figures were no less beautiful, however, and this new type of sculpture, the pieces larger than most of those produced by the *cire-perdue* method, was to be one of the cornerstones of Lalique's glass production for the rest of his life. These three-dimensional figures appeared as paperweights, bookends, seals, car mascots and box finials. The same basic image could be part of an ashtray, a free-standing figurine or, greatly enlarged, a fountain (as with the various models of the *Source de la fontaine* figure, elegant robed women accompanied by aquatic attributes or symbols).

FEMALE FIGURES

Lalique's glass creations of the 1920s were a tribute to the female sex – clothed and nude, languorous and active, brazen and shy, sacred and profane, classical and quasi-modern. Mythological creatures in frosted or opalescent glass, such as the 5in-tall *Naiade* and 4in-tall *Sirène*, both of whom are tucked into their bodies in somnolent, even shy, poses, also appear frequently. *Naiade*'s fin twists up and curls around itself at the bottom of the base, and *Sirène*'s non-human, vaguely fin-like extensions twine and curl around her.

One figure listed in Lalique's 1932 catalogue as *Grande nue (longs cheveux)* is over 16in high (including an ivy-molded glass base and a larger, pierced, ebonized one below it) and represents a voluptuous, mysterious nude. Her left arm covers her face and her right conceals her breast and extends up around her neck. From whichever angle the figure is viewed, she presents a powerfully erotic image, though not as aggressive as *Grande nue (bras levés)*, who holds up an offering but might just as well be offering her full body to the gods. Unlike the twisting nude, this figure is not free-standing, but is backed by a long, almost veil-like, segment of glass which becomes the squared-off base on which she stands. Both nudes rank among the tallest that Lalique produced (the one with upraised arms is 26in high).

A pair of medium-sized (6in-tall) figures, *Moyenne voilée* and *Moyenne nue*, present Lalique's versions of Goya's naked and clothed maja. Actually, both neoclassical women are completely covered; the nude's chiton (inner covering) is transparent, whereas the other woman's himation (outer garment) silhouettes her body in an overtly erotic manner. Both bodies have slightly distended stomachs, and their stance is straightforward and confident. Their thick, full hair-styles are not especially Greek, but Lalique was not bothered by such details of authenticity.

One 11in-tall female figure, *Voilée, mains jointes*, is a stunning veiled and draped maiden, especially in opalescent glass and proper light, when her body glows opaque yellow and her robe becomes diaphanous. The figure is not overtly sexual, but a more saintly, ethereal being, oblivious of her surroundings and her audience.

Without a doubt the best known of Lalique's female figures are *Suzanne* and *Thaïs*, glorious 9in-high representations of womanhood in an Art Déco setting, with perhaps a slight nod to the dancer of the Art Nouveau era, Loïe Fuller, whose veiled costumes swirled about her when she performed. Lalique's disrobed women are static in their pose, exotic, sensuous nudes holding up voluminous garments behind them in translucent rippling squares of molded glass. *Suzanne*,

151 *Cire-perdue* statue of a woman, *c.* 1901–05, 17⅜in (44cm), without base. Kagan/ Waller; photo courtesy Sotheby's, New York.

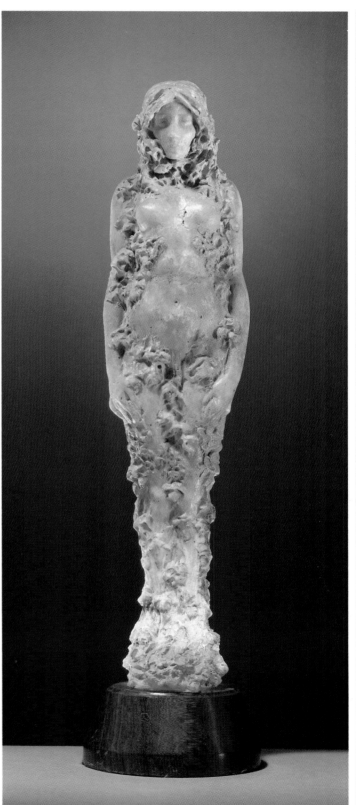

151

This lovely Symbolist figure, the woman covered by leafy tendrils and her long hair, has a sepia *patine* and lightly painted facial features. It was unknown until 1987.

also known as *Suzanne au bain* and loosely based on the Biblical story of Susannah and the elders (though it is probably not coincidental that Lalique's daughter's name was Suzanne), perches on her left foot, her right knee crooked sideways and her head looking to her right. Her robe drapes so as to create two openwork sections under her arms. This figure was available in frosted, opalescent or, occasionally, colored glass (an amber model is known), at first with a decorative bronze illumination stand incised with a design of leaves and two stylized peacocks. Such stands were quite costly and eventually abandoned in favor of simple metal bases. *Suzanne* and her companion piece *Thaïs* were both made for at least ten years, from about 1922 until the mid-1930s. *Thaïs'* pose is much more erotic than *Suzanne*'s (the statue is also the rarer of the two), with her head thrown back farther over her left shoulder, her breasts thrust upward and her visage more rapturous. Such translucent figures as these were ideally shown off when lighted from underneath or behind (they were offered with optional illuminating bases).

A very different feeling from that of *Suzanne* and *Thaïs* is conveyed by the *Source de la fontaine* figures, which were available in frosted glass in 13 different models in three sizes (18in, 25in and 28in), as well as an even tinier one (just under 5in-tall) on an ashtray. These water maidens are almost inhuman in their stance, gesture and countenance. Though elongated and veiled like the *Voilée, mains jointes* figure, they are more rigid and decorative. Nearly all of them wear elaborate, Oriental headdresses and most of them hold some aquatic attribute (a fish or waterlily, for instance); stylized representations of flowing, rippling or bubbling water extend down their gowns.

Two unusual 15in-high figures in relief on floral-bordered oval plaques are *Tête penchée* and *Joueuse de flute*. The tilted-headed woman and the flute player are pretty, classically draped figures, much like many who appear on Lalique's boxes and rock-crystal and glass pendants. Their sentimentality, however, cannot hold a candle to shimmering figures like *Suzanne* and the *Grandes nues*.

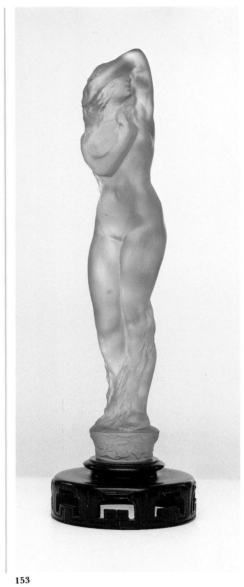

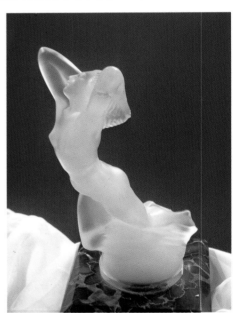

154

152 *Naiade* statuette/car mascot, *c.* 1925, 5¼in (13cm). The Pickard-Cambridge Family Collection, National Motor Museum, Beaulieu, Hampshire.

153 *Grande nue, longs cheveux, c.* 1910, 16½in (41cm). Collection S. and E. Khachadourian, England.

154 *Vitesse* car mascot, 1929, 7½in (18.5cm). Collection André Surmain, Paris; photo Alfieri, Cannes.

152   **153**

LALIQUE

155

155 *Thaïs, c.* 1923, 9¼in (23cm). Galerie Moderne.

The sensuous poses on all of these voluptuous statues are, except for the mysterious demeanor on the *cire-perdue* figure – full of abandon and ecstasy. Note the stylized, almost geometric hairstyle on *Vitesse*, and the incongruous flapper-like short hair on *Thaïs*.

158

157

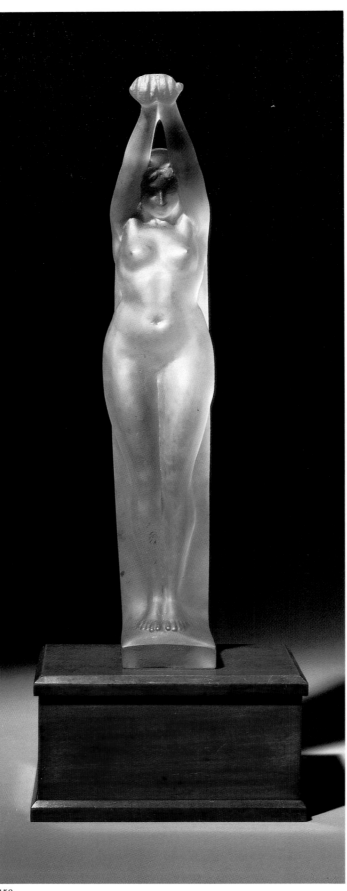

158

156 *Moyenne voilée* and *Moyenne nue*, *c.* 1912, 6in (15cm). Private collection, London.

157 *Voilée, mains jointes*, *c.* 1920, 11¼in (28cm). Galerie Moderne.

158 *Grande nue (bras levés)*, *c.* 1920, 26½in (66cm). Collection S. and E. Khachadourian, England.

159 *Sirène* car mascot, *c.* 1928, 4in (10cm). The Pickard-Cambridge Family Collection, National Motor Museum, Beaulieu, Hampshire.

159

ANIMAL FIGURES

Several large animal sculptures were made in glass by Lalique and offered in his 1932 catalogue under the umbrella term, *Motifs décoratifs*. (The three-dimensional *motifs* are discussed here; the relief *surtouts* and other panels are treated in the chapter covering lamps and interior furnishings.)

Two monumental foot-high deep-sea fish were offered on bronze illuminated stands, one base incised with a *japoniste* wave motif, the other with one of seaweed. *Gros poisson vagues* and *Gros poisson algues*, dating from *c.*1923, were both available in clear glass (an earlier version, simply called *Gros poisson*, came in opalescent glass as well, but its production was discontinued after a year). Fish were common motifs in both the fine and decorative arts of Japan.

A flock of individual sparrows (*Moineaux*) was available, with or without bases, at just under 5in-high. Often called table ornaments, these little glass birds were frequently stained with sienna *patines* and came in a variety of poses – pecking, preening, feeding, etc. Pigeons were also available in different poses. As Lalique's figurines go, they are among his least ambitious and innovative, but they no doubt attracted a clientele who were able to afford their price (as low as 125 francs).

Gabriel Mourey, in a tribute to Lalique, extolled his virtues as an animal sculptor in the highest terms:

[Lalique] gave life to the "menagerie" which, it appears to me, was quite worthy of a place in the glass-cases of the collectors and on the shelves of cultured amateurs . . . Lalique reveals himself . . . as a sculptor of animals amongst the very best. None was able, better than he, to fix in their essential lines the general and typical gait, the familiar and characteristic gestures of those of our inferior brothers towards which he has felt more particularly drawn . . . Amongst the winged tributes, let us mention the presence of pigeons and sparrows, plump gluttons, so well reproduced, so lifelike that one would expect them to coo and to chirp.[1]

AUTOMOBILE MASCOTS, PAPERWEIGHTS AND BOOKENDS

Paperweights preceded car mascots in Lalique's design history – they were fashioned as early as 1914 – but within ten years mascots became the rage. Thus, even though a certain design was available as a *presse-papier* (or in a pair of bookends, or *serre-livres*), it was better known and more plentiful as an automobile accessory.

Some designs were intended only as paperweights and, to a far lesser extent, as bookends (some of these same subjects, generally in a much smaller size, were also used for seals or ashtrays). Christopher Vane Percy has written that most paperweights, which were feather-light, were "clearly intended to be decorative rather than practical; but Lalique excelled himself in providing each one of them with a personality of its own."[2] A very early paperweight (*c.*1914) in clear glass, called *Lézards*, depicts two lizards biting each other's tails. It has a simple rectangular shape, with two minute "handles" at the sides, and is signed *Lalique* in script on one side of the thick sides. It is

a rare and wonderful design, Art Nouveau in its feel. *Double marguerite* (also made as a small seal) is a stunning glass blossom which "melts" at the bottom to form a base; it was available in clear glass and several colors, including amber and red.

Nicholas Dawes concludes that "Lalique's most commonly successful desktop accessory of the 1920s was the paperweight, of which more than forty models were put into production between 1925 and 1930".[3] The fact that these *presse-papiers* were multi-purpose and could be made into bookends when attached to a black-glass base appealed to Lalique the businessman. As Dawes remarked, they "helped to increase his range of ware, and thus his sales, while keeping production overhead to a minimum".[4]

Figural paperweights were the most common and the most easily transformed for another use, but *2 Aigles* seems to have been a model that was not made into a mascot. Two facing eagles' heads, highlighted with dark blue or black *patine*, share a cabochon-glass "pearl" between their open mouths. This is an Oriental motif which Lalique has used several times – on the *Cock's Head* diadem, for instance – and its rigid stylization even reminds one of the Egyptian winged sun disc. Two small rectangular paperweights, 4in long, are molded with two and three *Sardines*. *Barbillon* is another aquatic subject; a stylized diamond-pattern covers the body of the barbel fish and the top fin looks like a squared-off Mohican haircut. Also available are *2 Tourterelles (Turtle Doves)*, beaks touching and perched on a conical base strewn with blossoms (this pair also appears as the top of the vase *Tourterelles*); six sparrows (three of them described as proud, bold and timid) and a barn owl. Two *biches* were modeled as paperweights, *Antilope* and *Daim (Deer)*, the former standing proudly at attention, the other lightly spotted and feeding; and there was also a motley herd of *Renne (Moose)*, *Bison*, *Taureau (Bull)* and *Rhinocéros*. Two different-sized elephants were also modeled as paperweights, as well as a crouching *Chat (Cat)*.

Bookends were usually two of the same paperweight used together. But Lalique designed several paperweights as a pair with the idea of bookends in mind. In the 1932 catalogue, for example, are shown *Serre-livre amours*, two seated putti with stylized ringlets and wings, both in a decidedly tilted or support position. The very stylized *Coq Houdan*, designed as a single free-standing paperweight or mascot, was also sold in a pair with thick frosted-glass supports behind the fowl (this same pair also became the sides of a mantel clock of *c.*1930).

Lalique automobile mascots, collected by both antique car buffs and glass collectors, are probably the most sought-after of all Lalique's figural works, perhaps of all his creations. They are also some of his most dramatic and geometric Art Déco designs, especially *Cinq chevaux*, *Comète*, *Epsom*, *Vitesse* and *Victoire*, whose images suggest, embody or, in one case, personify grace, movement and speed.

The history of the motor car is not much older than that of the mascots which have adorned its hood or bonnet. If one takes into account an English visionary's 1827 drawing of a three-wheeled steam carriage, called a Docudep, then the two were conceived as one:

1. Mourey, "A Great French Craftsman", 109.
2. Vane Percy, *The Glass of René Lalique*, 77–78.
3. Dawes, *Lalique Glass*, 69.
4. *Ibid.*

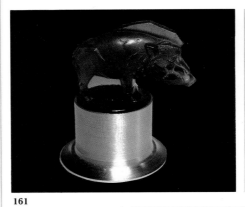

161

162

160 *Coq houdan* car mascot, *c.* 1928, 8in (20cm). The Pickard-Cambridge Family Collection, National Motor Museum, Beaulieu, Hampshire.

161 *Sanglier* car mascot, *c.* 1928, 3¾in (9.3cm) long. Private collection, Switzerland.

162 *2 Aigles* paperweight, *c.* 1911, 4in (10cm). Galerie Moderne.

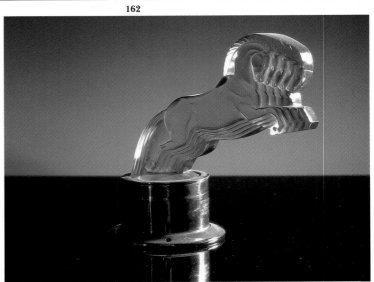

160

163

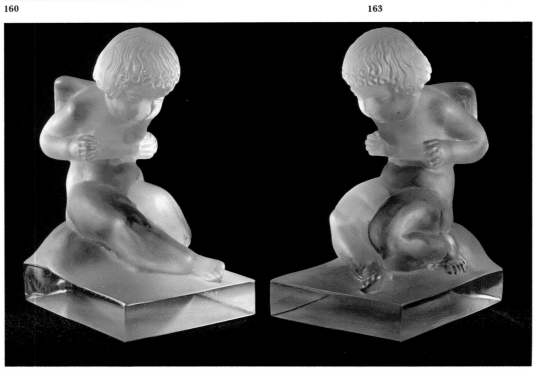

163 *Cinq chevaux* car mascot, *c.* 1927, 4½in (11.5cm). Collection Lord Montagu of Beaulieu, National Motor Museum, Beaulieu, Hampshire.

164 *Serre-livre amours* (bookends), *c.* 1930, 5½in (13.5cm). Galerie Moderne.

164

165

166

The sharply angled
extensions on these
two mascots – the hair
of *Victoire* and the tail
of *Comète* – are fine
examples of stylized
Art Déco; both convey
a sense of speed as
well, appropriate to
their intended use on
an automobile's hood.
The androgynous
head of *Victoire*, also
known as *Spirit of the
Wind*, has become an
icon of sorts of the Art
Déco period.

165 *Victoire* car
mascot, *c.* 1928,
10½in (26cm) long.
Collection R. V.
Craig, London.

166 *Comète* car mascot,
c. 1928, 7½in (19cm)
long. The Pickard–
Cambridge Family
Collection, National
Motor Museum, Beaulieu.

167

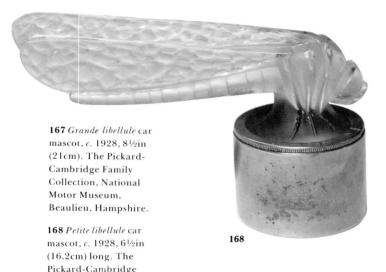

167 *Grande libellule* car mascot, *c.* 1928, 8½in (21cm). The Pickard-Cambridge Family Collection, National Motor Museum, Beaulieu, Hampshire.

168 *Petite libellule* car mascot, *c.* 1928, 6½in (16.2cm) long. The Pickard-Cambridge Family Collection, National Motor Museum, Beaulieu, Hampshire.

168

Perched upon its tiller bar pivot was a golden bird with outstretched wings – the first recorded use discovered to date of a mascot on a motorized vehicle.[5]

The actual first use of a mascot can also be attributed to an Englishman, Lord Montagu of Beaulieu, who placed a bronze statuette of St. Christopher, patron saint of travelers, on the radiator cap of his 1896 4-cylinder Daimler (he created a sensation by driving to the House of Commons in 1899). Soon the idea spread throughout Europe and America, where in 1909 the likeness of "Gobbo, God of Good Luck" was copyrighted by L. V. Aronson for use as a mascot. There followed in 1910 Aronson's *Speed Nymph*, a graceful female diver, and in no time a wide array of mascots flooded the marketplace:

> It was bound to happen. With a mode of transport as individual as the automobile, it was inevitable that man would wish to make a motorcar uniquely his own, to personalize it, to differentiate it in some way from that of his neighbor.[6]

Or the matter could be put another way:

> Mechanically [mascots] had no *raison d'être*, but they played a singular and vital role: they added a personal touch to cars . . . [and they embodied] every possible human aspiration, superstition, hope, fear, expectation, pretention and obsession as well as man's sense of fantasy and humour.[7]

Although Rolls-Royce's *Spirit of Ecstacy* (by Charles Sykes) was available from 1911, along with several other manufacturer-approved mascots, it was not until the 1920s that such mascots as Chrysler's winged hat of Hermes (1924), Pontiac's Indian (1926) and the Vauxhall wyvern (1927) became widely accepted. Before long, car manufacturers offered an approved mascot as standard equipment or a deluxe accessory.

The history of mascots in France is slightly less mundane. Animal sculptors in that country produced custom-made bronze mascots in the Belle Epoque – often figural, usually bestial. The 1920s provided a ripe opportunity for sculptors to produce outrageous, fantastic, one-of-a-kind mascots, or *bouchons de radiateur*. The rage for things Egyptian was strongly seen in mascots, and the primitive African and pre-Columbian worlds also provided stylized motifs.

Lalique's mascots were some of the most handsome so-called "fantasy" mascots, probably the most handsome. They were intended for the very rich, automobiles being status symbols beyond the means of everyone but the wealthiest class. Lalique's first bona-fide mascot was commissioned by the Citroën Company in 1925, "the banner year", according to Nicholas Dawes, "of the golden age of French motoring".[8] Deluxe motorcars had been displayed at the 1925 Paris Exposition (to the scorn of some automobile purists, who felt they were more decorative art than transport vehicles), and no doubt Lalique had seen them. The collaboration with Citroën came soon afterward, in the form of *Cinq Chevaux* (Five Horses), the name of the automobile for which it was designed (it was often simply called the 5 CV). Molded on the side with five stylized, rearing horses in dramatic profile, the mascot was at once both very modern and undeniably classic.

5. William C. Williams, *Motoring Mascots of the World*, Osceola, Wisconsin, 1979, 12.
6. *Ibid.*
7. Giuseppe di Sirignano and David Sulzberger, *Car Mascots*, London, 1977, 7.
8. Dawes, *Lalique Glass*, 71.

169

171

170

169 *Longchamps* car mascot (earlier model), *c.* 1928, 6¼in (15.5cm). The Pickard-Cambridge Family Collection, National Motor Museum, Beaulieu, Hampshire.

170 *Longchamps* car mascot (later model), *c.* 1928, 6¼in (15.5cm). The Pickard-Cambridge Family Collection, National Motor Museum, Beaulieu, Hampshire.

171 *Epsom* car mascot, *c.* 1928, 7¼in (18.2cm). The Pickard-Cambridge Family Collection, National Motor Museum, Beaulieu, Hampshire.

172 *Lévrier* car mascot, *c.* 1928, 8in (20cm) long. The Pickard-Cambridge Family Collection, National Motor Museum, Beaulieu, Hampshire.

LALIQUE

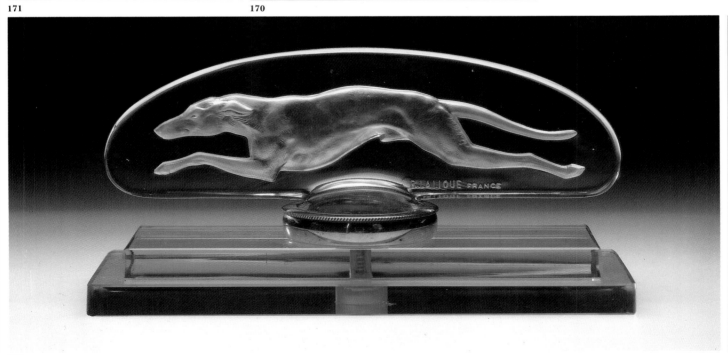

172

Cinq Chevaux was the first of more than 20 mascots that Lalique designed before 1930. Besides the one for Citroën, the designs which were made into hood ornaments only were *Comète, Petite libellule* and *Victoire. Comète* is a glistening, faceted and clear-glass star, out of which shoots a stylized tail. There is an interesting anecdote, possibly apocryphal, concerning *Comète*'s genesis. The Citroën firm had its name spelled out vertically on the Eiffel Tower from 1925 to 1936, at the time almost assuredly the largest advertising sign in the World. Each letter was two stories high, and half a dozen hues were used in the advertisement's 250,000 light bulbs, which could be seen for 20 miles. At the top of the sign, a lighted comet went off, and this supposedly so impressed Lalique that he designed the *Comète* with it in mind.[9]

Petite libellule (a small dragonfly with its wings folded) is a stunning creature whose beautifully detailed wings extend in a perfectly straight line. The design implies flight and movement, and both the motif and its naturalistic rendering hark back to Lalique's Art Nouveau period. The Lalique signature molded in the glass of the base is unusual because the "Q" bears a double tail.

Victoire, which could easily be called one of the symbols of the Art Déco style – it certainly is an immediately recognizable image – represents an androgynous female head in profile, the mouth open as if in a scream, the long, windswept hair streaming out behind her in the shape of a crystallized wing. Viewed from head on, the face has a horrific aspect and the hair resembles a Native American headdress (in the United States this mascot is sometimes referred to as "Seminole", whereas in the United Kingdom it is often called "Spirit of the Wind"). The image is incredibly powerful, even unsettling, especially when lit from within. The amethyst tint which permeates one version of the sculpture gives it a strong, talismanic appearance. In its design, impact, weight and balance, *Victoire* is a truly artistic automobile mascot, as well as a symbol of Art Déco.

Lalique mascots were often illuminated from within, if the client so desired, and a glowing *Victoire* or dragonfly must have alarmed some oncoming drivers. The Breves' Galleries booklet was high in its praise:

> The motor mascots designed by Lalique achieve a rare combination of beauty and distinction. They are moulded from a special glass, untarnishable and almost unbreakable. At night, their charm is enhanced by concealed illumination in soft colours.[10]

Most people mounted Lalique mascots by screwing their bases on to the radiator cap of the auto. But the mascot could be placed further back by boring a hole directly through the hood and bolting the metal mount to it. Mascots could be illuminated in an assortment of rainbow hues by an interchangeable light filter (Breves' supplied one disc with every illuminated mascot, but additional ones were available at extra charge in red, green, blue, mauve, amber and white). The filter was placed into the mount between the mascot and a clear light bulb, which could be activated by a dynamo system to intensify the light when the car picked up speed.

Although Lalique's own company supplied mounts for the mascots at a minimal charge, retailers could decide how best to attach the ornament to a customer's automobile. Breves' brochure included a page of suggestions on how to fit them; it also made and patented its own mounts in nickel-plated and cadmium-plated brass.

Five types of mount were available to clients. The three produced by Lalique were always done in chrome-plated French bronze. There was the large size for illumination purposes only, followed by a large and a smaller collar. These two collars were used for general-purpose mounting (for cars, paperweights or bookends) and did not light up. Breves' produced several types of large and small bases, each of which was available in nickel or cadmium.

Three other equine mascots (in addition to the *Cinq Chevaux*) were produced by Lalique, each of them consisting of a majestic single horse's head. In fact, there were only two names for the three, *Epsom* and *Longchamps*, because a second updated design of the *Longchamps*, more stylized and altered in size to fit better into its base, was not given a new name. Named after the famous French racecourse, the first *Longchamps* had a mane consisting of two rows of regular ribs and it was less angular than the later, now more commonly seen, *Longchamps*. The later *Longchamps* also had a mane more akin to the hair of *Victoire* than to the fluted mane of the original model (although each is shaped to form an almost perfect semicircle). *Epsom*, named after the English racecourse, lunges forward in a straining position and is modeled realistically all over, especially around the mouth. Its mane is cropped shorter and is much more natural in appearance than that of the *Longchamps* models.

Grande libellule is a larger dragonfly mascot with upraised wings. It was made in clear glass, although one vivid purple-glass version, probably custom-made, exists. The subject is Art Nouveau, but the treatment is stylized and closer to Art Déco. When illuminated, the wings of this insect must have looked especially dramatic.

Archer (c.1928) depicts on a clear-glass roundel an intaglio-molded, frosted-glass nude in a neoclassical vein. The half-kneeling archer, his bow taut and his arrow aimed, is a sinewy Sagittarius-like figure. The molded-intaglio technique is one in which Lalique reigned supreme. The hollowed-out form of the nude is actually contained in the glass mold, although at first glance it might appear to be engraved on the glass. Proper lighting gives this type of statuette an almost three-dimensional look. There are two other examples of the type, both of them, like *Archer,* available also in paperweights. *Saint-Christophe* represents the bearded saint in his usual pose, carrying the infant Jesus on his back across water, and a dazzle of bright rays radiates from the child's halo to the edges of the roundel. *Lévrier* is sleek greyhound frozen in a graceful running position. Another greyhound mascot, with a dramatically arching body forming the outline of its fan-like shape, was made for His Royal Highness Prince George of England in 1931 or thereabouts.

Birds' heads were the subject of a number of Lalique's mascots. The best known (for unfortunate reasons) is probably *Tête d'aigle.* This sometimes amethyst-tinged mascot may have been the one that Hitler gave to the generals of the Third Reich for their personal use. The eagle's head is sharply outlined, its gaze is piercing and its beak is threatening. *Tête d'aigle* is a powerful, right-angled image which harks back to other aquiline subjects in Lalique's repertory. A personal seal, or signet, also called *Tête d'aigle*, dates from c.1905–07.[11]

9. Clendenin, "The Hood Ornaments of Lalique", 50–51.

10. Breves' Lalique Galleries, *The Art of René Lalique*, 9.

11. Sigrid Barten, *René Lalique, Schmuck und Objets d'art, 1890–1910*, Munich, 1977, 553, no. 1732.

173

173 *Tête d'aigle* car mascot, *c.* 1928, 4¼in (10.7cm). The Pickard-Cambridge Family Collection, National Motor Museum, Beaulieu, Hampshire.

The amethyst-blue shade of this mascot is especially rare. The stark eagle-head motif also appeared on Lalique seals and paperweights.

174 *Tête de bélier* car mascot, *c*. 1928, 3½in (9cm). The Pickard-Cambridge Family Collection, National Motor Museum, Beaulieu, Hampshire.

175 *Tête d'épervier* car mascot, *c*. 1928, 2½in (6.1cm). The Pickard-Cambridge Family Collection, National Motor Museum, Beaulieu, Hampshire.

176 *Tête de coq* car mascot, *c*. 1928, 7¼in (18cm). Collection D. Gill, USA.

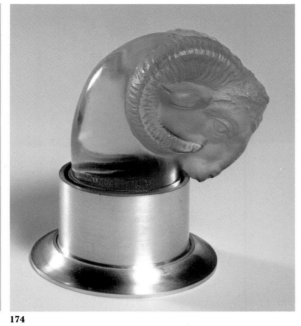

174

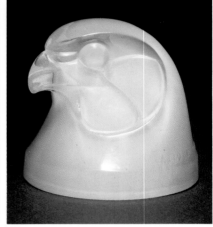

175

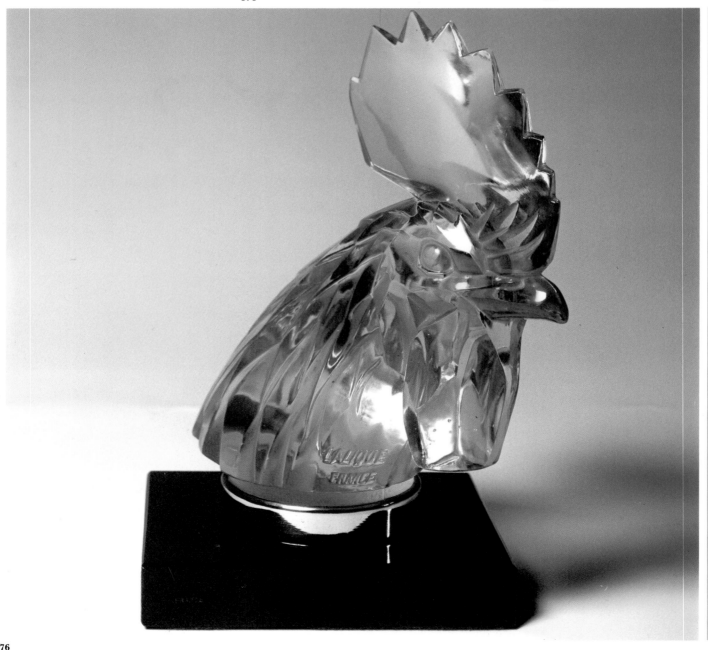

176

177 *Hirondelle* car mascot, *c.* 1928, 6in (15cm). The Pickard-Cambridge Family Collection, National Motor Museum, Beaulieu, Hampshire.

178 *Hibou* car mascot, *c.* 1928, 3½in (8.6cm). The Pickard-Cambridge Family Collection, National Motor Museum, Beaulieu, Hampshire.

The owl mascot is one of Lalique's rarest. In 1987, one sold at auction in Paris for some FF340,000 (around £35,000, or $60,000).

177

178

Animal heads predominate on Lalique's mascot designs, which could be opalescent, as in the Egyptian-like *Tête* *d'épervier;* frosted, as in the serene *Tête de bélier*, or clear, as in *Tête de coq*. Bright colors were far rarer in the mascots.

107

179

180

181

The yellow opalescent version of the fish mascot, *Perche*, is very rare. Note the angular body of the fox (*Renard*), quite a contrast with the realistic scales on *Perche*.

179 *Renard* car mascot, *c.* 1928, 8½in (21cm). Collection André Surmain, Paris; photo Alfieri, Cannes.

180 *Perche* car mascot, *c.* 1928, 7¼in (18cm) long. The Pickard-Cambridge Family Collection, National Motor Museum,

181 *Perche* car mascot, *c.* 1928, 7¼in (18cm) long. The Pickard-Cambridge Family Collection, National Motor Museum, Beaulieu, Hampshire.

182 *Pintade* car mascot, *c.* 1928, 4½in (10cm). Collection Edmund Ruffin, USA.

183 *Grenouille* car mascot, *c.* 1928, 2½in (6.6cm). The Pickard-Cambridge Family Collection, National Motor Museum, Beaulieu, Hampshire.

184 Two *Tête de paon* car mascots, *c.* 1928, 4¾in (11.7cm). The Pickard-Cambridge Family Collection, National Motor Museum, Beaulieu, Hampshire.

Note the subtle color variation on the two peacock-head mascots.

185 *Faucon* car mascot, *c.* 1928, 9½in (23.5cm). Collection D. Gill, USA.

182

183

184

185

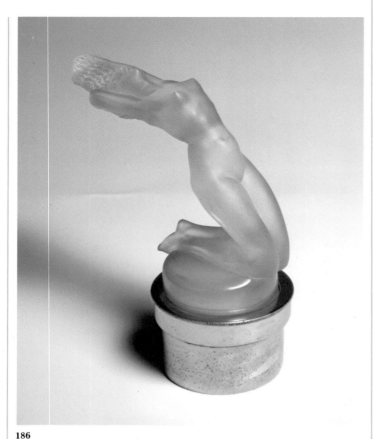

186

187

186 *Chrysis* car mascot, *c.* 1928, 5½in (13.5cm). The Pickard-Cambridge Family Collection, National Motor Museum, Beaulieu, Hampshire.

187 Part of the display of the Pickard-Cambridge Family Collection of Lalique car mascots, at the National Motor Museum, Beaulieu, Hampshire, one of the finest and most complete collections of its kind.

Although the bird's feathering is more realistic than that of the mascot, it has the same stark angularity. The rock-crystal seal is directly related to the 3in-high glass seal offered in Lalique's 1932 catalogue, an interesting use of a similar image across the space of two decades.

The heads of three other avian creatures were also available as mascots. *Tête de paon* shows the proud peacock's head in stark profile, a crested feather emerging at the crown like a stylized lotus, the neck bowed back slightly and the beak pointing downward. This mascot came in clear and vivid blue glass; its subject, of course, was a popular one with Lalique throughout his career. *Tête d'épervier (Sparrowhawk's Head)* is minimally articulated, a very rounded form which resembles ancient Egyptian images of their falcon-headed god, Horus. *Tête de coq* treats the plumage around the cock's head in a stylized manner akin to the feathering on *Tête d'aigle*, and its zig-zag comb and squared-off goiter are all the more pronounced because of the absence of veining or striation. This mascot has retained its popularity and is produced today as a paperweight.

Coq nain, the full-length dwarf cockerel with its tail pluming up and outward and its head bending down, was also a very popular design. The angular stylization of the cockerel's feathers is similar to that of the *Hirondelle* mascot, which depicts a swallow leaning forward, its stylized wings and tail feathers forming an almost abstract vertical design. The falcon was also represented in full size, its breast jutting forward in pride, its head very similar to *Tête d'épervier*.

Tête de bélier (Ram's Head) is a lovely mascot whose curling horn forms a near-perfect circle with its lowered head. It might almost have been taken from Mycenaean or Minoan representations of the beast.

Perche is an attractive fish mascot, which was available in a rare example in a deep yellow-orange hue (there is also an opalescent fish, and a clear model, the latter of which is still made today). Other full figural mascots – all very rare – include *Pintade (Guinea Hen)*, *Renard (Fox)*, *Grenouille (Frog)* and *Hibou (Owl)*, the latter two realistically modeled in the round, the first two more geometric and angular. *Sanglier* is an angular figure of a standing boar. (The hunt of the boar, which has long appealed to French huntsmen, was depicted on the walls of the dining room that Lalique designed for Sèvres in the 1925 Exposition.) *Sanglier* was available in brown, charcoal-grey or clear glass.

Two other figural mascots are *Vitesse*, the sensuous personification of speed, and the kneeling *Chrysis* (Agamemnon's lover in Greek mythology), whose back arches at almost 90 degrees. Both figures were available in clear and colored glass, and both have stylized ripples of hair, *Vitesse's* falling down her back and *Chrysis's* streaming out behind her as if it were a stiff cloud. *Chrysis* was a commercial success and continues to be made by Cristal Lalique today.

The mascot, *Weeping Siren* (the same female statuette, *Sirène*, which was discussed earlier), was offered by Breves' Galleries. It is believed that *Naiade* was also offered as a mascot. These two figures are much more sentimental and static than *Vitesse* and *Chrysis* and they lack the dramatic energy of the more exhibitionistic nudes. They therefore lend themselves less to automobile adornment.

Lalique also designed a 6½in-high commemorative piece for the French national railways, the Compagnie des Wagons-Lits (whose insignia it bears). The base includes an inscription commemorating the inauguration of the Côte d'Azur Pullman Car in 1929 (Lalique designed figural glass panels for this train). The statuette itself is of a nude woman caught in an ecstatic moment.

Lalique's mascots were very popular, especially in Great Britain, where they were enthusiastically offered by the Breves' Galleries, which used a "blurb" from a satisfied customer on the back of one of their brochures:

> I bought from you last spring one of your "Falcon" Mascots for cars. It has toured over 10,000 miles in Central Europe over the worst roads imaginable and it is in as good a condition as it was when it was new. This, I think, is pretty good, as the vibration must have been terrible.[12]

Numerous collectors seek out Lalique mascots and since Lalique designed only a relatively small number of them (in comparison with his other glass objects), the determined collector can acquire almost the whole range. The Pickard-Cambridge Collection, on display at the National Motor Museum in Beaulieu, England, is one of the best collections in the world.

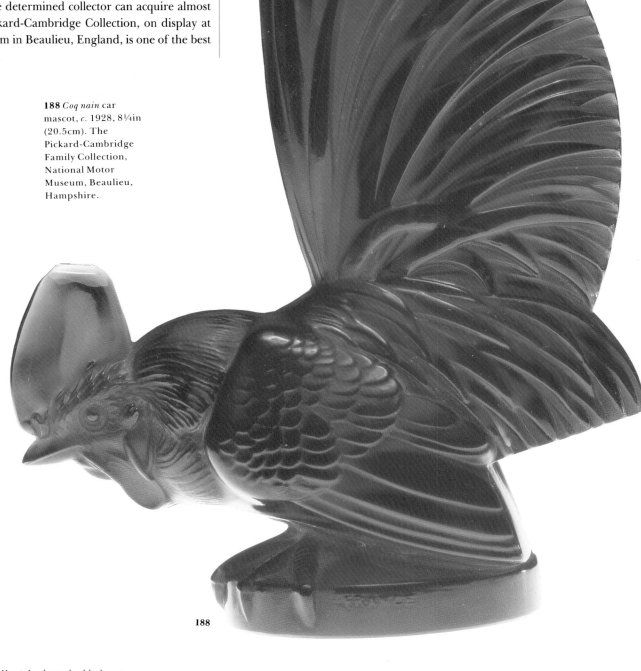

188 *Coq nain* car mascot, *c.* 1928, 8¼in (20.5cm). The Pickard-Cambridge Family Collection, National Motor Museum, Beaulieu, Hampshire.

188

12. Breves' Lalique Galleries, *Lalique Car Mascots*, London, undated, back cover.

DECORATIVE FURNISHINGS

9

lass is perhaps the medium which best communicates with, relates to and exploits light. Whether transparent, translucent, opalescent, frosted or colored, it reacts to light, not merely passively, as any opaque surface, whether matt like ceramic or shiny like brass, does, but actively, responding dynamically to the rays of light which penetrate it and play along its surface. Crystal, especially when faceted, explodes into a rainbow of colors, and opalescent glass undulates in rich, milky shades of blue or yellow.

Lalique was aware of the dramatic properties of glass, and he exploited them doubly by illuminating many of his works in glass and making glass lamps and lighting fixtures of glass. The material did not react only to natural light, but also to an artificial light source from within, producing a dazzling effect. Some of the works which have already been discussed could be lit from within. The statuettes, *Suzanne* and *Thaïs*, were often mounted on light bases, as were *Gros poisson vagues* and *Gros poisson algues;* and, of course, his automobile mascots could be illuminated from below. This chapter will deal with other decorative pieces, such as his magnificent *surtouts*, which could be lighted, and with lamps, chandeliers and other lighting fixtures. It also treats mirrors, picture frames and clocks – the remainder of Lalique's non-tableware and non-architectural glass which has not been discussed in earlier chapters.

MIRRORS, PICTURE FRAMES
AND CLOCKS

The earliest mirrors were made of highly polished metal. The ancient Egyptians, Chinese and Greeks all used polished-bronze mirrors. The Romans and Etruscans made disc-shaped mirrors, often with decorative handles; these were usually of bronze but occasionally of silver. In the Middle Ages, small mirrors, of metal or glass, were set in ivory frames adorned with reliefs of chivalric subjects. Glass convex mirrors were being made in small quantities at Nuremberg by the 15th century, their shape determined by the bubble of glass from which they were blown. Around the beginning of the 16th century, Venetian glassmakers discovered the art of making flat mirrors by the "broad" or "Lorraine" process – blowing the glass with a pipe into a cylindrical form which was then slit along its length, and placing the semi-molten tube in a heated chamber where it was rolled open and flattened under heat with a wooden tool. The glass was then annealed and polished to make the surface even. Finally came the silvering or "foiling" process: mercury was poured on to a sheet of tin foil, the plate of glass was laid on it, and the surplus quicksilver was drained off over a few days. Venetian glass mirrors made metal mirrors more or less obsolete by the mid-16th century.

In the late 17th century the method of making mirrors of plate glass (with its evener surface) was developed by the Frenchman, Bernard Perrot; it was then further advanced at the Saint Gobain Glasshouse in Picardy (coincidentally, the factory where two centuries later the glass panels for the front doors of Lalique's Cours la Reine townhouse were cast). In the plate-glass process, the molten glass was poured on to iron tables covered with sand, where it was rolled, cooled and finally ground and polished with abrasives to obtain a perfectly flat surface. In 1835 a German chemist invented a process of depositing a thin layer of pure silver on to the surface of the glass and this method soon superseded the mercury-and-tin silvering process.

Small hand mirrors were used almost exclusively in the Middle Ages. It was not until the 16th century that wall mirrors began to be hung in rooms. Toilet-glasses for use on dressing tables were in constant demand from the 16th century; late-17th-century examples were framed in silver, needlework, wood or *faux*-lacquer (sometimes the silver ones matched a lady's *garniture de toilette*). By the late 19th century, mirrors in the neoclassical and rococo styles were popular, and then the Art Nouveau style made its mark, and frames with whiplash curves proliferated. A succession of styles followed in the 20th century and Lalique's mirrors sported frames with both Art Nouveau and Art Déco motifs.

Although the majority of Lalique's mirrors and frames were made of glass, some stunning metal ones dated from his Art Nouveau period. One such was displayed at the 1900 Paris Exposition. The Gulbenkian Collection houses an early standing mirror, a 5½-ft-high rectangle of reflecting glass which has as its frame a pair of bronze serpents. The open jaw of each serpent grasps an upper edge of the mirror and their bodies stretch down the sides, coiling and intertwining to form the largely openwork stand. *Serpents* dates from *c.*1899–1900; photographs taken about five years later of Lalique's Cours la Reine gallery show such a mirror on display.

Drawings exist for some 10 hand mirrors, all of whose frames and handles depict Art Nouveau subjects: snakes, flowers, dragonflies, butterflies, etc. They date from the first decade of the 20th century, as does a drawing for a mirror of *c.*1906–08, *Narcisse couché*, in which Narcissus is enclosed in a tiny rectangular plaque at the space where the top of the handle meets the bottom of the round mirror. The handle and the gradating-crescent border around the mirror are covered with a design of skeletal leaves. The actual frosted-glass mirror itself was illustrated in *Art et Décoration* in 1912,[1] thus dating it to that year or earlier; and since Sigrid Barten has dated the drawing some five years earlier, the mirror may have been made during the first decade of the century, making it one of Lalique's earliest glass mirrors. Narcissus, the beautiful youth of Greek mythology who, upon seeing his own reflection in a clear pool, fell in love with himself, is an appropriate subject for a mirror, and the piece was evidently popular, since it was still in production two decades later (it was offered in the 1932 catalogue). There it was listed as *Narcisse couché*. Gustave Kahn's article in *Art et Décoration* did not give it a title, but merely said it depicted the "very fine figure of a seated nymph",[2] that is, a *female* figure. Sigrid Barten, on the other hand, refers to the earlier drawing as "Gefallener Krieger," a fallen *warrior!*[3] Perhaps Lalique gave the name to the mirror some time after he started making it in large quantities, that is, considerably later than 1912, when it was illustrated in *Art et Décoration*. Another early mirror, backed in silver (others were backed in bronze), has a handle on which two elongated, draped, symmetrical women stand.

Most of Lalique's mirrors were produced in the 1920s. One large

1. Kahn, "Lalique Verrier", 153.
2. *Ibid.*, 156.
3. Barten, *René Lalique, Schmuck und Objets d'art*, 557, no. 1746.

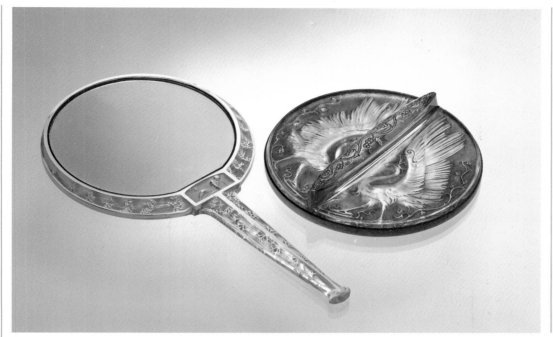

190 Two hand mirrors: left, *Narcisse couché, c.* 1908, 14in (35cm) long; right, *2 Oiseaux, c.* 1912, 6½in (16cm) dia. Collection Glenn and Mary Lou Utt, USA.

round model was in his *garniture de toilette* pattern, *Epines (Thorns)*. Seventeen inches in diameter, it consists of six separate sections of molded glass interspersed with twig-like bands. There is a foil backing under the glass and silver-plated terminals attach the frame to its wooden backing. The same mirror also came in an *Eglantines (Wild Roses)* pattern, and the two, at 2,800 francs each in the 1932 catalogue, were costlier than every vase but one in the same price list.

Another round standing mirror was also of clear glass backed with foil, its recesses highlighted with a pale-blue *patine*. The delicate blossom-and-branches pattern all around the border continues at the top, where a fan-shaped "extension" depicting a crown juts up (suggesting that it was custom-made for a royal or noble personage). Lalique did design a circular hand mirror for Princess Victoria of Baden, wife of the King of Sweden, in about 1924. It was backed with a silver mount which bore a swallow, vine, and flower pattern on the handle. A huge flock of overlapping swallows (six in the foreground, about five dozen in the background) covered the round section; and on an extension at the top are more birds whose outlines form a crown surmounted with a globe and cross design.

Circular hand mirrors, a little more than 6in in diameter and heightened with colored staining, came in four patterns. *Muguet (Lily-of-the-Valley)* depicted a bouquet of flowers, with two holes where they bunched together, out of which came a braided tassel. *3 Paons* showed a frontal view of stylized peacocks in full plumage; its tasseled rope was gathered near the holes with a plump glass bead. The two other mirrors, *2 Chèvres* and *2 Oiseaux*, both have slender oval hand grips attached across their diameters. Aside the fruiting-vine-handle of the one face two symmetrical egrets with fully outstretched wings; the grape-decorated handle of the other centers on two goats, one with curved horns touching the edge of the circle, the other with straight horns aligned with the handle.

Four tiny mirrors (2¾in high), each with a metal border and a little eye affixed at the top, presumably for a silk cord or chain, were called *Sauterelles (Grasshoppers), Psyche, Narcisse debout (Narcissus Standing)* and *Tête*, a blossom-draped female head. These little mirrors were possibly kept in purses, or perhaps worn around the neck.

With the advent of photography in the 19th century, picture frames became an extremely popular item. They adorned humble mantelpieces as well as the boulle tables of the rich. From the Victorian era onward, as photography became a mania, the small-scale frame, usually with a backrest or stand, was produced in profusion and variety. In the 1920s and 1930s Lalique sold a number of lovely frames. Many of these, which were intended primarily for use on ladies' dressing tables, could also be fitted for mirrors, although the 1932 catalogue lists them all as picture frames. Mostly rectangular in shape, they depicted Lalique's flora and fauna. Two large, stand-backed frames were *Bleuets* and *Lys*, 10in and 9in in height respectively. The unusual cornflower pattern of *Bleuets* showed the imbricated stylized blossoms in three rows on the frame, resembling little wheels with zig-zag edges. The glorious, overlapping lilies of *Lys* were much more realistically drawn. *Etoiles*, 6½in high, was covered all over with a galaxy of tiny stars of all sizes, and the frame of *Hirondelles*, a little over 5in high, was aswarm with molded swallows in flight, their open-winged, conical-shaped bodies topped with tiny triangular heads and ending in squared-off tail-feather bases. *Bergeronettes* enclosed a tiny rectangle with a wide-border frame of six birds amid large, spade-shaped leaves.

Four square frames with round center openings, each about 4in tall, were illustrated in the 1932 catalogue. *Muguets* is strewn with relief lilies-of-the-valley, spiraling wildly around the middle, whereas *Guirlandes* has a controlled, geometric design of stylized daisies. *Inséparables* is a charming, often-used design with two pairs of close-

191

193

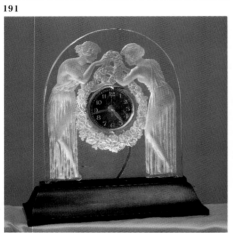

194

192

191 *Inséparables* clock, *c.* 1924, 4⅓in (11cm) square. Galerie Moderne.

192 *2 Colombes* clock, *c.* 1926, 8¾in (22.2cm). Galerie Moderne.

193 *Le jour et la nuit* clock, *c.* 1925, 14½in (37.5cm). Galerie Moderne.

194 *2 Figurines* clock, *c.* 1928, 14¾in (37cm). Collection Glenn and Mary Lou Utt, USA.

195 Demilune clock with birds, *c.* 1926, 6¼ x 8½in (15.5 x 21.5cm). Galerie Moderne.

196 *Le jour et la nuit* clock, *c.* 1925, 14½in (37.5cm). Galerie Moderne. This stunning round clock representing Night and Day came in several hues and was Lalique's most spectacular – and expensive – timepiece.

195

196

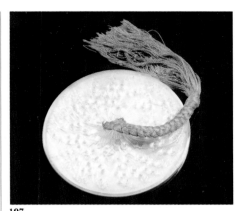

197

198

197 *Muguet* mirror, *c.* 1912, 6½in (16cm) dia. Galerie Moderne.

198 *Naiades* clock, *c.* 1924, 4½in (11.3cm) square. Galerie Moderne.

199 Picture frame, with bird design, *c.* 1922, 9¾in (24.5cm). Collection Laurie and Joel Shapiro, Detroit.

199

knit lovebirds perched on florid branches flanking the center, and *Naiades* represents a sextet of frolicking sea nymphs, their strands of hair depicted as arcs of bubbles. In contrast to this senuous aquatic group, the 5in-high *2 Figurines et fleurs* frame, a vertical oval, is decorated with floral garlands and two demure nudes.

Laurea grand modèle is a stunning 6½in-high mirror of clear and frosted glass, decorated with a maze of horizontal and vertical zig-zag lines extending around and within a 12-sided cruciform shape. Of all the Lalique's frames this was the most "masculine" in motif; perhaps it was intended for his male clientele.

Drawings exist for several earlier frames from Lalique's goldsmith period. One with a superb, curvilinear surround of two glorious peacocks whose full tail feathers terminate at the base of the frame and another of the birds (its neck and head sculpted in high relief) perched at the top center of the frame, was very much in the Art Nouveau style. Dating from *c.*1898–99, it was probably made of bronze. It belonged to Mme Waldeck-Rousseau, the wife of the politician. Other drawings show another frame with peacock, one with two lilies and an elaborate one with a wheat-stalk motif. There is also a drawing for a dramatic frame with stark, stylized branches bearing huge thorns.

The Picture and Art Trade Journal once commented that "the frame should always be unobtrusive – never so ornate as to make one exclaim, before noticing the picture, 'What a pretty frame!'"[4] Lalique's frames would not have met with the writer's approval!

Lalique also designed cases for desk clocks, table clocks and mantel clocks, both large *pendules* (from 8in to 14in high) and small *pendulettes* (about 4in to 6in high). Some models, such as *Inséparables*, were also picture-mirror frame subjects. Nineteen clocks were offered in Lalique's 1932 catalogue and several other designs are known.

Free-standing clocks had been in existence for a few centuries before Lalique started making his, the grandest and most ornate being those of the Louis XV period. The boulle work and ormolu which decorated those cases practically developed the making of clock cases into an independent art form, making the clock works themselves almost secondary to the design of the case. By the late 19th century small clocks were available in assorted shapes and sizes: delicate designs for a lady's dressing table, more substantial and rugged looks for a man's desk, and opulent, sometimes outrageous, confections to rest on a marble fireplace, to surmount an Art Nouveau sideboard, or, a bit later, to crown a sleek, lacquered Art Déco commode. The great turn-of-the-century and Art Déco designers applied their skills to create clock cases of distinction. Among them were Charles Rennie Mackintosh, Josef Olbrich, Charles F. A. Voysey, Jean Goulden and Albert Cheuret, whose silvered-bronze Art Déco clock case, designed as a stylized Egyptian head-dress, is one of that style's most memorable images (and not unlike Lalique's *Victoire* car mascot). The French jeweler, Cartier, designed exotic "mystery clocks" whose pendulums or hands seemed to be suspended in thin air, working without any visible mechanism; such clocks had been made by French and Swiss firms from the late 19th century.

4. Quoted in Patricia Bayer, "Enhancing the Image", *Connoisseur*, May 1982, 32.

It was only natural that Lalique should design decorative cases for this most prevalent of household accessories. Before the mass-produced, molded-glass models, he designed at least three clock cases in *cire-perdue* glass (they appear in the book, *Lalique par Lalique*)[5]. Of traditional mantel-clock shape – rectangular with arched tops – they are adorned with detailed floral and bird designs which are typically Art Nouveau in their naturalistic rendering and their profusion of subtle curves. One, with a pattern of gently curving roses on branches, was supposedly executed for the Queen of Egypt.

As for Lalique's later glass clocks, the smaller of these generally told time by means of winding movements made in Switzerland (usually the eight-day type). The larger ones were run by electricity, battery or mains, the majority of them with various faces bearing the mark of the firm ATO. Colored-glass clock cases were rarely executed; nearly all were of clear, frosted or opalescent glass.

The small clocks which Lalique designed tended to be the prettiest or the most "feminine", with delicate floral or charming avian designs. *Inséparables*, with its two pairs of lovebirds, was the smallest of his clocks at 4⅓in square. *Naiades*, with the same mermaid design as on the picture frame, was 4½in square. Both these clocks had openings for round faces and several different types of face could be used. The face of *Inséparables* could be of simple white enamel with black numerals or of ivory with a colorful painted scene of birds and branches on it (and a Greek-key border around the numerals). *Naiades* could also have either a simple gilt-metal or white face with black numerals, or a Greek-key border and a painted-ivory design. This polychrome face depicted a trio of sea nymphs echoing those cavorting on the clock's case. (There was another, larger clock – 11in square – with the same design of six sea maidens, called *Sirènes*.)

Pierrots (5in high) and *Antoinette* (6in high) have simple round frames, disc feet and a pair of plump birds perched on their tops. *Antoinette's* hands are attached directly to the frosted-clear glass face, whereas *Pierrots's* face is separate and of white enamel with simple black numerals. Five other eight-day clocks, larger than the two above, also have the numbers and hands affixed directly to the glass front of the case. *Marly* has three stems of lily-of-the-valley arching around its face, *Muguet* has a wide band of a dozen lily-of-the-valley surrounding the face, and *Rossignols* and *Papillons* depict, respectively, a dozen stylized little birds and overlapping butterflies around their numerals. *Pendule roitelets*, 8in high, is bordered by a flock of wrens whose angular wings form a zig-zag relief pattern around the circumference.

Two clocks of demilune, arched shapes are *Feuilles*, with a stylized leaf pattern, and another with two pairs of birds amid stylized foliage. Another arched-form clock, waisted at the base, has a deep case covered all over with scrolling, florid foliage. Its face sometimes sported geometrical numerals and a center roundel covered with stylized leafy forms; the electric movements of the face are marked "ATO". Another square case clock has the same ATO face (another model has a plain face), and its four corners are adorned with chubby birds similar to those of the arched clock with the two avian pairs.

Two cuddling doves are depicted over the face of *2 Colombes*, a tall (nearly 9in high) table clock with an arched top, and *Hélène*, an inch shorter than *2 Colombes*, has an unusual design of three female nudes molded at the top, one standing in the middle, the other two kneeling beside her, and floral garlands strewn amid them, extending down the case of the clock. The clock's numerals are glass and molded with minuscule blossoms.

Four clocks are similarly shaped, 6in-high rectangles on flared bases with round faces. All are reverse molded, and their designs are *6 Hirondelles* (three pairs of swallows on florid branches), *4 Perruches* (two pairs of long-tailed budgerigars on limbs, with a flowering tree in between), *5 Hirondelles* (a quintet of swallows in flight, their wide sweeps of feathers deeply stained with a midnight-blue or black *patine* which is reminiscent of the calligraphic strokes brushing the birds and berries on the *Roger* box) and *Bouquet de marguerites* (perky stylized daisies irregularly dotting the top and sides of the case).

The two most elaborate clocks made by Lalique were figural ones, both measuring nearly 15in high. *2 Figurines* depicted a pair of graceful neoclassical women in frosted glass leaning over a floral-wreathed face, all contained within a clear arched form (this design was also available as a lamp, with clear glass in place of the clock face). *Le jour et la nuit (Day and Night)*, Lalique's costliest clock at 3,500 francs, had a circular form on a trapezoidal base and was available in smoked purple, red-amber and blue glass. Its design was quite unusual for Lalique. It depicts a man and a woman, their nude bodies curving around the clock face. Heterosexual couples were quite rare in Lalique's repertory – a gilded-silver, amethyst and opal belt buckle with the same name as this clock depicted the personifications of Night and Day as two young women. The two sensuous figures on the clock are all the more spectacular because the long-tressed woman is molded in relief on the reverse of the glass and appears a darker shade, whereas the man, intaglio-molded also on the back of the glass is of a lighter, in the case of the blue clock almost lavender, hue. They seem so close, and indeed two of their hands meet at the top and their feet overlap at the bottom, yet by their very natures (as well as by being molded in opposing ways on the same side of the glass) they are destined, sadly, never to meet.

SURTOUTS AND OTHER
MOTIFS DECORATIFS

The two large fish sculptures, *Gros poisson vagues* and *Gros poisson algues*, fit into this category of Lalique's glass *objets*, which were termed *motifs décoratifs*. The umbrella term was used in Lalique's 1932 catalogue, and it covered the two big fish, the large *surtouts* and several other decorative plaques, centerpieces and table-top ornaments, most of which could be illuminated.

The two largest *surtouts* (the word means "above all") measured nearly 3ft in length and cost 8,000 francs each. *Deux cavaliers (Two Knights)* depicted an unusual subject for Lalique as a glassmaker, although an early enamel, gold and glass chest ornament, *Tournament* (*c.*1903–04; Gulbenkian Collection), was very similar in motif. Armored knights on galloping steeds are shown on both pieces, but

5. *Lalique par Lalique*, 179.

whereas the brooch's riders flank a gaping-mouthed mythological beast on a central plaque, the *surtout's* two horsemen themselves ride fantastic horses, hybrid beasts whose legs terminate in dragon-like webbed feet. Both monsters are dramatically depicted in rearing positions toward the center of the crescent-shaped bowed glass panel. Well over three-quarters of the length of the piece is taken up by seaweed-like forms emerging from the jousting knights' helmets, perhaps implying an aquatic conflict. The bronze base of the *surtout* was decorated with a pattern of cobwebs and trailing tendrils, and it was mounted for electricity.

The other 3ft-long *surtout* was decorated with one of Lalique's favorite subjects, peacocks. The *3 Paons* panel was mounted for electricity on a bronze base, engraved with a simple vine motif, and, like *Deux cavaliers,* was of clear and frosted glass nearly an inch thick. The magnificent avian trio stand in different positions, their stylized tail feathers trailing behind them and occupying most of the space on the glass. There is a gray *patine* highlighting their feathers.

An exquisite, 17in-high *surtout* is *Oiseau de feu (Firebird),* a fan-shaped piece of molded clear and frosted glass on a bronze block base fitted for electricity. The stand is cast with various-sized moths, and the panel itself its molded with the exotic firebird, with a human head and torso attached to a feathered bird's body which nicely fills the demilune of glass. This panel has also been referred to as a screen, a lamp, a *luminaire* and a *motif décoratif.* However it is described, it is an object which no doubt would have impressed Igor Stravinsky, composer of the *Firebird,* performed by the Ballets Ruses in Paris several years before this panel was made in the mid-1920s.

Tulipes and *Caravelle,* two demilune *surtouts* both over 25in long, represent distinctive images. *Caravelle,* molded with a three-masted man o'war ship, has a rather restrained design, but the fact that a *surtout* with this motif was presented by the City of Paris to King George VI and Queen Elizabeth of England in 1938 has lent it considerable appeal (the same motif has also been depicted on ashtrays). A lovely bouquet of tulips, with both closed buds and open blossoms, covers the other large *surtout;* and the flowers' stems at the side gently bend to the shape of the glass.

Yeso, a smaller *surtout* molded all over with a shoal of tropical fish amid bubbles of glass, is a stunning image, far stronger than the *Nid d'oiseaux* demilune panel with its scene of two birds bringing food to their young in the nest. So many of Lalique's panels, vases, bowls, table ornaments and the like depicted charming domestic birds – quite a change from dramatic peacocks, cockerels and eagles and probably a sign of changing times and changing tastes.

The two sculptures of swallows *(Hirondelles),* one with two birds on a bronze base, the other with three on a glass one, are interesting in that they comprise cut-out images of the birds, not reliefs molded on panels of glass. The broad sweeps of the swallows' wings give them dramatic silhouettes, but made them prone to easy chipping.

Another *motif décoratif, 4 Danseuses,* is likewise of the cut-out type, and its quartet of billowing-robed dancers presents a marked contrast to the high-stepping *Suzanne* and *Thaïs.* Mounted on a bronze base engraved with stylized daisies (which could be illuminated), the neoclassical figures are a sensuous group, clad in diaphanous, pleated gowns which reveal their silhouettes.

200 *4 Danseuses, c.* 1920, 8¾in (22cm). Private collection, Paris.
This is a very rare *motif décoratif;* only one example is known, although it is illustrated in the 1932 catalogue.

201 *Oiseau de feu. c.* 1920, 17¼in (43cm). Galerie Moderne.

202 *Fauvettes A, c.* 1928, 15¼in (38cm) long. Collection Glenn and Mary Lou Utt, USA.

203 *Gros poisson algues, c.* 1923, 12½in (31cm). Courtesy Christopher Vane Percy.

200

All four of these sculptures were known as *motifs décoratifs*, and were intended as decorative objects, such as table centerpieces. Most of these works could be illuminated at the base for dramatic effect.

201

202

203

204 *Paons* lamp,
c. 1908, 16½in
(41.5cm). Courtesy
Bonhams
Auctioneers, London.

205 *Dandelion* lamp, *c.*
1924, 6½in (16.5cm).
Collection Glenn and
Mary Lou Utt, USA.

204

205

206 *Japanese Hawthorn*
lamp, *c.* 1920, 16in
(40.6cm). Private
collection, Paris.

The overflowing
shades on the
Dandelion and *Japanese
Hawthorn* lamps are
reminiscent of
Lalique's perfume
bottles with crescent-
shaped stoppers.

Although several of the statuettes, mascots and *motifs décoratifs* came equipped with lighting devices, their primary purpose was not illumination; the lighting merely enhanced their purely decorative function. Lalique did, however, make many lamps, chandeliers and *plafonniers* (bowl-shaped lighting fixtures which could be hung from or attached to the ceiling). Indeed, from the candelabra and candlesticks he designed for dining tables to the table lamps of assorted shapes and sizes and the massive *lustres* he created for the tall ceilings of large rooms, Lalique was concerned with all aspects of electrical lighting. Domestic electricity developed at a quickening pace after World War I, and Lalique provided a plethora of attractive products in the significant field of lighting, just as he was on the cutting edge of the burgeoning scent-bottle industry. (The 1932 catalogue did not contain any lamps or lighting fixtures *per se*, although it did offer an extensive range of illuminated *surtouts* and *motifs decoratifs*. Breves' Galleries in London, however, produced two booklets on Lalique's lamps, *Lalique Lights* and *Lalique Lights and Decorations* and the English titles used for the various lamps and lighting fixtures in this chapter came from them.)

Some of Lalique's lamps, though described as lamps in various brochures, qualified more as *motifs décoratifs*. These included the several models whose bases (usually frosted glass with fine vertical ribs) were surmounted by elaborate, decorative "stoppers" which echoed the smaller scent bottles of the same type (these stoppers ended in a central lug and sat loosely in the bases). *Apple Blossom* was a stunning example of this kind of lamp, with its overflowing crescent of glass molded with blossom-heavy apple boughs. *Cupids*, with a putti pair embracing amid floral garlands, and *Pigeons*, with two birds on blossoming branches, were both 16in high (as was *Apple Blossom*) and had similar horseshoe-shaped stoppers.

This type of lighting device with overhang was often referred to as a *Tiara veuilleuse* table lamp, and smaller models – the 7in-high *Roses*, *Carnation* and *Almond Blossom* – were also made, their bases usually of a tapered-cylindrical shape as on the larger models, but with a different vertical pattern. In all, five types of bases were made for seven such small *luminaire* models (which were most likely used in the boudoir or dressing room).

The three pairs of lovebirds on the 17in *tiara veuilleuse* called *Inséparables* echo the quartet of birds on the clock case of the same name. The stopper on this lamp differs from that on most Lalique lamps in that it is not curved at the top, but rises to a subtle point; its bottom edges are straight, not pointed. The same is true of *Dandelion* which represents seven full puffs of the flower on a small stopper-panel, with two stems bereft of their fluffy balls drooping down at either side.

Other table lamps produced by Lalique included some rare ones with Art Nouveau subjects and later examples with starkly geometric motifs. Among the former, *Paons* is a 16½in table lamp in clear and frosted glass, highlighted with dark *patine* overall. Four flowing-

207

208

tailed birds are articulated on the square-sectioned stem which tapers from a spreading base with bracket-type feet, and another quartet, with showy, outstretched feathers, adorns the top of the circular shade, which has a leaf-and-branch pattern on the rim. Another table lamp, *Serpents,* depicted one of Lalique's favorite Art Nouveau motifs. This lamp, whose inverted circular shade was designed to give off indirect light, also came with designs of neo-classical figures and leafy forms. All three motifs were confined to a small collar (or *bague*) below the frosted-glass, which flared into a circular foot.

The *moderne* lamp designs were stylized confections quite removed from most of the statuettes and *motifs décoratifs* which Lalique created at the same time, but they were no doubt perfect touches for many of the fashionable interiors which were being designed in the 1920s and 1930s. *Cardamine,* its stem a long, wide rectangle molded with a tree trunk of stylized scrolling branches, was topped by a simple rectangular shade with vertical stripes. The stem was set into a chromed-steel base, which was a departure from the ornate bronze bases usually favored by Lalique. The same shade and base surrounded a lamp whose body was made up of two interlacing, openwork rectangles which were perpendicular to each other. Another lamp, pictured in a desk-top vignette in the 1932 catalogue, had a similar shaped shade, but its body was a rectangular clear-glass plaque molded with a long-haired, stylized female nude in frosted glass. It was enclosed in a chrome frame on a metal stem and foot. Another lamp of this same type, but with a tapered rectangular shade, depicts a nude female holding grapes and dancing in a bacchanalian frenzy.

Anemones, a stunning *lampadaire,* or table lamp, featured a highly stylized bouquet of flowers held together by metal bands at the bot-

207 Chandelier, eight-armed, with berry and leaf design, *c.* 1930, 32in (81.3cm) overall dia. Kagan Collection, USA.

208 Wall sconce, with peach and leaf motif, *c.* 1930, 9¾in (24.7cm) square; one of a set of four. Galerie Moderne.

209 *Stalactite* chandelier, *c.* 1928, 10½in (26.7cm). J. Lyons, London.

209

tom of the stems and just beneath the blossoms. This lamp did not have a true shade – the light was diffused through the thick frosted-glass, cut-out floriform top. Breves' Galleries' brochure, *The Art of René Lalique,* illustrated a handsome frosted-glass lamp with a thick pillar-like stem on a circular foot, and a hemispherical shade covered all over with rigid, stylized leaves, heavily molded so as to jut out at various angles. The same brochure showed a lamp called *Grapes,* which took the form of a tree of rectangular outline bearing stylized grape clusters amid openwork sections; this lamp was also displayed at the 1925 Paris Exposition.

Lalique vases appear on the market today transformed into lamp bases, with shades in complementary motifs. Lalique himself never intended the vases to be used as such (nor did most of his retailers – the customers themselves often altered them), but some of these hybrids are attractive enough despite their added elements. One such lamp base ("transformed" by Breves') is the *Ceylan* vase, a tapering cylinder of frosted, opalescent and turquoise-stained glass depicting four pairs of parakeets perched on branches all along its top. The clear celluloid shade is painted with similar birds.

Lalique designed two lighted wall plaques – near-circular in shape but for their flattened bottoms – which were attached to frosted-glass bowls holding incandescent bulbs. One had a tulip design, the other depicted a flock of sparrows in flight. There were also other lighting fixtures which could be attached to walls, including an elegant pair of sconces in clear and frosted glass, each with four elongated flowerhead shades placed on stylized-leaf supports. The Breves' brochure, *Lalique Lights,* includes *Mistletoe,* an *applique,* or wall light, of inverted demilune shape, as well as two semi-conical wall lights, *Leaves and Bracken* and *Dahlia,* a shade available in brown, green or white for use in corners.

Beech and *Shell* were two other wall lights, 13in and 11¾in high, respectively, which were semispherical and molded with stylized leaves (in green, white or brown) and scallops (opalescent only). *Berries* was a highly stylized wall light whose geometric pattern comprised three sets of squares, each consisting of four rows of four relief hemispheres, or berries; this dramatic and starkly modern light was available in white frosted glass.

Lalique's hanging globes and *lustres* (chandeliers) were perhaps his greatest contribution to interior lighting. From geometric globes to pendant bowls to futuristic, multi-armed concoctions, these lighting devices were not only handsome and popular designs, they also contributed significantly to Lalique's design schemes.

Lalique's hanging bowls, or *plafonniers,* as Christopher Vane Percy has written, were remarkable for:

> ... diffusing the light through the molded surfaces of the glass and using the ceiling as a reflector ... in order to create a two-tone effect; a relief of leaves or fruit ... would act as a lens, concentrating the light into bright patches that contrasted with the surrounding soft glow. This fashionable device was a twentieth century innovation, and Lalique exploited it to great effect.[6]

Lalique's ceiling lights were *plafonniers* decorated with both realistically floral and boldly geometric nature-inspired motifs. The former were not as true-to-life as the few *cire-perdue* shades that Lalique created in the first decade of the century, but they were handsome nonetheless: *Acanthus,* with stylized, folded-over leaves occupying three tiers on a dome of clear and frosted glass; *Dahlia,* molded with large flowerheads, each surrounded by pinnated leaves; and *Beech Leaves* (as Breves' called it), made of stylized leaves whose design was repeated on small molded-glass panels attached to the silk cords from which the bowl hung.

6. Vane Percy, *The Glass of René Lalique,* 105.

210

211

210 *Etoile* or *Bracken* chandelier, *c.* 1925, 30¾in (78cm) dia. Galerie Moderne.

211 *Saint-Vincent* plafonnier, *c.* 1930, 13¾in (34.5cm) dia. Galerie Moderne.

This same design could be found on a bowl of the same name.

212 *Grande boulle de gui* chandelier, *c.* 1925, 36in (90cm). Galerie Moderne.

The giant ball of mistletoe often came stained with various *patines*, including green and sepia. The sphere comprises ten pieces: top, bottom and eight curved central segments.

More stylized reliefs appear on *Coquilles,* with its overlapping-shell motif (popular also on bowls, vases and other Lalique tableware), and on *Eglantines,* a plain frosted-glass dome with six attached volutes encrusted with wild roses. Breves' brochure also illustrated *plafonniers* designed with *monnaie du pape* (the honesty plant), with swallows, with attached bunches of mulberry (as in *Eglantines*) and with stylized grape clusters in three gradating concentric circles. There was also an unusual figural example with a solitary siren in opalescent glass.

Pure geometric designs on ceiling lights were found on a 14in-high globe with frosted, diamond-shaped recesses (this also came as a vase with flat base) and on a stunning *plafonnier* that was molded on the inside with radiating crescents (available in clear or amber glass).

Lalique's chandeliers, or *lustres,* differed from traditional chandeliers (which depended on their faceted-glass components to reflect a great amount of light) in that, like all his lighting devices, they were designed to diffuse and project light *through* the glass, thus making the best use of its translucence and achieving, in Nicholas Dawes' words, "a soft, warm radiance".

Lalique's chandeliers were sometimes of traditional designs, with *tulipes,* or lamp shades, capping branched chandeliers; at other times they took on extraordinary shapes, like the one that resembled a multi-winged, upside-down rocket (conventionally called *Bracken* in Breves' brochure and *L'Etoile à huit branches* in a 1925 French article[7]). There was even a hanging fixture which resembled a formation of pendant stalactites – appropriately, Breves' listed its availability "in ice colour".

Lustre Paris, as Breves' brochure termed it, was a traditional chandelier design, 43in in height, consisting of a cluster of right-angled arms at different levels, each topped by a cylindrical *tulipe* with inside-out scallop edges. *Lustre Bucarest,* the "centerfold" in Breves' brochure, also had a conventional chandelier shape: eight of its scrolling foliate arms terminated at the top in conical lamp shades.

A most unusual chandelier, in the *Mistletoe* pattern, was called a *Grande boulle de gui.* Its panels of clear and frosted glass formed a sphere, and this "caged" lighting device – which, along with other Lalique chandeliers and lighting fixtures, was displayed at the 1925 Paris Exposition – was essentially a puzzle of curved-glass panels. Eight panels, plus two domes for the top and bottom, were attached to each other by metal loops to form one giant, 36-in high globe. Appropriately, these mistletoe balls came highlighted with, among other hues, green.

Also unconventional was a cylindrical chandelier whose surface was covered all over with at least five dozen extensions in the shape of little stepped pyramids. Another of basic cylindrical shape (called *Lantern pointu* by Breves') was decorated with eight rows of squares-within-squares out of whose centers jutted square pegs of glass.

Lalique's contributions to the lighting industry were indeed many and diverse, as an article in *La Demeure Française* of 1925 stated:

Every year there are new chandeliers, new candelabra, globes, fountain bases, in which every type of flora finds its use: mistletoe like a chestnut tree, stars whose every point is a luminous jet; a thousand combinations, a thousand discoveries.[8]

7. Raymond Cogniat, "Un Maître Verrier, M. René Lalique", *La Demeure Française,* Spring 1925, 22.
8. *Ibid.*

212

VASES
AND
TABLEWARE

10

ne would not generally attach the words "art" and "drama" to a household accessory as mundane and humble as a vase, but in the designing eye of René Lalique, ordinary flower holders were wondrously metamorphosed into *objets d'art* of great appeal to discerning clients living in the *de luxe* world of the 1920s and 1930s. Today, Lalique's vases appear to be his most spectacular monumental creations – not to mention the most desired by collectors – and most have never held a stem, a blossom or a drop of water!

Lalique began to create vases and other such vessels in the late 19th century. A serpent-mounted, tall glass vase (*c*.1898) was exhibited at the 1900 Paris Exposition and a number of *cire-perdue* vases were produced through the 1920s. For the most part, such vases were adorned with organic Art Nouveau motifs – leafy forms, swarms of butterflies, delicate blossoms – or with mythological or classical figures; but in the early 1920s *cire-perdue* vases of an intriguingly symmetrical and stylized nature began to appear, signaling a change to the starker, more controlled designs of Lalique's Art Déco vases. One such *cire-perdue* vase (*c*.1921; Gulbenkian Collection) has four pairs of long-tailed parakeets perched on its top, just below the thick rim. Their lower halves are naturally enough realized, but their facing heads and necks form an unnatural 90-degree angle, hugging the rim and thus creating a near-square shape. Likewise, a vase at whose bottom protrude the heads of two pairs of facing bull-headed fish is rigidly symmetrical and untrue-to-nature, almost grotesque. These vases contrast greatly with *cire-perdue* vessels of a decade earlier, such as the covered vase whose top rim and lid are decorated with lovely, long-haired female heads, and a vase in the Musée des Arts Décoratifs, which is molded with leafy rhubarb stalks. But there were vases even in the second decade of the century which pointed to the stylized turn Lalique was to take by the mid-1920s. One very unusual example is a cylindrical vase decorated with open-mouthed fish heads which emerge halfway through the surface of the vase in an extraordinary pattern of three rows of contiguous relief diamonds. Such strange and wonderful creations in *cire-perdue* were rare. Most of the vases which Lalique produced by that method up to the 1920s were of restrained, mostly symmetrical, floral and foliate designs. All of them are very rare today.

The majority of Lalique's vases, *jardinières*, bowls and other such containers from the 1920s are of mold-blown and press-molded glass. A mold-blown vessel is created by blowing a bubble of glass (either by mouth or automated means) into a mold, and a press-molded piece is produced by pressing or forcing molten glass into a mold with a plunger. The latter method was introduced at Lalique's Wingen Glassworks and proved economical, efficient and capable of producing great quantities of massive, solid vessels with bold Art Déco motifs, as well as thinner-walled vases with busier, gentler designs.

Lalique's vases – he designed some 200 in all – were of myriad colors, surfaces, shapes and sizes, the latter ranging from *Laiderons*, just over 3in high, to *Naiades*, 18 in high. They were of clear, frosted, stained, enameled, opalescent and colored glass, with hues ranging from the mellowest butterscotch and lushest jade green to the rubiest red and deepest black. Some mold-blown vases had two or three layers of cased glass; others were delicately thin-walled. There were cylindrical, ovoid and spherical forms; there were vases molded partly or overall in high or low relief, with narrow necks or flaring rims, with ornate handles or other projections or extensions. The subjects and motifs depicted would fill several books on ornament. There were birds and fishes of all species, done in all degrees of realism and fantasy; there were flowers and leaves, both botanically accurate and purely imaginative; there were geometric designs; and there were, to a lesser extent, human figures in both a classical vein, à la *Suzanne*, and a more stylized geometric manner. The colors of certain motifs could be wildly unrealistic – turquoise cockerels, for instance, or amber turtleshells or blue-tinged squirrels – but the effect was all the more exciting and dramatic.

Gabriel Mourey wrote admiringly of Lalique's "vases, flower-cups, basins, nosegay-horns and urns" which seemed "to have been carved and modeled out of blocks of precious stones". He continued:

> The glass sometimes becomes as firm and sharp as metal; at places, it has the dense and clean-cut opacity of some minerals or it takes the aspect of an unknown, mysterious, indefinable matter which reminds one of the rind of a fruit or the flesh of a flower; sometimes, it flashes out into an unheard-of radiance, an almighty splendor which rivals the pomp and the gorgeousness of the most dazzling shells – though we are never allowed to forget that all this is made of glass.[1]

One of the earliest known non-*cire-perdue* vases of Lalique's, made in the second decade of the 20th century, is a highly unusual hybrid vessel of blue glass with inlaid floral panels in frosted glass. This mold-blown vase, nearly a foot high, was exhibited at the Pavillon de Marsan in 1912, as was a squat-globular vase (8¼in high) of clear glass molded with bas-relief lily pads and adorned with applied green-glass frogs. Nicholas Dawes refers to these elaborate vessels (which were made in ceramic molds) as transitional pieces, and he believes the frog vase is unique, whereas the floral-panel example is one of "a limited series, each differing slightly from another in color or hand-applied work".[2]

Following in the wake of these two singular vases were true production pieces, probably made in metal molds and available in a wide variety of colors. Made from around 1913 to 1920, these early mass-produced vases included *Gui (Mistletoe)*, *Courges (Gourds)*, *Monnaie du pape*, *Ronces (Briars)* and *Hirondelles (Swallows)*. All depicted subjects from nature which had long been in Lalique's design repertory. *Gui*, whose pattern covered one side of the medallion-invitation for Lalique's 1912 glass exhibition, was a compressed-ovoid vessel which was available in a range of colors, including opalescent, blue and green, and frosted with sienna or blue *patine*. *Monnaie du pape*, cylindrical and tapering at the rim and neck, was covered all over with the honesty plant. This motif also was seen on a large jewelry box that Lalique produced, and it is at its loveliest in opalescent glass with a sienna *patine* – very much resembling the pearlescent pods of the plant (which is also called "Japanese pennies").

1. Mourey, "A Great French Craftsman", 109.
2. Dawes, *Lalique Glass*, 28.

214

215

216

217

218

214 *Cire-perdue* vase with rose blossoms, 1926, 6in (15cm); engraved: *R. Lalique 594 26.* Private collection, London.

215 *Cire-perdue* vase with fish amid frothing waves, 7in (17.5cm); wheel-cut: *R. LALIQUE 272-21.* Private collection, London.

216 *Cire-perdue* vase with large leaves, 1920, 6½in (16cm); wheel-cut: *R. LALIQUE 164-20.* Private collection, London.

217 *Laiderons* vase, *c.* 1932, 3¼in (8cm). Private collection, Switzerland.

218 *Grande boulle lierre* vase, *c.* 1921, 13½in (35cm). Private collection, London.

Lalique continued creating one-of-a-kind *cire-perdue* pieces while mass-producing vases of all sizes in the hundreds. *Laiderons,* one of Lalique's smallest mass-produced vases, is one of a later series whose photographs are appended to the back of the 1932 catalogue. *Grande boulle lierre* is a frosted-glass piece whose ivy-leaf design is sparse yet quite dramatic; it is one of Lalique's largest vases.

219

220

219 *Ronces* vase, *c.* 1913-20, 9in (23cm). Galerie Moderne.

220 *Monnaie du pape* vase, *c.* 1913-20, 9¼in (23cm). Galerie Moderne.

221 *Gui* vase, *c.* 1923, 6¾in (17cm). Galerie Moderne.

222 *Eucalyptus* vase, *c.* 1922, 6¾in (17cm). Galerie Moderne.

223 *Mimosa* vase, *c.* 1920, 6¾in (17cm). Galerie Moderne.

224 *Palmes* vase, *c.* 1926, 4¾in (12cm). Galerie Moderne.

Courges, with its highly curvilinear arrangement of squash amid ribbony tendrils, harks back to Art Nouveau motifs, as does *Ronces,* with interlacing briars covering its slim oviform body. *Hirondelles* depicts a thick flock of overlapping swallows covering the upper three-quarters of the vase (the bottom and rim are undecorated); it came in red, grey, blue and clear glass.

The five vases named above were all made in the decade before 1914, and *Monnaie du pape, Courges* and *Gui* were listed in the 1932 catalogue, evidence of their long-lasting popularity. The 1920s and early 1930s marked the apogee of Lalique's vase production – as it did his career as a glassmaker – quite amazing when one considers that he was already past the age of 60.

FLORAL/FOLIATE VASES

These motifs are predominant throughout Lalique's career as both a goldsmith and glassmaker, but nowhere are they represented with such boldness and verve as on his vases. For instance, a simple featherlike leaf was shown starkly vertical on a cylindrical vase with everted rim and seed-pod-encrusted base *(Eucalyptus),* or streaming downward from the narrow neck of a teardrop-shaped vessel *(Mimosa),* or billowing and overlapping on a globular body *(Palmas).* One vase, *Fern,* has leaves so feathery-light that they resemble the real thing. The perfectly symmetrical, vertical leaves of *Acacia, (Mimosa),* or billowing and overlapping on a globular body *(Palmes).* realistic, leaves of *Sauge (Sage), Acanthes, Milan* and *Estérel.*

By far the most striking foliate vases are those whose leaves are almost unrecognizable as such, but create stunning semi-abstract designs. *Moissac's* leaves are thick, striated triangles arranged diagonally next to each other in vertical lines; *Languedoc's* scaly rows of mother-in-law's tongue (sansevieria), each leaf extending outward from the surface and finely denticulated, create a bold pattern, especially in its bright green version. Most of the vases come in clear and frosted glass, often with *patine,* as well as opalescent and colored glass.

Sophora presents a simple, but strong, design of large, spade-shaped leaves in bold relief against an often-frosted dark ground. *Violettes,* on the other hand, is almost architectonic with a frieze of large, overlapping violet leaves running along a tall, out-turned rim which overhangs a simple cylindrical base. *Lotus,* with the plant wholly occupying its tall cylindrical shape and flaring rim, is likewise a stately, subdued foliate form, quite in contrast to the ebullient *Charmille,* whose globular body is covered overall with a dizzying pattern of half-emergent, low-relief, skeletal leaves.

Two vases, though not depicting leaves *per se,* may be mentioned here. The wheat-stalk motif, with its gently fanning top, is seen on a lovely ovoid vase in a markedly stylized pattern consisting of seven rows of interwoven stalks of gradated sizes, the largest in the middle. An additional pattern of arching recesses where the tops of the fans are "gouged out" is equally strong, and almost totally abstract (there is another wheat vase whose all-over pattern comprises triangular half-stalks). *Chardons (Thistles)* is notable for wide bands of empty space which divide a pair of stylized thistle leaves.

221

222

223

224

225

226

227

225 *Malines* vase, *c.*
1922, 4¾in (12cm).
Galerie Moderne.

226 Vase with ferns, *c.*
1922, 7¼in (18cm).
Galerie Moderne.

227 *Acacia* vase, *c.*
1923, 8in (20cm).
Galerie Moderne.

This version has a
wider neck than usual.

228 *Acanthes* vase,
c. 1924, 11½in
(29cm). Collection
I. Chisholm, London.

228

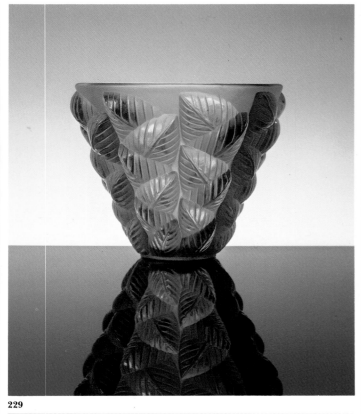

229

230

231

232

229 *Moissac* vase, *c.*
1925, 5½in (13cm).
Galerie Moderne.

230 Vase with
wheatsheaf design, *c.*
1924, 7¼in (18cm).
Galerie Moderne.

231 *Sauge* vase, *c.*
1924, 10in (25.5cm).
Galerie Moderne.

232 *Estérel* vase,
c. 1924, 6in (15cm).
Galerie Moderne.

233 *Plumes* vases, *c.* 1922, 8½in (21cm). Galerie Moderne.

234 *Languedoc* vase, *c.* 1925, 9in (22.5cm). Collection Glenn and Mary Lou Utt, USA.

235 *Violettes* vase, *c.* 1922, 6½in (16cm). Galerie Moderne.

These pages show more examples of leaf motifs on Lalique's vases. Even the feathers on *Plumes* are leaf-like in appearance, their billowy curves seeming to defy nature.

233

234

235

236

237

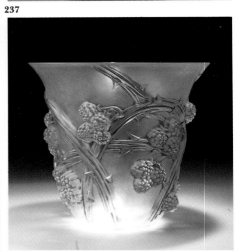

238

239

236 *Chamarande* vase, *c.* 1925, 7¾in (19.5cm). Galerie Moderne.

237 *Thistle* vases, in frosted and gray glass. *c.* 1922, 8in (20cm). Galerie Moderne.

238 *Graines* vase, *c.* 1930, 8in (20cm). Galerie Moderne.

239 *Mures* vase, *c.* 1924, 7½in (19cm). Galerie Moderne.

240

241

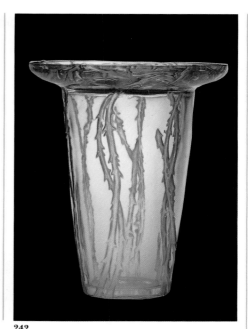

242

240 *Chardons* vase,
c. 1922, 8in (20cm).
Nicholas M. Dawes,
New York.

241 *Bordure bleuets*
vase, *c.* 1913, 6¾in
(17cm). Galerie
Moderne.

242 *Bordure épines*
vase, *c.* 1913, 8in
(20cm). Galerie
Moderne.

243 *Bleuets* vase, *c.*
1913, 7¼in (18cm).
Galerie Moderne.

243

LALIQUE

244

245

246

247

244 *Tulipes* vase, *c.* 1928, 8¼in (20.5cm). Galerie Moderne.

245 *Paquerettes* vase, *c.* 1933, 7¼in (18.3cm). Galerie Moderne.

246 *Oran* vase, *c.* 1925, 10½in (26cm). Galerie Moderne.

247 *Chevreuse* vase, *c.* 1933, 6¼in (16cm). Galerie Moderne.

248 *Rampillon* vase, *c.* 1926, 5in (12.7cm). Galerie Moderne.

249 *Prunes* vase, *c.* 1924, 7½in (18.5cm). Galerie Moderne.

250 *Cerises* vase, *c.* 1924, 8in (20cm). Galerie Moderne.

251 *Soleil* vase, *c.* 1912, 8in (20cm). Galerie Moderne.

Two simple vessels of tapered cylindrical shape with flat circular rims are also interesting for their minimal imagery and extensive blank spaces. *Bordure bleuets* depicts thin, interlacing stem-tendrils topped by unopened cornflower buds, most of which skim the top of the vase, just under the rim. Highlighted in blue *patine,* this asymmetrical, Art Nouveau image is touching in its desolation (much stronger than *Bleuets,* which depicts the cornflowers in full bloom). *Bordure epines* has a similarly uneven design of sinuous, thorny branches, climbing up the vase's sides.

Thorns also feature on *Mures,* but thick, luscious mulberry bunches tower over the bas-relief brambles. *Chamarande,* too, features, prickly branches, but they are barely discernible stems in low relief on the top of this thick-walled, clear-glass cylinder – whose only other decoration are two "handles" comprising floral clusters.

In contrast to the "top-heavy" floral-decoration vases are those whose wide-flaring, clear-glass rims emerge from boldly designed, high-relief lower halves. *Graines* is decorated with seven rows of plump seeds of graduated size (the tiniest at the bottom) and *Prunes* and *Cerises* are molded with thick leaf-and-fruit clusters.

Renoncules, on the other hand, has a bottom band of very stylized leaves and flowers, the latter scallop-edged concentric circles of the boldest design. Stylized blossoms cover the entire surface of other vases. *Rampillon* is one of the most handsome, with its three tiers of stark relief diamonds surrounded by little florettes. Although small in size (only 5in high), the bold design gives it an almost monumental appearance. *Tulipes* has fat relief blossoms, mostly unopened, all over its surface; and *Oran,* with its hemispherical chrysanthemums, is similarly stylized and striking, as well as one of the largest, and most beautiful and practical vases.

An unusual floral vase depicts cog-like daisies against a background of what one writer has called "crushed ice" (one book gives this vase the name *Paquerettes*). It has a machine-age regularity and coldness, and is a world apart from the narrow-necked *Soleil,* which has a pert, brightly enameled sunflower covering its heart-shaped body. Another crisply modern vase is *Chevreuse,* whose five high-relief hoops of stylized florette-friezes alternate with recessed, vertically striated bands.

248

249

250

251

141

252

252 Vase with floral-garland tiers, *c.* 1934-35, 6¾in (17cm). Galerie Moderne.

253 *Ormeaux* vase, *c.* 1922, 6¾in (16.8cm). Galerie Moderne.

254 *Poivre* vase, *c.* 1922, 10in (25cm). Galerie Moderne.

253

254

255

255 *Pinsons* vase, *c.*
1927, 7½in (19cm).
Galerie Moderne.

256 *Lézards* vase, *c.*
1908, approx. 14in
(35.6cm). Galerie
Moderne.

257 Vase with storks
in reeds, *c.* 1936,
approx. 11in (28cm).
Galerie Moderne.

256

257

ANIMAL VASES

Not surprisingly, Lalique's vases depict a menagerie of beasts and birds, from the familiar Art Nouveau snakes, lizards, beetles and peacocks, to the more innocent and decorative creatures used more frequently in the second half of his career, like parakeets, squirrels, antelopes, horses and fish. These animals were both realistically portrayed and stylized to such an extent that they are barely recognizable.

Lalique's depictions of fish on vases are instructive of the diversity of his animal imagery. Fish could be stylized and geometric, as on the earlier-mentioned *cire-perdue* fish-heads vase, or on the diamond-patterned *Penthièvre, Camaret* (with its bulging bubbles of fish), *Piriac* and *Monaco*. The latter two vases had piscine friezes on their lower sections, *Piriac's* fish riding on four ripples of water. But some designs were more textured and realistic, covering the entire shell of a vase, as on *Oléron* or *Salmonides*, swimming upstream toward the rim of the vase, as on *Marisa*, or gently skimming the face of the water, as on the *japoniste* and very popular *Formose*, which was available in jewel-like shades of opalescent, green, orange, yellow and red glass. *Poissons*, with a huge, rather ugly, but well-defined bull-headed fish, was reminiscent of the early *cire-perdue* vase which had four fish-heads serving as feet.

Representations of birds, too, range widely on Lalique's vases. *Borromée*, with its cluster of peacock heads, treats an Art Nouveau subject in an unusual way, passing over the birds' decorative tail feathers and depicting the clutch of gaggling heads instead. *Aigrettes*, with its flock of egrets in gentle flight amid tall, billowy reeds, is a lovely *japoniste* image, especially with a blue-green *patine*. A pair of vases with similar Orientalizing bird imagery is *Coqs et plumes* and *Coqs et raisins*. On the other hand, *Le Mans* and *Bresse*, two small vases (some 4in high) depicting calligraphic-like cockerels, are striking exercises in decorative symmetry and can be compared to *Coq houdan*, the more angular paperweight/mascot. Both *Le Mans*, whose frieze of cocks crow toward the rim, and *Bresse*, whose row of birds feed at the base, were available only in colors (including turquoise and butterscotch), and their recesses were often strongly frosted to make the relief strokes of the birds more prominent. *Canards*, with its diagonal rows of parading ducks receding toward the top, was also fashioned with bold figures, usually against a frosted ground.

In contrast to those two patterned avian designs were the depictions of such birds as parakeets and sparrows. The cylindrical *Ceylan* shows parakeet pairs as charming as those on the *Inséparables* frame, and *Perruches'* lovebird couples perch on diagonal flowering branches which cover the whole surface of the ovoid form. *Deux pigeons* roost on the round handles of a plain, clear-glass vase, quite different from the two pairs of more angular birds whose facing bodies, beaks clutching berries, form the square handles of the covered vase, *Sylvia*. Little birds hidden amid leaf and berry clusters appear on the thick, ornate handles of *Pétrarque* and *Margaret*, both of whose bodies are undecorated. But *Tourterelles*, with a close-knit pair of turtle doves perched atop the lid of a simple teardrop-shaped

vase, and *Bellecour*, with four sparrows overlooking the rim of its long-necked body, depict more substantial birds which do not get lost in the foliage. On the popular vase *Avallon*, which is molded all over its surface with a rich flora-and-fauna design, equal weight is given to both small birds and twisting berry-bearing vines on which they perch. *Alicante* is an unusual depiction of the heads and necks of massive tropical birds, their overlapping scaly feathers molded in fine detail, their breasts fading into the base.

Insects also appear on Lalique's vases and one of the most outstanding examples is *Gros scarabées*, mold-blown, of a deep amber hue and polished meticulously by hand to achieve a lustrous sheen. The popular *Sauterelles*, with its swarm of grasshoppers balanced on sweeping curves of grass, was available in a variety of colors, from green, blue and red to a fetching stained version with green-tinged insects on a cloudy blue ground. (There are also later non-Lalique copies of the vase in bright hues; these are said to have been made in Argentina from an original Lalique mold.) The serpent is used on one of Lalique's most memorable vases, the beast's thick, sinuous body coiling three times and forming the actual body of the vase itself. The snake's open-jawed head rests aside the raised rim of the vase, which was available in red-amber, grey, opalescent and (rarely) purple glass. Scrolling lizards scamper between flowering bouquets up the body of *Lézards et bleuets*, a richly designed vase which was one of the few available in black; an even rarer one resembling agate was made of triple-cased grey glass.

Other animals, although prominent on Lalique's ashtrays and mascots, appear less frequently on vases. When they do, they are often highly stylized, as in the frieze of gerenuks (a type of antelope) standing amid wintry trees which decorates a striking vase. The sleek beasts' huge, curling horns form a bold horizontal band of spirals which tower over their simply drawn bodies. Other *biches* gracing Lalique's vases include the dark-stained herd whose bodies curve over the clear-glass relief roundels on *Antilopes* (the motif resembles that of the bird-and-boss *Roger* box), as well as the three rows of impala on *Soudan*. Two *biches* form the handles of *Yvelines*, their bodies set amid gentle curling foliage which continues on to the sides of the undecorated body (as on *Chamarande*, with its florid handles). *Chamois* depicts two rows of the beasts with highly exaggerated interlocking horns (this vase is similar to *Le Mans* and *Bresse* in that the bodies are boldly displayed against frosted recessed grounds. These three vases, along with *Canards* and *Laiderons*, comprise a late series listed on a supplemental page in the 1932 catalogue; they are considered high-quality collectable pieces, and are still quite undervalued.

Camargue is a boldly stylized 1930s vase with ribbony rim and base and a frosted-glass body decorated with plaques of four rearing equine specimens. The horses are set against whirling clouds of smoke or dust often boldly stained in sepia. In contrast to the energy and movement of *Camargue* is the serene *Chevaux*, with its herd of bas-relief neoclassical horses marching along the base in front of tall leafy growths. Other animals that Lalique depicted on his vases were a band of leaping hare on *Lièvres*, rams on the handles of *Béliers* and tree-dwelling squirrels on *Senart*.

258

259

258 *Poissons*, blue, *c.* 1922, 9¼in (23.5cm). Collection Glenn and Mary Lou Utt, USA.

259 *Poissons*, yellow and red, *c.* 1922, 9¼in (23.5cm). Galerie Moderne.

260

260 *Poissons*, frosted with sepia *patine*, *c.* 1922, 9¼in (23.5cm). Galerie Moderne.

261

262

263

264

261 *Oléron* vase, *c.* 1926, 3½in (9cm). Galerie Moderne.

262 *Formose* vase, *c.* 1929, 7¼in (18cm). Galerie Moderne.

263 *Camaret* vase, *c.* 1928, 5½in (14cm). Galerie Moderne.

264 *Piriac* vase, *c.* 1928, 7½in (18.5cm). Galerie Moderne.

265 *Salmonides* vase, *c.* 1926, 11½in (29cm). Galerie Moderne.

266 *Aigrettes* vase, *c.* 1922, 10¼in (25.7cm). Galerie Moderne.

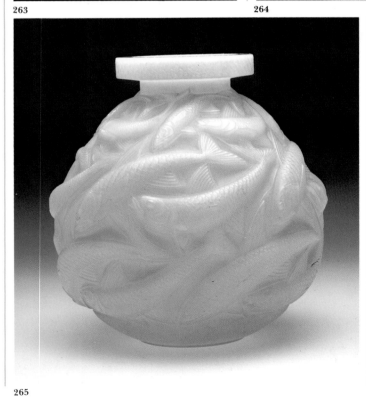

265

266

The fish design on the tiny *Oléron* and the huge *Salmonides* are exactly the same; the differences are their sizes and necks

267

267 *Tourterelles* vase
and cover, *c.* 1920,
11¼in (28cm).
Galerie Moderne.

268 *Tourterelles* vase
and cover, smoky gray
glass, *c.* 1920, 11¼in
(28cm). Kagan
Collection, USA.

268

147

LALIQUE

269

271 *Chevaux* vase, *c.*
1924, 7½in (18.8cm).
Galerie Moderne.

271

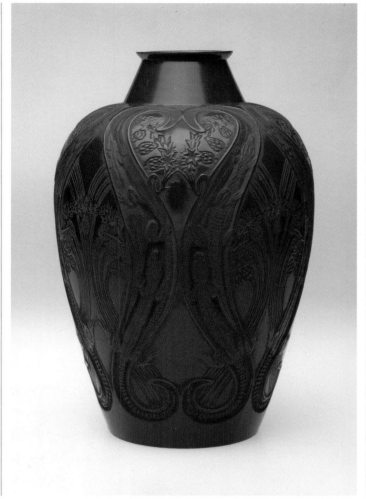

270

272

269 *Serpent* vase, *c.*
1924, 10½in (26cm).
Kagan Collection,
USA.

270 *Lézards et bleuets*
vase, *c.* 1922, 13¼in
(34cm). Kagan
Collection, USA.

273

272 *Perruches* vase, *c.*
1923, 10½in (26cm).
Galerie Moderne.

273 *Béliers* vase, *c.*
1924, 8in (20cm).
Galerie Moderne.

Animals of all kinds
appear on Lalique's
vases – sometimes as
shaped handles, i.e.,
the rams of *Béliers*, but
usually as part or all
of the body's design,
as with *Serpent*,
Chevaux and *Perruches*.

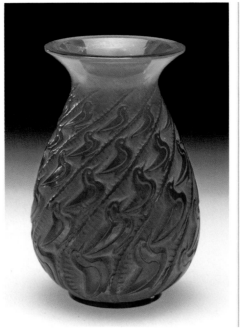

274 *Bresse* vase, *c.* 1932, 4¼in (10.5cm). Galerie Moderne.

275 *Canards* vase, *c.* 1932, 5½in (13.5cm). Private collection, Switzerland.

276 *Pétrarque* vase, *c.* 1925, 9in (22.4cm). Private collection, Paris.

277 *Gros scarabées* vase, *c.* 1924, 12in (30cm). Galerie Moderne.

274

275

276

LALIQUE

278

278 *Lièvres* vase,
c. 1922, 6in (15cm).
Galerie Moderne.

279 *Senart* vase,
c. 1932, 8½in
(21.4cm). Collection
Glenn and Mary Lou
Utt, USA.

280 *Senart* vase, *c.*
1932, 8½in (21.4cm).
Galerie Moderne.

279

280

281

281 *Yvelines* vase, *c.*
1924, 7¾in (19.5cm).
Galerie Moderne.

282 *Soudan* vase, *c.*
1928, 7¼in (18cm).
Galerie Moderne.

283 *Camargue* vase, *c.*
1935, 11½in (29cm).
Galerie Moderne.

283

282

FIGURATIVE VASES

Lalique produced *cire-perdue* vases with human subjects, including several whose bases displayed neoclassical nudes or chubby cherubs. He continued to mass-produce such vases in clear, frosted and colored glass well into the 1920s, when he made *Lutteurs*, with a band of male wrestlers on its tall, outcurved foot, *Farandole*, with a bottom frieze of putti amid floral garlands, and *Naiades*, with muscular sea sirens floating amid waves of water and their own long hair.

Other vases were molded all over with neoclassical figures: *Palestre* has a group of standing male nudes in various positions; *Archers* shows muscular bowmen aiming their arrows at huge flying birds swarming on the vase's top, and *Danaides* has highly stylized daughters of Danaos emptying their urns in vertical stripes of water. In contrast to the Danaides, the female nudes on *Bacchantes*, which was shown at the 1925 Paris Exposition, are highly sculptural, even Rodinesque, in their muscularity and erotic poses and pairings. The crusty background is also quite sculptural and, but for the smoothness of the skin on the nudes, the surface of this monumental piece could almost be mistaken for *cire-perdue* glass.

There were also vases whose figures, although not covering the entire exterior of a piece, nonetheless dominated the surface. One such vase is *Camées*, which has two rows of neoclassical nudes in oval surrounds. *Gobelet 6 figurines* and *6 Figurines et masques* represent full-length, elongated figures set in quasi-panels; *Gobelet's* saintly, robed and veiled women are recessed into stark rectangular niches, whereas the six erotic nude females (seen from the front and back) of the other vase stand on classical satyr-masks amid floral backgrounds, separated from one another by billowy vertical lozenges. Its essential roundness and voluptuousness are entirely opposite to the rigidity and angularity of *Gobelet*, although both exhibit a monumental, architectonic quality.

Another outstanding vase – closer in fact to a large covered bottle – is *Méplat sirènes*, which has bulbous sides adorned with curvy, neoclassical nudes and a half-kneeling nude acting as a "stopper" at the top. *Nadica* represents a pair of stylized, long-haired nymphs whose entwining legs turn into tails which scroll and become side-handles, terminating as volutes at both ends of the vase. *Terpsichore*, from the mid-1930s, depicts a quartet of dancing female nudes amid stylized diamond-pattern curtain-folds.

Classical masks are depicted singly in large roundels on several Lalique vases, among them the vaguely Orientalizing *4 Masques* and *Cluny*, the latter with handles terminating in highly stylized face masks.

284 From left to right, three vases: *Méplat sirènes, c.* 1922, 14¾in (37cm), Galerie Moderne; *Bacchantes, c.* 1920, 10in (25cm), Collection R. V. Craig, London, and *Ronsard, c.* 1926, 8¼in (20.8cm). Galerie Moderne.
This trio of vases depicts female nudes, which largely figured in Lalique's design repertory. *Méplat sirènes*, whose shape and top give it the appearance of a large perfume bottle, has bulbous sides molded with curvaceous neoclassical nudes, plus a half-kneeling figural stopper. The nudes on *Bacchantes* – one example of which was on view at the 1925 Paris Exposition – are highly sculptural, even Rodinesque, with their voluptuous shapes and sensuous poses.

284

285

286

285 Vase with border
of sirens and glass
cabochons, *c.* 1912,
8¼in (21cm). Private
collection, London.

The clear vase with
narrow neck and
decorative border is
quite early, and most
unusual. The
cabochon-glass
"jewels" embellish
the space around the
zigzagging border,
which is occupied by
sea nymphs with
interlacing tails.

286 *Archers* vase,
c. 1922, 10½in (26cm).
Collection Laurie and
Joel Shapiro, Detroit.

287 *Archers* vase, *c.*
1922, 10½in (26cm).
Private collection,
London.

287

288

289

LALIQUE

290

291

292

288 Vase with nudes
and garlands amid
zigzag ribbon borders.
c. 1938, approx. 12in
(30.5cm). Galerie
Moderne.

289 *Bouchardon* vase,
c. 1920, 5in (12.8cm).
Collection R. V.
Craig, London.

290 *Palestre* vase, *c.*
1928, 16¾in (42cm).
Galerie Moderne.

291 6 *Figurines et
masques* vase, *c.* 1912,
10in (25cm). Galerie
Moderne.

292 *Méplat sirènes*
vase, *c.* 1912, 14¾in
(37cm). Galerie
Moderne.

293 *Danaides* vase, *c.*
1920, 7½in (18.5cm).
Galerie Moderne.

Lalique's figural vases
mostly comprise
neoclassical female
figures, although
some, such as *Archers*
and *Palestre*, depict
male athletes. A
palestre (or palaestra
in English) was a type
of gymnasium where
athletes in classical
Greece and Rome
trained.

293

OTHER VASE DESIGNS

Some of Lalique's vase designs, though grounded in nature, are given startling, semi-abstract treatment. *Tortues* has such a design. Its billowing, almost breathing body is covered with the shells of a score of tortoises, whose stylized heads, peeking out, are barely discernible. This stunning 10½in-high vase was produced in clear and frosted glass, stained in brown and green; and it was also available in gold and alexandrite, the latter a rare orange shade (actually, a greenish hue which changes to reddish-brown under transmitted light).

Marine patterns were frequently depicted on Lalique's vases. *Coquilles* is an oviform vase covered with huge fanning scallops, finely molded down to every vertical striation on the shell. *Oursin* takes the beautiful symmetrical shape of the sea urchin, *Palissy's* surface is irregularly covered with tiny snail shells of assorted sizes, and *Dordogne's* flattened sphere is dotted at the base with two rows of pointed snail shells. *Escargot*, available in shades ranging from orange and red to green and blue, is in the flattened circular shape of a giant snail shell; each curving line on the spiral is finely detailed and the vase is reminiscent of the perfume bottles, *Amphytrite*. *Escargot's* coiling pattern is repeated down the sides of *Amiens,* a thick-walled, clear-glass vase with a trio of scrolling handles; the same coiling pattern appears on *Spirales,* whose scallop-edged coils rise inward from shallow to high relief. *Méduse's* thick vertical tails coil in small spirals that could be dragon's tails or perhaps the arms of an octopus.

The bold design on a lush milk-white vase called *Picardie* resembles both a shell and a flowerhead pattern. Molded in relief on the underside of the body, the eight perfectly symmetrical forms are at once dramatic and delicate.

One of Lalique's best-known vases, *Tourbillons (Whirlwinds),* is also one of his most perfectly executed pieces – and a bold Art Déco statement. The thick-walled body (varying from ¼in to 2in) is molded in high relief and the vase was available in clear glass with a black-enameled surface, as well as in several colors, including a rich honey-amber shade and a deep sapphire blue. *Tourbillons'* prickly-vortical design is echoed on the huge decorative handles of the plain-bodied, bucket-shaped *Pierrefonds,* which was available in clear and colored glass.

Several Lalique vases depicted water or had water-like or bubbly surfaces that mimicked the liquid properties of glass (unlike the bold Art Déco creations of Maurice Marinot, which exploited the actual bubbles within the glass). *Fontaine* was the most literal of Lalique's watery vases. An early swollen-cylindrical vase with cover (it was illustrated in a 1912 article in *Art et Décoration*[3]), it had an uneven surface that resembled a still pond, or perhaps condensation on the side of the glass. Somewhat incongruously, its neck was molded with a border of devil masks.

Davos, an astonishing design of bubbles in rows of regular clusters, resembles, as Nicholas Dawes has written, "the arrangement of molecular structure as seen under microscope conditions".[4] Dawes has suggested that Lalique may have taken his inspiration for *Davos* from well-publicized discoveries in nuclear physics, for example, the positron and neutron, in the 1930s.

Purely geometric shapes cover the surfaces of a number of vases. *Nanking* has concentric triangles angling off its surface; *Actinia* has billowing, denticulated curves; *Nimroud* has tall triangles enclosing zig-zags and straight lines, and *Koudour* has its top covered with molded zig-zag lines in black *patine.* The geometric patterns of the last two vases may have been inspired by American Indian art, as may have been the six tiers of stick-figure or hieroglyph-like marks against the black-enameled ground of *Lagamar.*

The press-molded vases of the later 1930s were simplified geometric products of the machine age. Crisp, cool, elegant and with only a hint of opalescence or other color, they signaled the end of an era – one in which Lalique's vases had scaled new heights in terms of color, decoration and drama.

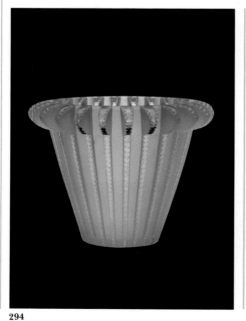

294

295

296

3. Kahn, "Lalique Verrier", 150.

4. Dawes, *Lalique Glass,* 101.

297

294 Vase with zigzag geometric design, *c.* 1936, approx. 7in (18cm). Galerie Moderne.

295 *Marignane* vase, *c.* 1935, 9½in (23.5cm). Private collection, Paris.

296 *Meander* vase, *c.* 1935, 6½in (16.3cm). Galerie Moderne.

This trio of vases was designed in the 1930s; they do not appear in the 1932 catalogue.

297 *Méduse* vase, *c.* 1922, 7in (17.5cm). Galerie Moderne.

298 *Pierrefonds* vase, *c.* 1925, 13½in (34cm) long. Galerie Moderne.

The curling tendrils of *Méduse* could be the scaley arms of an octopus, whereas the spiraling handles that overwhelm *Pierrefonds* are much more stylized, reminiscent of the vortices on the vase *Tourbillons*.

298

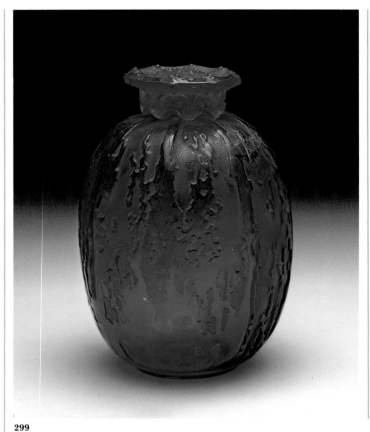

299

300

301

299 *Fontaine* vase, *c.* 1912, 6¼in (15.5cm). Collection Christopher Vane Percy.

300 *Escargot* vase, *c.* 1920, 8¾in (22cm). Kagan Collection, USA.

301 *Nanking* vase, *c.* 1928, 13in (33cm). Collection Lynne and David Weinstein, New York.

302 *Lagamar* vase, *c.* 1925, 7½in (18.5cm). Collection Laurie and Joel Shapiro, Detroit.

The geometric design of *Nanking,* which upside-down appears as a lamp shade (with a different neck, however), is very much Art Déco. The hieroglyph-like motifs on *Lagamar* are also in the 1920s style, perhaps influenced by American Indian or Mayan art.

302

303 *Baies* vase, *c.*
1925, 10½in
(26.5cm). Private
collection, London.

304 *Oranges* vase,
c. 1925, 11½in
(29cm). Collection
Glenn and Mary Lou
Utt, USA.

303

304

162

JARDINIERES

Three long *jardinières* were created by Lalique, ranging from 18in to 21in in length and having canoe-shaped bodies with massive, decorative handles. *Saint-Hubert's* C-scroll handles are molded and pierced with a leaping deer amid a tangle of foliage; *Acanthes'* are upward-pointing wings lightly molded with overlapping acanthus leaves (which extend on to the body of the piece), and *Mésanges* has two chubby birds acting as its handles.

TABLEWARE

Into this expansive category – comprising the majority of Lalique's commercial production in the 1920s – fall a full range of bowls, platters, decanters, carafes, glasses, candlesticks and odd assortments like menu and place-card holders, pepper mills and knife rests. These and other molded-glass objects met a post-war demand for economically priced, non-crystal pieces:

He has designed and produced many wares of this kind, such as decanters, water-bottles, tumblers, preserve-dishes, cream-jugs, fruit- and cake-dishes – all of very high artistic merit, and at an economic price, no higher than that of the ordinary inferior glassware obtainable anywhere.[5]

So wrote Gabriel Mourey, who praised Lalique's combination of originality and practicality. He continued:

What is strangely amazing is that Lalique manages to create, after so many others, a table set and yet remain original. The reason is that he always sticks to reason and logic and abhors eccentricity; that he always clings to nature, as far as it is possible to do so.

His dinner-sets, liqueur, port, beer, or dessert-sets, his fruit and cake-plates, stewed-fruit dishes and cream-bowls are always inspired, whatever may be the ornamentation that clothes them by the practical conditions of their very existence. Thanks to the assembling of the two techniques . . . of cut glass and cast glass, there is practically no liberty that is forbidden to him; thus for instance, he has succeeded in incorporating to the foot of a wine-glass of cut crystal tiny figures made of cast glass which give to the object a supplementary charm. He discreetly sets off others with dots of enamel and thus makes them more precious still.[6]

305

305 Bowl with applied floral handles, *c.* 1908-12, 10in (25.5cm) wide. Collection Glenn and Mary Lou Utt, USA.

306 Bowl with applied handles with lily-of-the-valley design, *c.* 1908-12. Private collection, London.

306

5. Mourey, "Lalique's Glassware", 34.
6. Mourey, "A Great French Craftsman", 109.

307

309

308

LALIQUE

307 *Lotus* glasses,
c. 1930, 3¼in (8cm).
Galerie Moderne.

308 *Saint-Denis* goblet,
c. 1925, 6¾in (17cm).
Galerie Moderne.

309 Goblet with grape
design on stem,
c. 1933, approx. 5in
(12.7cm). Galerie
Moderne.

310 *6 Figurines* carafe,
c. 1910, 14in (35cm),
and four *Coquelicot*
glasses, *c.* 1930, 2in
(5cm). Galerie
Moderne.

310

311

312

311 *Coquilles* carafe,
c. 1912, 13½in
(34cm). Galerie
Moderne.

312 *2 Danseuses*
carafe, *c.* 1920, 13¾in
(34.5cm). Galerie
Moderne.

Lalique's jugs, carafes
and decanters came
with a variety of
figural, faunal and
abstract designs.

313 *Nippon* tray, *c.* 1930, 13½in (34cm) dia. Galerie Moderne.

314 Decanter with grape design on stopper, *c.* 1933. Galerie Moderne.

315 *Hagueneau* decanter, with Greek-key design on stopper, *c.* 1933. Galerie Moderne.

LALIQUE

314

315

316 *Acanthes*
jardinière, *c.* 1926,
18¼in (45.5cm) long.
Galerie Moderne.
Lalique designed at
least three such
jardinières, all with
canoe-shaped bodies
and massive,
decorative handles.

317 *Mésanges*
jardinière, *c.* 1926,
21½in (53.5cm) long.
Galerie Moderne.

316

LALIQUE

317

318

319

318 Left, pair of caryatid table decorations, *c.* 1910, 11¾in (30cm); right, pair of candlesticks, *c.* 1910, 11in (28cm). Private collection, London.

319 Right, *Thionville* plate, *c.* 1924, approx. 7in (17.8cm) dia. Left, *Unawihr* goblet, *c.* 1930, 4½in (11.5cm). Galerie Moderne.

Lalique produced a great many sets of tableware, comprising goblets and decanters, as well as bowls and platters. The *Thionville* and *Unawihr* patterns are especially elegant and *moderne*, the goblet's checkered motif reminiscent of Viennese turn-of-the-century design.

320

320 Charger with spiraling sardines surrounding a bubbly center, *c.* 1928, 13in (32.25cm) dia. Galerie Moderne.

321 *Trépied sirène* footed charger, *c.* 1925, 14½in (36cm) dia. Galerie Moderne.

Marine patterns were found on many of Lalique's *coupes*, as all the bowls, chargers and platters were termed in the 1932 catalogue – from the ubiquitous siren, alone or in a pair or groups, to various species of fish.

321

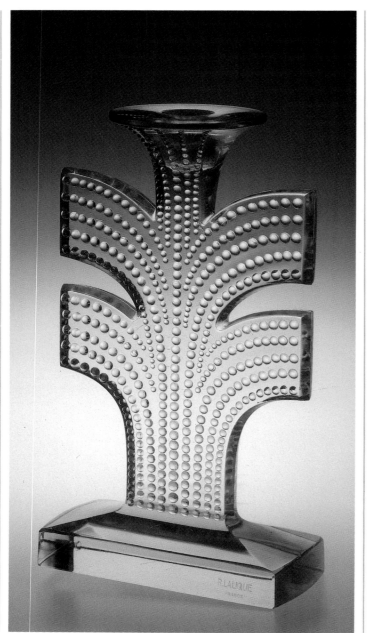

322

323

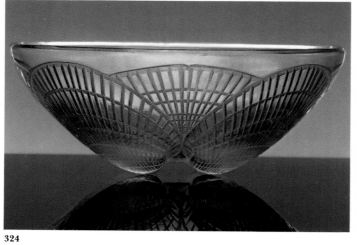

324

322 *Tokio* candlestick, *c.* 1933, 8½in (21cm). Galerie Moderne.

323 Assortment of *Coquilles* bowls and platters, *c.* 1930. Galerie Moderne.

324 *Coquilles* bowl, *c.* 1930, 7½in (19cm) dia. Galerie Moderne.

325

325 *Phalènes* bowl,
c. 1929, 15½in (39cm)
dia. Galerie Moderne.

326 *Eléphants* bowl,
c. 1929, 15½in (39cm)
dia. Collection Lynne
and David Weinstein,
New York.

326

327

328

329

330

LALIQUE

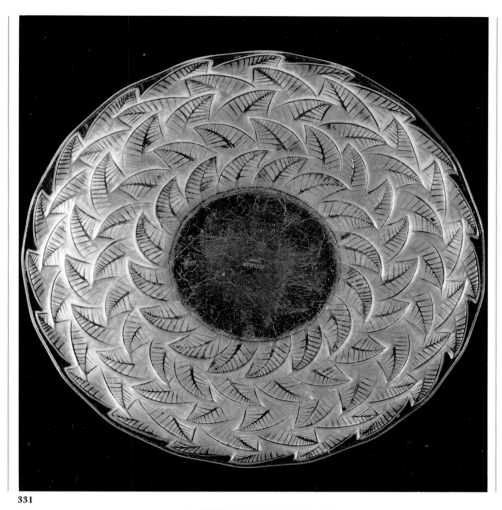

331

327 Left, *Gui* bowl, *c.* 1924, 8¼in (20.5cm) dia; right, *Volubilis* bowl, *c.* 1924, 8½in (21cm) dia. Galerie Moderne.

328 Bowl with frieze of parakeets *(Perruches), c.* 1924, 10in (24.7cm) dia. Galerie Moderne.

329 Charger with swirling fish, *c.* 1933, 9¼in (23.5cm) dia. Galerie Moderne.

330 *Nemours* bowl, *c.* 1931, 10in (25.5cm) dia. Galerie Moderne.

331 Bowl with overlapping leaves, *c.* 1933, 13in (33cm) dia. Galerie Moderne.

332 *Anvers* bowl, *c.* 1929, 15½in (39cm) dia. Galerie Moderne.

332

333

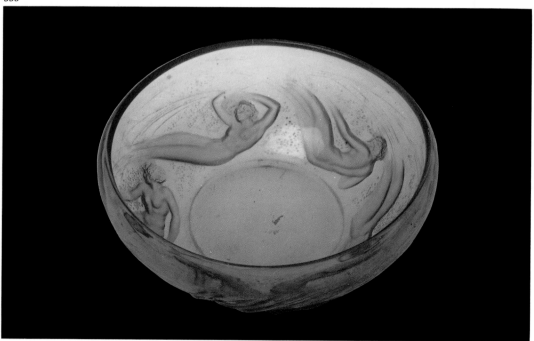

334

333 *Ondine ouverte* bowl, *c.* 1920, 8½in (21cm) dia. Galerie Moderne; photo by Zeljan Pavicevic.

334 *Ondines refermées* bowl, *c.* 1920, 7½in (19cm) dia. Galerie Moderne.

335 *Calypso* bowl, *c.* 1928, 12in (30cm) dia. Galerie Moderne.

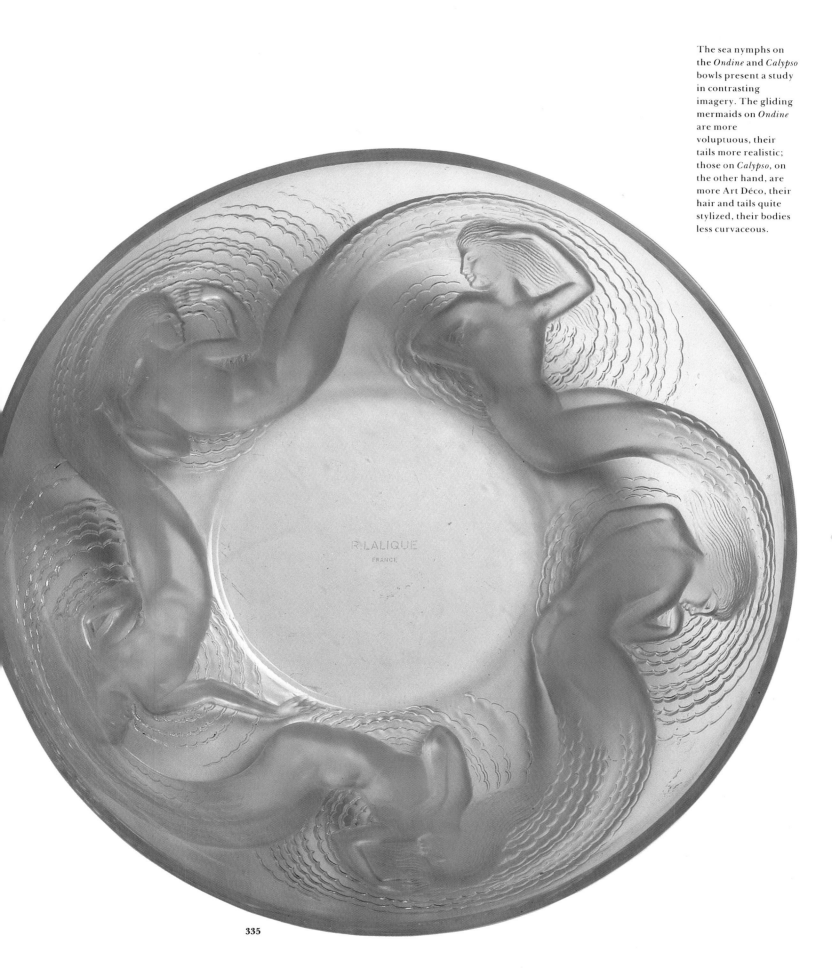

The sea nymphs on the *Ondine* and *Calypso* bowls present a study in contrasting imagery. The gliding mermaids on *Ondine* are more voluptuous, their tails more realistic; those on *Calypso*, on the other hand, are more Art Déco, their hair and tails quite stylized, their bodies less curvaceous.

335

336

336 Bowl with wheatsheaf design, *c.* 1936, approx. 13in (33cm) dia. Galerie Moderne.

337 *Jaffa* bowl, *c.* 1936, approx. 13in (33cm) dia. Galerie Moderne.

338 *Chicorée* bowl, *c.* 1924-25, 9½in (24cm) dia. Galerie Moderne.

337

338

339

339 Bowl with lily-of-the-valley design, *c.* 1922, 9¼in (23cm) dia. Collection Mr. and Mrs. Conti, Chicago.

340 *Ondes* bowl, *c.* 1936, approx. 7 in (17.8cm) dia. Galerie Moderne.

340

Lalique had begun to produce limited numbers of decanters, carafes and stemware in the early 20th century, including the monumental and purely decorative sculptural goblets and chalices incorporating metal, ivory and glass. Before 1915 he was creating utilitarian, tall-necked carafes such as *Sirènes* (c.1911), with its additional decoration of frogs, and *Plate 2 danseuses* (c.1913). Both of them have bodies not very different from his later carafes such as *Masque, 6 Figurines, Reine marguerite, Aubépine (Hawthorn)* and *Plates épines*. Most of his carafes were beaker-shaped, but some, like *Vrilles de vigne*, were spherical and others, like *Dundee* (hexagonal) and *Pyramidale*, were multi-sided. Their bodies were variously molded with simple medallions (*Masque*), or all-over geometric patterns (*Dundee*, with its Aztec-like squares-within-squares comprising tiny triangles), or with bodies and necks of the same pattern (*Aubépine* and *Plates epines*). Some carafes, such as the *Raisins, Strasbourg, Wingen* and *Ricquewihr* patterns, came with matching glasses; others were single pieces.

There were also goblets available on their own without carafes, such as *Bague lézards* (with a band of molded lizards above the foot), *Frise personnages* (with a tall ring of classical figures in the same spot) and *Chasse chiens No 1* and *No 2*, both with hunting dogs in relief on their everted feet. Most glasses were traditionally shaped, with molded bold relief on their rims or, less frequently, a light design all over their bodies or in vertical designs separated by blank spaces.

In 1924 Lalique received a commission to create two carafes for the wine merchant, Cusenier; the two that he made were both of similar tall-teardrop shapes, one with bramble-design, the other with satyr-motif, handles. Later Lalique designed table glass for the Compagnie Général Transatlantique, the French steamship firm (for whose ship, *Normandie*, he did some interior design).

Among the many other "useful wares" which Lalique designed were colorful soft-drink services comprising pitcher, glasses and tray, all similarly decorated overall (termed *services à orangeade* in the 1932 catalogue, the five sets were exotically named *Sétubal, Jaffa, Bahia, Blidah* and *Hespérides*). There were also wine services, including spherical carafes, glasses and trays (designs included *Coquelicot, Bambou* and *Nippon*), and elaborate *caves à liqueurs*, made up of three flacons in carry-all metal frames (one set had a central bottle depicting a pipe-playing Pan, the companion pieces adorned with dancing Bacchantes).

Other tablewares designed by Lalique included hemispherical menu holders (usually with floral, fruit or bird designs); an elaborate *moulin à poivre* (pepper mill), covered all over with leaves; cocktail shakers; candlesticks and candleholders in figural, floral, foliate, avian and abstract designs; flower- and dragonfly-molded knife-rests, and ornamental glass birds and flowers which, as Gabriel Mourey wrote, completed the ensemble of a dinner table when "harmoniously scattered in the vacant spaces".[7] Also, there were bowls, platters and other dinnerware available in patterns to match the *Nippon, Bourgueil, Unawihr* and *Hagueneau* glassware sets. Then there was a special tableware set decorated with flying swallows (including candlesticks and four sizes of glasses), which was presented by the City of Paris to King George VI and Queen Elizabeth of England in 1938; there were also dinner plates in the same service, their rims decorated with the arms of both the House of Windsor and the City of Paris.

The bowls were adorned with a variety of floral, faunal and figurative motifs; the later ones also had purely geometric patterns. Some animal bowls depicted motifs which had not been seen on any other Lalique pieces. These included *Madagascar*, molded with a dozen stylized monkey masks, and *Eléphants*, the inside of which was molded with a parade of pachyderms (the bowl is shaped like an upside-down, wide-brimmed hat).

There were the usual pretty-bird designs: the *Perruches* bowl, with its frieze of parakeets perched on florid branches; *Nonnettes*, a dish whose underside is molded with three pairs of open-winged, cooing doves; and *Cristal 2 oiseaux moqueurs*, on whose wide rim perches a pair of three-dimensional mocking birds. A brilliant opalescent bowl is covered over all with stylized molded "eyes" of peacock feathers, diminishing in size toward the center.

Fish, too, decorated the rims and bodies of assorted plates and bowls. *Martigues* is decorated with 12 interlocking fish; its supports are the fins of the three middle fish. Another bowl is molded on the underside with a school of carp dramatically swimming amid a watery vortex, and yet another (these last two without names) is decorated with a dozen sardine-like, open-mouthed fish, their curving bodies radiating around a bubbly center.

Three *Gazelles* are molded under the broad rim of a circular dish, and another bowl is molded with hounds jumping through stylized foliage. *Phalènes* depicts a central florette on its bowl and a swarm of overlapping butterflies on its wide rim, some above, others below.

An unusual figural design depicts eight pairs of genuflecting angels radiating around a rose-window central medallion (*Anges*). Ubiquitous sea nymphs figure on several *coupes* (circular dishes) and *assiettes* (plates) from the solitary mermaid on *Trépied sirène*, to the five on *Calypso* and the half-dozen swimmers on *Ondines* (which comes in two versions, one with everted, the other with inverted rim). Another marine creature, a highly stylized scallop shell, appears on five different-sized *Coquilles* platters. This popular design was also available as a *plafonnier* (hanging-light fixture).

Floral and foliate designs predominate on Lalique's bowls and platters. They include *Chicorée*, a salad bowl molded with curly, curved chicory leaves, another bowl with a dandelion-leaf design, and yet another with a radiating pattern of stylized overlapping leaves. *Nemours* is a thick-walled bowl molded with deep-set graduated flowerheads in concentric circles; *Vernon* is a dish molded with flowerheads, the center three of which form feet; *Volubilis* is molded underneath with three convolvulus blossoms, their stems also fashioned as feet, and *Lys* is an elegant bowl with a design of four lily blossoms, their outstretched centers acting as feet. The bottom of the *Marienthal* bowl is molded with a bold design of thick berries and scrolling vines, and a similar double-tiered, grape-and-stem motif covers the exterior of the bowl *Saint-Vincent*.

There are also unnamed bowls and platters with starkly geometric designs which echo the machine-age patterns on some of Lalique's later vases. On the whole, however, the designs on Lalique's bowls and plates are much gentler and less daring than those of his vases.

---

7. *Ibid.*

341 *Martigues* bowl,
c. 1924, 14½in (36cm)
dia. Galerie Moderne.

342 *Lys* bowl, *c.* 1925,
9½in (23.5cm) dia.
Galerie Moderne.

Several Lalique bowls,
or *coupes*, were
molded with feet,
such as *Lys*, whose
flowerheads
metamorphose into
three-dimensional
supports on the
bottom of the piece.

341

342

343 Panel for a
Pullman car on the
Côte d'Azur train,
1929, glass and
sycamore, frame 36¾
x 31½in (93.3 x
79.4cm). The Virginia
Museum of Fine Arts,
Richmond, Gift of
Sydney and Frances
Lewis.

ARCHITECTURAL WORK

11

LALIQUE

ené Lalique applied his skills to an extensive range of work and it is not surprising that he should have been drawn to interior and architectural design.

The first major architectural project with which he was associated was his own Paris atelier and living quarters at 40 Cours la Reine. He had previously been involved with design aspects of his Rue Thérèse headquarters (occupied from 1890–1902), but that was a limited project in comparison with the Cours la Reine complex, and details of the Rue Thérèse interior are not known, except for what his family wrote about it:

> Helped by two relatives, René Lalique personally decorated his residence, covering walls and ceilings with frescoes, paintings, relievo motives. He designed his own furniture, combining functional and decorative purposes.[1]

Lalique was in great part responsible for the design of the façade, interior fittings and even furniture and lighting fixtures in the multistory Cours la Reine building, which, with the architectural firm of Feine, he renovated to suit his production, residential and display needs. His descendants have written:

> Sculptor as well as architect, René Lalique erected . . . a building as revolutionary for the time as his jewels were. Daring, original, were the terms which fully described the architectural realization whose sober lines were ornamented with a fir and pine tree decoration. The glass panels of the main door entrance revealed, in the finest details, the sensiblity and elegance of the artist's work.[2]

The ground level and first floor served as exhibition space. Vintage photographs of the impressive area show a spacious room with wood and glass display tables, four striking opalescent blown-glass chandeliers (a 1902 article described them as "electric chandeliers of bronze and blown glass, in the forms of snakes and chameleons and hung from the ceiling by means of heavy, wrought-iron chains"), bronze capitals of marble pillars molded with the pine design and an elaborate wooden staircase, again with the pine motif, leading to a mezzanine which also held a variety of vitrine-tables. The walls were covered with a beige fabric and were decorated with a pine-and-branch frieze.

The work table, desk, and their chairs, from Cours la Reine, have been described earlier, as have the exterior glass panels and façade of his *hôtel*. Also of interest was an etched-glass interior double-door. Its surface was covered with a simple, vertical leafy-stem motif and the architrave continued this motif, broken up by diaper work of berry roundels. The door to the display room on the ground floor was decidedly different. It incorporated four horizontal glass panels depicting classical male nudes, most in forward-thrust positions, almost literally pushing open the door. Tristan Destève wrote of this door in 1902:

> The wrought-iron and glass door which he wished to place between the outside world and himself clearly denotes his innermost predilections. Mr. Lalique is a recluse and a shy man who lives, admittedly without losing interest in life, in a kind of work-oriented dream; the sturdiness and at the same time the fragility of this barrier which he has decorated, as if symbolically, with the gestures of nude men seeking to force access in order to penetrate the sanctuary of his work and of his dreams, will seem to all refined men deeply expressive of the idea which he has allowed to be made of his character, both according to the works of the artist and according to the business of the man.[3]

A multitude of fleur-de-lys elements comprised the door's wrought-iron, largely vertical, grillwork.

This door and the exterior pine-bough-laden door were roundly praised as outstanding technical feats and led to Lalique's receiving architectural commissions (although the bulk of them were not until after World War I). The Cours La Reine project was above all significant, as one writer put it, for providing a "precise measure of the encyclopedic ambition that characterized the great artists of the early 20th century. Like the Renaissance masters they put their hands to every form of plastic expression, their goal being a synthesis of the arts – the supreme result of the effort at unification to which the stylistic system of Art Nouveau bears witness."[4]

One of Lalique's pre-war architectural assignments was the design and production of windows with a floral motif for the New York branch of François Coty's perfume business, located at 714 Fifth Avenue. The Manhattan premises opened in 1913 and the frosted-glass panels – which are still intact – were manufactured at Clairfontaine under the auspices of the Union Centrale des Arts Décoratifs (an organization which was established at the end of the 19th century to give voice to the industrial arts reform movement). In 1913 panels were designed for a pair of wrought-iron gates designed by Bellery Desfontaines; they were decorated with two muscular, neoclassical male and female figures representing the seasons (the man is sowing seed, the woman picking fruit from a tree's branches) and molded on roundels which were enveloped by curving, wrought-iron wheat stalks.

Lalique's next interior-design project was the creation, in 1922, of the dining room for the Exposition des Artistes Décorateurs, held in the Pavillon Marsan of the Musée des Arts Décoratifs. As with the snow-covered pine branches of the Cours la Reine door, he employed a wintry motif. Christopher Vane Percy paraphrased Gustave Geffroy's rather hyperbolic description of the Lalique projection:

> The effect (of Lalique's stand) is at once strange and simple, bizarre and serene. Glass partitions appear to reproduce that foliage with which the winter hoar frost adorns the most ordinary of glass window-panes . . . In the middle, a chandelier – very plain and very bold – evokes the far-off softness of a star suspended over some place of mystery . . . Light plays the role of colour, replacing it and rendering it superfluous. All the nuances which the glass assumes, all the dream-like visions which it reflects, are rigidly defined by the surrounding darkness.[5]

The 1925 Paris Exposition marked a high point for the French decorative arts, which were to become known as Art Déco. And Lalique's presence was felt throughout the exhibition – in his own pavilion, in his designs in the Parfumerie Française and Sèvres sections, in his contributions to the entrance gate and, most of all, in the massive outdoor fountain on the Esplanade des Invalides. The fountain, consisting of 136 *Source de la fontaine* sculptures, was

1. *Lalique par Lalique*, 21.
2. *Ibid.*, 22.

3. Destève, "La Maison de René Lalique", 165–66 [authors' translation].
4. Yvonne Brunhammer et al., *Art Nouveau Belgium/France*, Houston, Texas, 1976, 394.
5. Vane Percy, *The Glass of René Lalique*, 15–16. Part of this statement was quoted by Maximilien Gauthier to describe the dining room for the 1925 Sèvres pavilion.

344

345

illuminated from within and below and water jetted out from the top to the bottom. In Christopher Vane Percy's words, it looked "like a fantastic crystal pagoda – a magnificent assertion of Lalique's mastery of his medium and of the moment".[6]

At the 1925 fair, as Gabriel Mourey, a longtime Lalique champion, wrote, Lalique "made the most brilliant demonstration of the innumerable applications of glass to architecture and interior design".[7] From his impressive Cours la Reine beginnings, Lalique had managed, without any formal training as an architect, to work his way up to a prominent place in the privileged hierarchy of Art Déco designers.

Following the 1925 Exposition came more design projects, as well as the continued production of decorative glass panels which could be purchased separately in the Place Vendôme showroom. Plaques and panels were produced for use as architectural and furniture elements, the latter a new field which Lalique took up in the mid-1920s. Most of his furniture projects were specific commissions, although some tables were made in limited quantities (Cristal Lalique still markets glass tables today, in the *Cactus* design). Lalique had, in fact, designed furniture while in his goldsmith period, notably at the Rue Thérèse and Cours la Reine premises. Furnishings which have recently come to light attest to his limitless inventiveness, for instance, the lovely tooled, painted, and gilded leather screen from around the turn of the century described in Chapter 2.

Later glass furniture projects were much more stylized and veered sharply away from the richness and natural content of that screen. A massive, rectangular liquor cabinet, for example, whose wooden frame was inlaid with 10 glass panels of prancing putti among grapes and vines, is much more in keeping with 1920s taste.

There were also the several glass tables which Lalique designed – elegant, sophisticated pieces, usually adorned with stylized leaf motifs and either circular with rounded pedestal bases or rectangular with column-like feet attached to a glass base. One, a breakfast table of glass and metal produced in 1937 for the fashion designer, Jeanne Lanvin, was a rare collaboration between Lalique and one of his competitors, Sabino; its thick, round stem was formed by two contiguous pillars, which were lighted from within to produce what must have been a subtle, early-morning glow. In 1935 there was a large, round bathtub on view at the Salon des Décorateurs, made up of vertical panels, each molded with a design of curving leaves which formed a fountain-like pattern.

Lalique also designed several outdoor fountains in the 1920s and 1930s, among them one for the City of Paris which was dominated by frosted-glass sculptures of pigeons, and another for the City of Marseilles with clear-glass fish which seemed to be leaping out of bubbly water jets (the stylized bubbles were very much like those which terminate many a siren's hair and fins on boxes, platters and the like). There was another fountain (completed in 1926) inside Paris's Arcades des Champs-Elysées (Lalique also designed four large outside lamps and 50 inside lights for the Arcades); its central section consisted of four tiers covered with a stylized foliate pattern, and above this stood four female figures (more restrained than the *Source de la fontaine* statuettes) beneath an inverted, flattened dome. On the whole, this fountain was more controlled and less exuberant than that of the 1925 Exposition. Another fountain was exhibited in London, at the Daily Mail Ideal Home Exhibition of 1931, and yet another one in Paris, at the 1937 Exposition Universelle. This last fountain was even more subdued than the Champs-Elysées one,

6. *Ibid.,* 111.
7. Mourey, "A Great French Craftsman", 116.

346

made up as it was of panels molded with simple arcs of bubbles – essentially the Marseilles fountain without fish, and stretched to quite a height.

In the year after the 1925 Exposition, Lalique provided much of the architectural and interior-design work on the House of Worth's Cannes showroom. Besides the frosted-glass door frame and the shop sign (both illuminated), he also devised a new type of cornice lighting – glass panels of quarter-round sections with ornamented molding on the outwardly curving exterior. Such cornice lights took the place of hanging-light fixtures, but they did not prove popular, despite their "throwing down into [a] room a diffused light of the utmost charm".[8] Five floral/arboreal designs were available on the cornice lights: acacia, dahlia, grapevine, hornbeam and thistle.

Lalique worked on lighting and interior-design projects throughout the 1920s, including fixtures for the French ocean liner, *Paris,* launched in 1920, and for the Paris nightclub, *Le Lido,* finished in 1929. In the United States, Lalique was involved with interior designs for the Alexander and Oviatt department store in Los Angeles (1927), including the entrance door, vitrines, an illuminated ceiling, panels for the penthouse, and elevator doors.[9] A year later he completed designs for the entrance salon and "crystal room" of the Jay Thorpe Building in New York. (He had also designed perfume bottles for both these American retailers.)

The crowning glories of the architectural/design arm of Lalique's career came in the 1930s, in the form of two rather unusual projects – one marine, the glass paneling and lighting of the dining room of the French ocean liner, *Normandie,* and the other ecclesiastical, the renovation of St. Matthew's Church at Millbrook, on the Isle of Jersey.

Lalique had already designed an altar before the Jersey commission – La Chapelle de la Vièrge Fidèle in Caen, installed in 1930 –

and following that commission, he had displayed variations of the altar at two salons. That valuable exposure gained him the commission for the Jersey chapel project, which dates from 1934. Lalique collaborated with the British architect, A. B. Grayson, on the renovation of the early Victorian church, a project sponsored by the local resident, Florence, Lady Trent, in commemoration of her late husband, Jesse Boot, 1st Baron Trent of Nottingham. Lady Trent knew Lalique personally. They had adjacent villas in the south of France and she had already commissioned a pair of doors from him for her Jersey residence.

Lalique's contributions to the renovation of St. Matthew's included a new high altar with illuminated cross behind it, side walls of glass panels surrounding a vestry and a small chapel (also with an altar), an altar rail, windows, font and other smaller fittings such as door handles. The chapel can still be viewed today in its crystalline purity and tranquillity, dominated as it is by the huge frosted-glass cross flanked by two glass pillars (with simple stem motifs similar to those of the interior door of Lalique's Cours la Reine premises). Both the tall cross and the two pillars are adorned at their tops with molded blossoms of the Regal lily *(lilium regale),* popularly known as the "Jersey lily". The columns, though monochromatic, are reminiscent of the multicolored glass-tile and ceramic columns with floral capitals which Louis Comfort Tiffany had several decades earlier installed in his Laurelton Hall estate on Long Island, New York.

The four screen walls (in stainless-steel frames) and windows are also adorned with the Jersey lily (in bud form on the windows); the altar rail is decorated with the Madonna lily *(Lilium candidium).* The lily, being a symbol of purity, is the ideal ecclesiastical motif, although it was not a new one for Lalique, who had used it on several bowls and in his glass jewelry.

The reredos of the smaller Lady Chapel of St. Matthew's is constructed of tall relief panels of monumental angels with hands folded over their breasts and eyes closed in prayer. The chapel's glass font, of frosted and clear glass striations, has a simple, but handsome, chalice form with a geometric pattern; its wide bowl is decorated with a chevron design at the top and rests on a thick, pillared stem which in turn stands on a square platform. The refurbished St. Matthew's was a fitting tribute to Lord Trent. Lalique and Grayson subtly transformed "the austere Chapel of Ease"[10] into a distinctive, modern house of worship.

Lalique's other great commission in the 1930s was for the luxurious ocean liner, the *Normandie,* which has been called "the last great expression of French Art Déco".[11] The French government underwrote the building of the ship, which was to be the biggest, fastest and handsomest at sea and which, despite the Depression, was intended to lure wealthy Americans to France. The greatest designers of the day were enlisted to furnish and decorate this floating palace. Lalique was commissioned to design the lighting for the first-class

8. Mourey, "Lalique's Glassware", 36.

9. Lalique seems to have had difficulty in getting paid for this commission, and it is almost certain that not all of his designs for Alexander and Oviatt were realized. Apparently the work was stopped due to non-payment by Oviatt, and Lalique's designs are thought to have been produced by another company.

10. Jane Ashelford, "Lalique's 'Glass Church'," *The Journal of the Decorative Arts Society,* IV (1980), 28.

11. Hunter-Stiebel, "Twentieth Century Decorative Arts", 34.

347

346 *Le Parfum des Anges* flacon, 1927, 3¼in (8.2cm). Collection Mary Lou Utt, USA.

347 General view of high altar, St. Matthew's Church, 1934, Millbrook, Isle of Jersey, showing Lalique cross and stem pillars, and altar rail and screen walls with lily designs.

348 Parlor door designed by Lalique, *c.* 1932, for the home of Lady Trent, Jersey.

349 Detail of parlor door, showing plump bird amid berries.

350 Detail of St. Matthew's, showing part of screen with lily design.

351 Holy-water font from St. Matthew's.

348

349

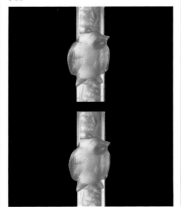

350

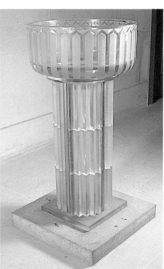

351

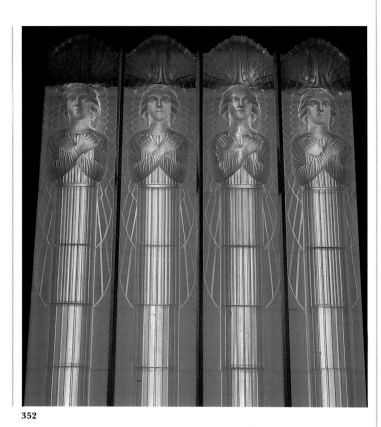

352

352 Detail of reredos from Lady Chapel of St. Matthew's, showing frieze of monumental angels.

353 Central rectangular section of maquette showing chorus of six angels, *cire-perdue* bronze, *c.* 1900, 5½ x 8⅞in (14 x 22.5cm), Kagan Collection, USA. This maquette was a preliminary model for at least two actual pieces, one a small gold brooch, the other a large frosted-glass relief plaque. The four profiles resemble many of the women in Lalique's goldsmithswork.

dining room, which was located in the ship's center and measured 300ft long × 46ft wide × 25ft high. Its walls were simply covered in rough, unpolished glass; the coffered ceiling was inlaid with lighted panels; and the room was bordered on the entire length of each side by six free-standing "monoliths of light", elaborate, four-tiered, temple-like sculptures each 23ft high. A huge chandelier, almost an upside-down version of the standing light fixtures and consisting of four tiers of vertical panels molded with zig-zag lines, hung at the entrance. The glittering jewels of the diners and the shimmering columns of light installed by Lalique must have provided a dazzling display of wealth and beauty and made the room, designed by the architects, Paton and Pacon, a latter-day version of the mirrored hall at Versailles. The ship's maiden voyage took place in 1935; seven years later the liner was sunk in New York harbor. It had just been seized by the United States government and was in the midst of being stripped for use as a troops carrier when an acetylene torch started a fire in the Grand Salon; firefighting efforts caused her to capsize.

Other Lalique design projects in the 1920s and 1930s included a commission in 1923 from the Compagnie des Wagons-Lits to decorate the sleeping car of the French president, Alexandre Millerand. The panels were molded with a simple, but handsome, laurel motif. Six years later Lalique designed figurative glass panels for a Pullman Car on the Côte d'Azur train, rich designs of neoclassical nudes amid stylized grapes and vines. One set of these panels is on view at the Virginia Museum of Fine Arts in Richmond.

Lalique also produced panels depicting classical nude athletes in various action poses to be set above Byron Inison's wrought-iron elevator doors in London's Claridge's Hotel (Oswald Milne was the architect responsible for using the panels, which, unfortunately, are no longer in place). They were described in an article of 1927:

> Purely classic in conception are the overdoor plaques . . . in which the athletes are facing towards the right, placed over a bronze door at Claridge's Hotel, London. It is not too much to claim that such virility of treatment, such perfection of modelling has never before been achieved in such a medium. Certain it is that pieces of such size have never before been moulded, they measure four feet in length.[12]

Lalique also provided custom-made lighting for the huge Maples furniture store in Tottenham Court Road, London.

Lalique completed an interior-design project for the entrance of John Wanamaker's department store in Philadelphia in 1932. These huge clear-glass panels, with sand-blasted decoration and framed in bronze, depicted neoclassical figures amid foliage. One of them is today in The Corning Museum of Glass, New York.

Lalique was the consummate designer of the early 20th century, a genius who was attuned to the aesthetics of both small-scale and large-scale objects. On the one hand, he could imbue a diminutive vase with a monumental, architectonic quality, and on the other, endow a massive architectural element with delicacy.

Gabriel Mourey paid tribute to Lalique's inexhaustible energy:

> This is commercial art perfectly conceived and realised, which permits of the introduction of a really modern and living artistic note into the decoration of our private rooms and into the arrangement and decoration of public buildings such as tea-rooms, hotels, cafés, dance-halls, shops, banks, theatres, concert-halls, and so forth. It frankly bears the mark of our complicated civilization, athirst for elegance, novelty, comfort and luxury.[13]

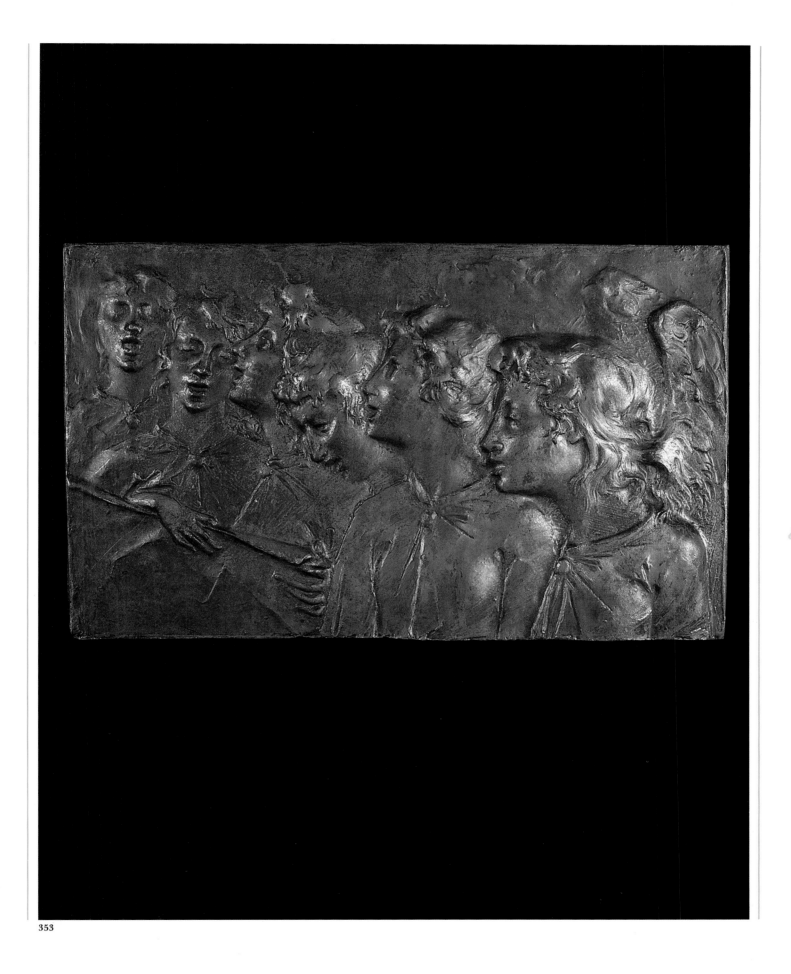

353

12. Gordon-Stables, "Lalique", 34.

13. Mourey, "Lalique's Glassware", 36.

Lalique's signature appears in a variety of permutations on virtually all of his output. The goldsmithwork is engraved discreetly with "LALIQUE" or "R. LALIQUE," whereas the glass pieces – vases, statuettes, tableware, jewelry and other work – may be wheel-engraved, impressed, etched, molded or acid-stamped with the designer's name, as seen on these two pages, accompanied very often by "FRANCE" in the same script.

Below are sixteen known Lalique signatures. In the main, they cannot be ascribed to any certain time period, and therefore no dates are mentioned.

Wheel-cut signature, with our without "FRANCE", marking pieces *c.* 1925 through the mid 1930s.

Wheel-cut signature.

Engraved script facsimile of René Lalique's signature.

R.I.AI.IQUE

FRANCE

Stenciled mark made by sand-blasting.

Very early pieces, i.e. those produced before 1914, bear a very fluid version of this mark, generally with the "R" omitted.

Important late pieces (e.g. *Palestre, Borromée* and *Languedoc* bear a more heavily stenciled sand-blasted mark.

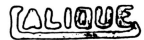

Engraved mark in diminutive script marking tableware.

Similar engraved signatures, on slightly later pieces, often appear in conjunction with the word "France" and the model number in conforming script.

Extended "L" intaglio stamped signature appearing on early works; occasionally, the die used to stamp this mark slips, resulting in multiple impressions.

188

Molded marks are cast as integral parts of the objects, with varying degrees of success in the quality of definition.

Molded marks may be in relief or intaglio.

R.LALIQUE

This mark appears in relief and intaglio, as evidenced on a range of vases and scent bottles.

Relief molded mark with distinctive doubled-tailed "Q".

This double-tailed "Q" signature in linear configuration without the "R" marks some mascots and early vases.

"VERRERIE D'ALSACE" (VDA) mark used briefly after 1921 when the factory opened.

Ball mask device rarely used, which appears on some powder boxes; probably another VDA mark.

Thin diamond-pointed-incised signature. Traditionally considered spurious, this mark was often added at the factory to those works bearing a molded mark of poor legibility.

BIBLIOGRAPHY

Countless books and articles have been written on the career and works of René Lalique by his contemporaries as well as by later admirers and experts. The list below is by no means exhaustive, and includes those works that are readily available, either in libraries or in bookshops. Of course, general books on Art Nouveau and Art Déco devote lengthy sections to the output of René Lalique, and can also be consulted.

Abdy, Jane. "Sarah Bernhardt and Lalique: A Confusion of Evidence". *Apollo*, May 1987.

B. Altman and Co. *René Lalique: Sculptor in Glass.* New York, 1935.

Anon. "L'Exposition de l'Oeuvre de René Lalique au Pavilion de Marsan". *Mobilier et Décoration*, March 1933, pp. 95–102.

Anon. "A Great and New Craftsman in France", *The Craftsman*, October 1912, p. 75.

Anon. "An Interview with Marie-Claude Lalique". *Collector Editions*, Summer 1983, p. 25.

Anon. "The Lalique Exhibition (at Agnew's)". *The Studio*, August 1905, pp. 127–134.

Anon. "Lalique Glass". *The Studio*, June 1919, pp. 126–27.

Anon. "La Presse à L'Exposition des Oeuvres de René Lalique au Pavilion de Marsan". *La Renaissance de l'Art et des Industries de Luxe*, February/March 1933.

Anon. "René Lalique". *Mobilier et Décoration*, January 1927.

Anon. "Sand into Glass". *Fortune*, May 1930.

Anon. "Les Verreries de René Lalique". *Mobilier et Décoration, September 1925, p. 32.*

Anon. "Les Verreries de René Lalique". *Mobilier et Décoration*, December 1932, pp. 213–19.

Armand-Dayot, Madeleine. "Le Maître Verrier René Lalique". *L'Art et les Artistes*, No. 26, 1933, pp. 273–77.

The Art of René Lalique. Breves Galleries, London, c. 1930.

Arwas, Victor. *Lalique.* New York, 1980.

Ashelford, Jane. "Lalique's Glass Church". *Journal of the Decorative Arts Society*, No. 4, 1980, p. 28.

Barten, Sigrid. *René Lalique: Schmuck und Objets d'art 1890–1910.* Munich, 1977.

Bayle, Paul. "Chez Lalique". *L'Art Décoratif*, May 1905, pp. 217–24.

Becker, Vivienne. *The Jewellery of René Lalique.* London, 1987.

Bley, Alice. *A Guide to Fraudulent Lalique.* Ohio, 1981.

Catalogue des Verreries de René Lalique. Paris, 1932; reprinted New York, 1982.

Clendinin, Dorothy. "The Hood Ornaments of Lalique". *Road and Track*, June 1974, pp. 50–52.

Clouzot, Henri, "Le Flaconnage Artistique Moderne". *La Renaissance de l'Art et des Industries de Luxe*, January 1919, pp. 28–32.

Courville, Paul. "L'Industrie de Verre en France". *L'Européen*, June 1, 1934.

Cresswell, Howard S. "Modern Glass". *Good Furniture and Decoration*, September 1929, pp. 160–161.

Dawes, Nicholas M. "Lalique Alert". *Connoisseur*, March 1984, pp. 20–21.

Dawes, Nicholas M. *Lalique Glass.* New York and London, 1986.

Demoriane, Helene. "Verres signé Lalique". *Connaissance des Arts*, April 1970, pp. 112–17.

Destève, Tristan. "La Maison de René Lalique". *Art et Décoration*, November 1902, pp. 161–66.

Gauthier, Maximilien. "Le Maître Verrier René Lalique à L'Exposition." *Le Renaissance de l'Art et des Industries de Luxe*, September 1925, pp. 414–19.

Geffroy, Gustave. "Des Bijoux": à propos de M. René Lalique. *Art et Décoration*, December 1905, pp. 177–88.

Geffroy, Gustave. *René Lalique.* Paris, 1922.

Gere, Charlotte. "René Lalique and His Patrons". *Apollo*, May 1987.

Felice, Roger de. "Les Arts Appliqués au Salon d'Automne". *L'Art Décoratif*, September 1905, pp. 209–19.

Gomes-Ferreira, Maria Theresa. "René Lalique at the Calouste Gulbenkian Museum, Lisbon". *Connoisseur*, 1971, pp. 241–49.

Haraucourt, Edmond. "René Lalique et La Verrerie d'Alsace". *Revue de l'Alsace Française*, August 18, 1923.

Haraucourt, Edmond. "A Salon of French Taste". *Arts and Decoration*, December 1921, pp. 91–4.

Hayot, Monelle. "L'Atelier de René Lalique". *L'Oeuil*, March 1977, pp. 22–9.

Important Lalique Glass. Christie's Auctioneers, New York, October 1980.

Important Lalique Glass. Christie's Auctioneers, New York, December 1980.

Important Lalique Glass. Phillips Auctioneers, New York, February 1980.

Important Lalique Glass and Lalique Jewelry. Phillips Auctioneers, New York, June 1980.

Kahn, Gustave. "Lalique Verrier". *Art et Décoration*, September 1912, pp. 149–58.

Kahn, Gustave. "L'Art de René Lalique". *L'Art et les Artistes*, Spring 1905, pp. 223–26.

Kahn, Gustave. "Les Verreries de René Lalique". *L'Art et les Artistes*, Winter 1921, pp. 101–106.

Kahn, Gustave. *Works of René Lalique.* London, 1905.

Lalique, Marc and Marie-Claude. *Lalique par Lalique.* Paris, 1977. (Note: the Lalique family is expected to bring out a new book on the works of René Lalique and his descendants in 1988.)

Lalique. Phillips Auctioneers, New York, October 1979.

Lalique at C.V.P. London 1974.

Lalique Car Mascots. Breves Galleries, London, c. 1930.

Lalique Encore. Dyansen Gallery, New York, March 1984.

Lalique Lights and Decorations. Breves Galleries, London, c. 1930.

Last D.W. "Car Figureheads: The Development by René Lalique of a Modern Field for Illuminated Glass". *The Studio*, February 1931, pp. 129–30.

Lauvrik, Nilsen J. *René Lalique: Master Craftsman.* New York, 1912.

Malevski, Mirek, and Waller, Mark. "Les Mascottes de Lalique". *Automobiles Classiques, Summer 1985, pp. 114–122.*

Marx, Roger. "Les Maîtres Décorateurs Français: René Lalique". *Art et Décoration*, June 1899, pp. 13–22.

McClinton, Katharine Morrison. *An Introduction to Lalique Glass.* Iowa, 1978.

McClinton, Katharine Morrison. *Lalique for Collectors.* New York, 1975.

McClinton, Katharine Morrison. "René Lalique: Sculptor". *Connoisseur*, October 1980, pp. 119–26.

Mourey, Gabriel. "Lalique's Glassware". *Commercial Art*, July 1926, pp. 32–7.

Mundhenk, B. L. "Lalique and Lalique-type Glass Ornaments". *The Classic Car*, Winter 1963, pp. 27–31.

Munn, Geoffrey. "René Lalique and Japanese Art". *The Antique Collector*, May 1987, pp. 80–88.

Percy, Christopher Vane. *The Glass of Lalique.* New York, 1977.

René Lalique. Parco Gallery, Tokyo, December 1982.

René Lalique. Museum Bellerive, Zurich, 1978.

René Lalique Glass: The Charles and Mary Magriel Collection. Fitchburg Art Museum, Massachusetts, 1975.

The Roger J. Mouré Collection of Lalique. Phillips Auctioneers, New York, March 1979.

Sale of Lalique Glass. Bonhams Auctioneers, London, September 1984.

Stables, Mrs. Gordon. "Lalique". *Artwork*, May 1927, p. 33.

Tisserand, Ernest. "L'Art de René Lalique". *L'Ilustration*, November 1932, pp. 223–26.

Zamacoïs, Miguel. *Chez René Lalique.* Paris, 1928.

INDEX

LALIQUE